CAMBRIDGE LIBRARY COLLECTION

Books of enduring scholarly value

Perspectives from the Royal Asiatic Society

A long-standing European fascination with Asia, from the Middle East to
China and Japan, came more sharply into focus during the early modern
period, as voyages of exploration gave rise to commercial enterprises such
as the East India companies, and their attendant colonial activities. This
series is a collaborative venture between the Cambridge Library Collection
and the Royal Asiatic Society of Great Britain and Ireland, founded in 1823.
The series reissues works from the Royal Asiatic Society's extensive library
of rare books and sponsored publications that shed light on eighteenth-
and nineteenth-century European responses to the cultures of the Middle
East and Asia. The selection covers Asian languages, literature, religions,
philosophy, historiography, law, mathematics and science, as studied and
translated by Europeans and presented for Western readers.

Christianity Contrasted with Hindu Philosophy

While living in India for sixteen years, James Robert Ballantyne (1813–64)
taught oriental languages to Indian pupils and became fascinated by Hindu
philosophy, seeking to harmonise it with the Western tradition. He produced
grammars of Hindi, Sanskrit and Persian, translations of Indian linguistics,
and a science primer in English and Sanskrit (also reissued in the Cambridge
Library Collection). Intended for the inexperienced missionary and published
in 1859, this work offers a summary of Hinduism (covering the Nyaya,
Sankhya and Vedanta schools) and argues for the truth of Christianity, while
acknowledging certain shared ideas. It contains a facing Sanskrit translation
(with redactions of parts considered to be of no importance to 'those whom
the missionary has to teach'). A valuable primary source for scholars
of orientalism, this work helps to illuminate the religious dimensions
of British imperialism.

Cambridge University Press has long been a pioneer in the reissuing of out-of-print titles from its own backlist, producing digital reprints of books that are still sought after by scholars and students but could not be reprinted economically using traditional technology. The Cambridge Library Collection extends this activity to a wider range of books which are still of importance to researchers and professionals, either for the source material they contain, or as landmarks in the history of their academic discipline.

Drawing from the world-renowned collections in the Cambridge University Library and other partner libraries, and guided by the advice of experts in each subject area, Cambridge University Press is using state-of-the-art scanning machines in its own Printing House to capture the content of each book selected for inclusion. The files are processed to give a consistently clear, crisp image, and the books finished to the high quality standard for which the Press is recognised around the world. The latest print-on-demand technology ensures that the books will remain available indefinitely, and that orders for single or multiple copies can quickly be supplied.

The Cambridge Library Collection brings back to life books of enduring scholarly value (including out-of-copyright works originally issued by other publishers) across a wide range of disciplines in the humanities and social sciences and in science and technology.

Christianity Contrasted with Hindu Philosophy

An Essay, in Five Books, Sanskrit and English

James R. Ballantyne

CAMBRIDGE
UNIVERSITY PRESS

CAMBRIDGE UNIVERSITY PRESS

Cambridge, New York, Melbourne, Madrid, Cape Town,
Singapore, São Paolo, Delhi, Mexico City

Published in the United States of America by Cambridge University Press, New York

www.cambridge.org
Information on this title: www.cambridge.org/9781108056564

© in this compilation Cambridge University Press 2013

This edition first published 1859
This digitally printed version 2013

ISBN 978-1-108-05656-4 Paperback

CHRISTIANITY

CONTRASTED WITH

HINDŪ PHILOSOPHY.

CHRISTIANITY

CONTRASTED WITH

HINDŪ PHILOSOPHY:

AN ESSAY,

IN FIVE BOOKS,

SANSKRIT AND ENGLISH:

WITH PRACTICAL SUGGESTIONS TENDERED TO

THE MISSIONARY AMONG THE HINDŪS.

BY

JAMES R. BALLANTYNE, LL.D.,

PROFESSOR OF MORAL PHILOSOPHY, AND PRINCIPAL OF THE GOVERNMENT COLLEGE AT BENARES.

LONDON:

JAMES MADDEN, LEADENHALL STREET.

MDCCCLIX.

STEPHEN AUSTIN,

PRINTER, HERTFORD.

To the Memory

OF

JOHN RUSSELL COLVIN,

LATE LIEUTENANT GOVERNOR OF THE NORTH-WEST PROVINCES OF INDIA,

TO WHOSE CORDIAL APPRECIATION OF HIS EDUCATIONAL AIMS

THE WRITER OWED IT

THAT THE DEATH OF THE LAMENTED THOMASON

DID NOT CRIPPLE THE RESOURCES OF THE BENARES COLLEGE,

THIS ESSAY IS INSCRIBED,

WITH SORROWING GRATITUDE,

BY

JAMES ROBERT BALLANTYNE.

SYNOPTICAL TABLE OF CONTENTS.

PAGE

ADVERTISEMENT... i

PREFACE.. iii

INTRODUCTION vii

Interference in matters of Religion requires Delicacy and
    Address .... *ib.*

The importance of the End derogates not from the import-
    ance of the Means.. *ib.*

Rude attacks on False Religions, why unadvisable............ viii

The Propagation of Christianity, how to be Hoped from the
    Dissemination of Knowledge .... *ib.*

Desirableness of Converting the Learned ix

How it is Reasonable to suppose that Christianity should be
    Propagated otherwise now than at its First Introduction *ib.*

Evidence of the Truth of the Christian Religion furnished by
    the Contrariety between the First and the Subsequent
    Order of its Propagation x

How St. Paul dealt with the Learned .... *ib.*

Hindū Philosophy to be mastered not merely for itself; and
    why xi

The Subject, notwithstanding the Depth of the Interests
    Involved, why to be treated here with Scientific Unim-
    passionedness.. *ib.*

We can most safely venture on Conciliation, where we best
    know the Errors which we must Avoid seeming to
    Countenance xii

Prejudices not Needlessly to be Awakened ....,........ *ib.*

The Confutation of Hindūism not the Primary indispensable xiii

An example of Lord Bacon's to be followed .... *ib.*

Bacon s example not to be Misinterpreted .... *ib.*

PAGE

GENERAL VIEW OF THE HINDŪ SYSTEMS OF
    PHILOSOPHY xv
  The Hindū Systems of Philosophy .... ib.
  Fundamental Agreement of the Three Great Systems ...... ib.
  How they Differ xvi
  The Nyāya Stand-point xvii
  The Sānkhya Stand-point .... ib.
  Precise Difference between the Nyāya and the Sānkhya
      Stand-point .... ib.
  The Vedānta Stand-point .... ib.
  Respective Subordination of the Systems xviii
  Corresponding Distribution of the Present Work............ ib.
SUMMARY OF THE NYĀYA PHILOSOPHY xix
  General Character of the Nyāya System .... ib.
  Meaning of the Name .... ib.
  The Nyāya Text-book... ib.
  Summary of the Topics xx
  Beatitude the Result of Knowledge .... ib.
  The Means of Right Knowledge...... xxi
  A Caution to the Missionary xxii
  Objects regarding which we are to have Right Knowledge xxiii
  Soul xxiv
  Mind .... ib.
  Activity xxv
  What the Nyāya reckons a Fault xxvi
  Transmigration .... ib.
  Pain and Final Emancipation.................................... xxvii
SUMMARY OF THE SĀNKHYA PHILOSOPHY .... ib.
  General Character of the System .... ib.
  Meaning of the Name... xxviii
  The Sānkhya Text-book .... ib.
  The Chief End of Man .... ib.
  Nature, What xxix
  Liberation, What and When xxx
  Annihilation not Sought... ib.
SUMMARY OF THE VEDĀNTA SYSTEM xxxi
  Its Great Tenet .... ib.

PAGE

The One Reality, how Designated xxxi
Possible Course of the Vedāntin's Speculations .... ib.
Why "Ignorance" must be Admitted xxxii
How "Ignorance" may have got its Various Synonymes... xxxiii
"Ignorance," how defined in the Vedānta xxxiv
Why "Ignorance" is held to Consist of Three Qualities... xxxv
The Operation of the Qualities Illustrated xxxvi
Means of Emancipation according to the Vedānta xxxvii

CHRISTIANITY CONTRASTED with HINDŪ PHILOSOPHY   1
BOOK I.—A PARTIAL EXPOSITION OF CHRISTIAN DOCTRINE...... ib.
    The Enquiry What 2
    Man's Chief End.. ib.
    The Rule for Man's Direction to his Chief End 5
    What the Scriptures Principally Teach 9
    What we are to Believe concerning God .... ib.
    The Unity of God 13
    The Trinity in Unity 14
    Creation 15
BOOK II.—THE EVIDENCES OF CHRISTIANITY 20
    Miracles the Credentials of a Religion 21
    The Christian Miracles worthy of Credit 22
    Sufferings of the First Christian Martyrs 26
    Unlikeliness that a Story so Attested should be False 28
    No Evidence of the Veracity of the Veda producible 29
    The Veda, how the result of Speculation, not of Revelation   33
    The Vedāntic Tenet does not justify the Vedāntic In-
        ference 38
    The Eternity of Human Souls, of What Kind 52
    Evidence of Christianity furnished by Prophecy 54
    That the Prophecies were really such 55
BOOK III.—NATURAL THEOLOGY 60
    Evidence of a Designer .... ib.
    The Sānkhya Theory of Unintelligent Design redargued... 61
    The Criterion of the Intelligent.............................. 65
    The Self-contradictory not Receivable on any Authority ... 66
    The Argument from Design Illustrated...................... 68

PAGE

BOOK IV.—OF THE MYSTERIOUS POINTS IN CHRISTIANITY   72
    Mystery of the Trinity in Unity ....   *ib.*
    The rule of "Excluded Middle"................................   75
    Mystery Explicable were no Mystery   78
    Mystery of the Incarnation   79
    Mystery of the Atonement   80
    The Freedom of the Will...........................   83
    Abortive Attempt of Hindūism to clear up the Mystery of
        Evil   86
    Mystery not Distinctive of Christianity   91
BOOK V.—THE ANALOGY OF RELIGION TO THE CONSTITUTION AND
        COURSE OF NATURE...   92
    Origen's Statement of the Argument ....   *ib.*
    Analogy Described   94
    Practical Value of Analogy   96
    In default of Certainty, Probability not to be Despised......   98
    Belief may be the Reward of Obedience.......................   100
    Belief may have Degrees of Assurance   101
    What the Divine Government of both Worlds implies,
        according to the Christian Doctrine   103
    Concluding Advice to the Inquirer   112

APPENDIX OF NOTES AND DISSERTATIONS   113
    A.—On the term "Matter" and its possible correspondents
        in the Hindū Dialects (a Dialogue)   114
    B.—On the Hindū employment of the terms "Soul" and
        "Mind"   138
    C.—On "Logic" and "Rhetoric" as regarded by the Hindūs
        (being a Remonstrance to Sir William Hamilton on
        his Injustice to the Hindū Logic)   140
    D.—On the "Vedas"   161
    E.—On "the Eternity of Sound" (a Dogma of the Mīmānsā)   176
    F.—On "Translation into the Languages of India"   195

ADVERTISEMENT.

THIS ESSAY, slightly modified subsequently, was submitted in competition for a prize of £300, offered by a member of the Bengal Civil Service. The prize was divided, and a moiety was adjudged to this Essay, the judges being gentlemen appointed by the Archbishop of Canterbury and the Bishops of London and Oxford. In the terms of the prospectus, the prize was offered "for the best statement and refutation, in English, of the fundamental errors (opposed to Christian Theism) of the Vedānta, Nyāya, and Sānkhya Philosophies, as set forth in the standard native authorities, in the Sanskrit language, treating of those systems; together with a demonstration (supported by such arguments, and conveyed in such a form and manner as may be most likely to prove convincing to learned Hindūs imbued with those errors), of the following fundamental principles of Christian Theism, viz. :—

"*First.*—Of the real, and not merely apparent or illusory, distinctness of God from all other spirits, and from matter; and of the creation (in the proper sense) of all other spirits, and of matter, by God, in opposition to the Vedānta.

1

"*Second.*—Of the non-eternity of separate souls, and their creation by God, in opposition to the Nyāya and Sānkhya.

"*Third.*—Of the creation of matter, in opposition to the tenet of its eternity in the shape of atoms (as maintained in the Nyāya and Vaiseshika Schools), or in the shape of Prakriti (as maintained by the Sānkhya).

"*Fourth.*—Of the moral character and moral government of God; and of the reality and perpetuity of the difference between moral good and evil with reference to such dogmas of the above systems as are opposed to these doctrines."

PREFACE.

THIS Essay, in its present shape, is but an imperfect sketch of what the writer would wish to offer as a help to the missionary among the learned Hindūs. Many topics, which might advantageously receive full treatment, are here scarcely more than indicated. With life and health, the writer will continuously prosecute his task towards its completion.

The five books " On Christianity as contrasted with Hindū Philosophy," which form the kernel of the following Essay, are given also in Sanskrit, with the omission of such incidental discussions as have reference exclusively to the missionary, and not to those whom the missionary has to teach.

There are some Sanskrit works, yet untranslated, which the writer must study before deciding upon his theological terminology for India. Among these works is the *Aphorisms of Sāndilya*. Sāndilya rejects the Hindū (gnostic) theory that *knowledge* is the one thing needful, and contends that knowledge is only the hand-

maid of *faith*.   Hence, however defective his views
may be in other respects, his work seems to promise
phraseology of which a Christian missionary may advantageously avail himself.   This remark might form
the text for an extended dissertation on the Christian's right to the theological language and the theological conceptions of his opponents.

If the present work were completed to the writer's
mind, he would next desire to be enabled to devote
himself to the translation and commentation of the
Bible in Sanskrit; taking book by book, not perhaps
in the order of the canon—for the completion of such
a work as is here intended is not to be looked for
in a lifetime—but in the order in which it might
seem most advisable to solicit the attention of inquirers,
from whom it would scarcely be advisable to withhold the New Testament till they should have threaded
all the historical details of the Old.   An occasional
watchword of Protestants, and a good one in its proper
place, is " The Bible without note or comment."   This
is right, when the design is to exclude such notes
and comments as those of the Douay version, and to
make appeal to the unbiassed judgment of Europeans,
as to the Romish and the reformed interpretations of
Scripture language.   But when, as in the case of the
Hindū inquirer, the question is not, *which* (of two or

more) is the meaning, but simply *what* is the meaning,—notes and comments become the helps or the substitutes of a living teacher. *English* clergymen have commentaries to refer to, and if we may ever look forward to an efficient native Christian clergy, these native clergymen also ought to be similarly supplied.

In speaking of a translation of the Bible in Sanskrit as a desideratum, the writer is very far indeed from ignoring the Sanskrit version of the Baptist missionaries; but his own investigations have shown him that this version—valuable as, in many respects, it is —was made at a time when Sanskrit *literature* had not been sufficiently examined to make a correct version possible. The mere mastery of the Grammar and the Dictionary does not give one the command of a language. As well might it be expected that the study of a mineralogical cabinet should make a geologist. Words, as well as rocks, to be rightly comprehended, must be studied *in situ*. A single example of our meaning will suffice, and we need go no further for it than the first verse of the first chapter of the Book of Genesis in the Sanskrit version of the Baptist missionaries. The Hindū is there told that, in the beginning, God created *ākāśa*[1] and *prithivī*.[2] Now in the dictionary, *ākāśa* will, no doubt, be found oppo-

[1] आकाश ॥   पृथिवी ॥

site the word "heaven," and *prithivī* opposite the word
"earth;" but if the books of the *Nyāya* philosophy
be looked into, it will be found that *ākāśa* is to be
regarded as *one* of the five elements (the five hypo-
thetical substrata of the five diverse qualities cognised
by the five senses severally), and that *prithivī* is another
of the five. Consequently, when the next verse proceeds to speak of the waters—a third one among the
five—the learned Hindū reader is staggered by the
doubt whether it is to be understood that the waters
were *uncreated*, or whether the sacred penman had
made an oversight. A Pandit once propounded this
dilemma, in great triumph, to myself; and he was
much surprised at finding that the perplexity could
be cleared up. But it is obvious what powers of mis-
chief we may place in the hands of unscrupulous opponents, by leaving our versions of Scripture thus needlessly open to cavil.

INTRODUCTION.

I CANNOT better prepare the reader to apprehend the design of this work than by submitting for his consideration the following remarks of the Rev. John Penrose, in his Bampton Lecture of the year 1808 :—[1]

"There is nothing which demands not only so much delicacy and address, but also so just and liberal a knowledge of human nature, as interference in matters of religion. It is manifest, however, from past history, and I know not that the experience of present times tends in any degree to invalidate the observation, that those persons who devote themselves to the missionary office, though often men of the most heroic disinterestedness, and sometimes of an acute and active genius, yet are rarely possessed of an enlarged and comprehensive intellect. In the immediate object which they are desirous of attaining—an object, indeed, of the highest worth and greatness—they appear somewhat too exclusively to concentrate all the faculties of their minds ; and, from want of an extended contemplation of human nature, to mistake the means by which that very object may be best

[Marginal note: Interference in matters of religion requires delicacy and address.]

[Marginal note: The importance of the end derogates not from the importance of the means.]

---

[1] Entitled,—"An attempt to prove the truth of Christianity from the wisdom displayed in its original establishment, and from the history of false and corrupted systems of religion."

attained. Eager to multiply conversions, they seem
naturally to fall into those imprudences which attend an
unenlightened spirit of proselytism. In some cases
[*e.g.*, that of the Jesuits], as we have seen, they accommodate Christianity to the idolatries of those to whom
they preach. In others, they forget that the same causes
Rude attacks on false religions, why un-advisable. which make religion necessary to mankind,
attach men to the religion in which they have
been bred, and that every rude attack serves only to
bind them to it more closely. These errors seem not to
imply any particular imputation of blame to individual
missionaries, but naturally to result from the constitu-
tional imperfection of mankind. Throughout India, and
other unconverted countries, they probably will extend
to all teachers of Christianity, whether of native or
European extraction. We rarely can find accuracy of
judgment united with that warmth of character which
is necessary to induce men to undertake the difficult and
dangerous office of promulgating Christianity to idolaters;
however useful they may esteem that office to be, however sublime. Those varied studies which discipline and
correct the mind lessen the intensity of its application to
any one pursuit. To improve reason has a tendency to
diminish zeal. I speak only of what usually is the tendency of such improvement, without examining whether
it is capable of being, or ought to be, counteracted.

The propaga-tion of Christi-anity,—how to be hoped from the dissemina-tion of know-ledge. "Should these observations be admitted,
they probably may lead us to infer that it is
not so much to the exertions of missionaries
that we must look for the future propagation
of Christianity, as to the general dissemination of know-

ledge. The indiscretions which it can scarcely, perhaps, be hoped that missionaries will be able to avoid, impede the end which they propose; but when those persons to whom our religion is offered shall be enabled to determine for themselves, concerning *its* records and evidences, they will learn to admit its truth on rational principles. When they shall add to the possession of our Scriptures, the sagacity to understand their meaning, and the judgment to appreciate their value, they will believe the doctrines which are taught in them. This belief, we may expect, will naturally Desirableness of converting the learned. descend from the more intelligent to the comparatively ignorant. Sound learning and just argument will triumph over fanaticism or error; will first convince the reason of the wise, and, by this means, will, in due time, overcome the prejudices of the vulgar; and thus Christianity will eventually be established by a progress contrary, indeed, to that which it experienced at its origin, but probably not less aptly suited to the altered circumstances of mankind.

"If this, in truth, be likely to be the case, How it is reasonable to suppose that Christianity should be propagated otherwise now than at its first introduction. so extraordinary a revolution in the manner of propagating our religion deserves serious consideration. It is an historical fact, entirely independent of the miraculous means by which it is said to have been effected, that Christianity was introduced into the world by low and uneducated men, and that men of rank and learning were afterwards, by degrees, converted to it. This fact appears, manifestly, to be an inversion in the ordinary progress of opinions, which are usually communicated from the wise to the ignorant, instead of being adopted from the ignorant by the wise. It accordingly has been considered by Christians as an important argument for the belief of a Divine interference in the original establishment of the Church. And

Evidence of the truth of the Christian religion furnished by the contrariety between the first and the subsequent order of its propagation. if it appears that things have now reverted to their natural order, even in the advancement of that very religion, in the foundation of which this order was interrupted; if it is to abilities and learning that we must now look for the extension and support of a religion which was first propagated by a few unlettered fishermen of Galilee; we have the stronger reason to admire the peculiarity of its origin, and to conclude that none but God could ever have enabled 'the foolish things of the world to confound the wise, and the weak things of the world to confound the things which are mighty.'"

How St. Paul dealt with the learned. In another place Mr. Penrose says:— "Once, at least, in the course of his ministry, St. Paul addressed himself to a learned, to an Athenian tribunal. He wisely adapted to local circumstances the mode in which he declared the existence of the Supreme. He alluded to a received theology: he quoted a philosophical poet."

I borrow these passages from Mr. Penrose instead of attempting to convey the same sentiments in my own words, the more readily, because the testimony thus borne to the importance of certain branches of learning, as subservient to the spread of Christianity, is not so liable as my own testimony, in respect of Hindū philosophy, might perhaps seem, to the· suspicion of a bias received from a favourite pursuit. It is not on the

ground of its intrinsic value (though I may have my own private opinion of its value), that I recommend the Hindū philosophy to *Hindū philosophy to be mastered not merely for itself—and why.*
the missionary among the Hindūs, as a thing to be mastered, not merely to be dipped into. It is in order that he may be under no temptation splenetically to turn his back upon the learned of the land, and to act as if only the uneducated had souls to be saved. I should wish that when the Missionary has occasion to address the learned of India, he should, like St. Paul, be able "wisely to adapt to local circumstances" the mode in which he declares his message. I should wish that here his "allusions to a received theology" should be such as tend to facilitate apprehension rather than such as are calculated to offend prejudice without altering conviction. I should wish his quotations from the philosophers to be more frequently, like St. Paul's, the winning advances of conciliation.

If the reader should glance at random over any part of the following work, it may perhaps seem to him that my practice differs from my precepts; for, instead of showing always how to conciliate, I have done my best to expose the errors of Hindūism, and, moreover, I have dealt with these in the dry dispassionate manner of a writer on Pathology. Let us attend first to the latter branch of this remark. The feelingless character appropriate to a pathological treatise is not proposed as a model to the physician in his practice; and just as little is it intended that the soul-slaying errors, here treated barely as if matters of scientific *The subject, notwithstanding the depth of the interests involved, why to be treated here with scientific unimpassionedness.*

examination, are to be regarded by the missionary in the calm spirit of speculation when he comes to deal with practical cases. In the fashioning and the tempering of a sword-blade, military ardour is not called for; nor even when we are studying the way to wield the weapon. But as nobody would suppose that we undervalued military ardour in the field of battle, because we employed caution and calmness in the previous tempering and exercising of our weapon, so nobody who reflects will probably fail to see that the consistent exclusion of passionate declamation throughout the following work implies no disparagement of passionate declamation in its proper place. Then, again, as to my having applied myself to the exposing the errors of Hindūism, while at the same time I urge the missionary more particularly to cast about for points of agreement, with a view to conciliation, there is here no real inconsistency; because he that best understands both the errors of his opponent and the means of refuting them, is the man who can most safely venture on making advances in the way of conciliation. I would have the missionary know well the errors of Hindūism, and also the means of their refutation, and yet I would have him reserve this knowledge till it is unmistakeably called for; lest, by provoking a contest on ground where he flatters himself he is certain of a victory, he should only needlessly awaken prejudices which had better, where possible, be left sleeping till they die.

We can most safely venture on conciliation, where we best know the errors which we must avoid seeming to countenance.

Prejudices not needlessly to be awakened.

There appears to be a growing conviction—in our

opinion a right one—that the confutation of *The confutation of Hindūism is not the first step, nor even the ism not the primary indispensable.* necessary preliminary, to the Christianization of India. This impression is akin to that under which Lord Bacon wrote the 35th aphorism of his *Novum Organum*, where, through a historical allusion to the expedition of Charles the Eighth into Italy, he explains how he seeks not contention, but a friendly hearing. "Borgia said, regarding the expe- *An example of Lord Bacon's to be followed.* dition of the French into Italy, that they came with chalk in their hands, that they might mark the inns, not with arms to break through. Such, in like manner, is our plan, that our doctrine may enter into fit and capacious minds; for there is no use of confutations when we differ about principles and notions themselves, and even about the forms of proof." But some of those who entertain this just impression, are apt to draw a wrong conclusion by coupling it with another premiss, which is by no means equally just. Bacon, as his readers are aware, did not *ignore* *Bacon's example not to be misinterpreted.* the opinions of those who differed from him. He was thoroughly versed in the opinions of those others; and this, while it enabled him, in pursuance of the conciliatory line of operations here adverted to, to avoid contention where contention would have been unprofitable, enabled him also to appropriate to the service of sound philosophy all the recognised truth which was not the less truth for having been embedded among the errors of an imperfect philosophy. The fact of Hindūism's not calling for confutation, does not imply that it may be safely neglected. Though not called upon to *volunteer* the confutation of Hindū errors, the missionary will do well to prepare himself to accomplish that task effectively when occasion imposes it upon him. The following work aspires to aid him in this preparation.

As invited by the suggester of this essay, we aim at refuting " the fundamental errors (opposed to Christian theism) of the Vedānta, Nyāya, and Sānkhya philosophies, as set forth in the standard native authorities in the Sanskrit language," etc. Let us commence with a general view of these Hindū systems of philosophy.

A GENERAL VIEW OF THE HINDŪ SYSTEMS OF PHILOSOPHY.

THE Hindūs have six systems of philo- The Hindū systems of philosophy. sophy, named the *Nyāya, Vaiseshika, Sānkhya, Yoga, Vedānta,* and *Mīmānsā.*[1] The *Vaiseshika* being in some sort supplementary to the *Nyāya,* the two are familiarly spoken of as one collective system, under the name of the *Nyāya* ; and as the case is somewhat similar with the two other pairs, it is customary to speak of Hindū philosophy as being divisible into the *Nyāya,* the *Sānkhya,* and the *Vedānta.*

These three systems, if we follow the com- Fundamental agreement of the three great systems. mentators, differ more in appearance than in reality ; and hence they are, each in its degree, viewed with a certain amount of favour by orthodox Hindūs. The partisans of one system may and do impugn the dogmas of another ; but, although every one in such a contest nerves his arm to the uttermost, and fights as if his character were staked upon the issue, yet the lances are lances of courtesy, and the blows are loving ones. It is a very different affair when the *denier of the Vedas* is dealt with. With the Buddhist,

[1] न्याय । वैशेषिक । साङ्ख्य । योग । वेदान्त । मीमांसा ॥

for example—though his notion of the chief end of man differs in no respect from that of the others— the battle is *a l'outrance*. The common bond of the others is their implicit acceptance of the Vedas, *which they explain differently*. According to the epigrammatic remark, that theological dislikes are inversely as the amount of disagreement, some might expect that these dissentient accepters of the Veda should be more bitter against one another than against the common enemy. But epigrams are not always to be trusted. As Dominican and Franciscan are brothers in asserting the infallibility of Rome ; so are the *Nyāya*, the *Sānkhya*, and the *Vedānta*, in asserting the infallibility of the Veda against the Buddhist.

How they differ.   Assuming, each of them implicitly, the truth of the Vedas, and proceeding to give, on that foundation, a comprehensive view of the totality of things, the three systems differ in their *point of view*. To illustrate this, suppose that three men in succession take up a cylindrical ruler : the one, viewing it with its end towards his eye, sees a circle ; the second, viewing it upright before his eye, sees a parallelo- gram ; the third, viewing it in a direction slanting away in front of his eye, sees a frustum of a cone. These three views are different, but nowise irrecon- cileable.   So far are they from being irreconcileable, that it might be argued that *all* of them must be accepted in succession, before any adequate concep- tion of the form of the ruler can be arrived at.   Now, in somewhat such a way the three Hindū systems differ mainly in their severally regarding the universe from different points of view,—viz., as it stands in relation severally to *sensation, emotion,* and *intellection.*

The *Naiyāyika,* founding on the fact that we have various *sensations,* enquires what and how many are the channels through which such varied knowledge flows in. Finding that there are five very different channels, he imagines five different externals adapted to these. Hence his theory of the five elements, the aggregate of what the *Nyāya* regards as the causes of affliction. *The Nyāya stand-point.*

The *Sānkhya,* struck with the fact that we have *emotions,*—with an eye to the question *whence* our impressions come,—enquires their *quality.* Are they pleasing, displeasing, or indifferent? These three qualities constitute, for him, the external; and to their aggregate he gives the name of Nature. With the *Naiyāyika* he agrees in wishing that he were well rid of all three; holding that things pleasing, and things indifferent, are not less incompatible with man's chief end than things positively displeasing. *The Sānkhya stand-point.*

Thus while the *Nyāya* allows to the external a substantial existence, the *Sānkhya* admits its existence only as an aggregate of qualities; while both allow that it really (eternally and necessarily) exists. *Precise distinction between the Nyāya and the Sānkhya stand-point.*

The *Vedāntin,* rising above the question as to what is pleasing, displeasing, or indifferent, asks simply, what *is,* and what is *not.* The categories are here reduced to two—the Real and the Unreal. The categories of the *Nyāya* and the *Sānkhya* were merely scaffolding for reaching this pinnacle of philosophy. The *The Vedānta stand-point.*

implied foundation was everywhere the same,—viz., the
Veda ; and this, therefore, we shall find is the field on
which the battle with Hindū philosophy must ultimately
be fought.

Respective subordination of the systems. The *Nyāya,* it may be gathered from what
has been said, is conveniently introductory to the
Sānkhya, and the *Sānkhya* to the *Vedānta.* Accordingly
in Hindū schools, where all three are taught, it is in
this order that the learner, who learns all three, takes
them up. The *Nyāya* is the exoteric doctrine, the
Sānkhya a step nearer what is held as the truth, and the
Vedānta the esoteric doctrine, or the naked truth.

Corresponding distribution of the present work. This view of the matter suggests the distribution of the following work. A separate
account of each of the three systems is first given; and
then a summary of Christian doctrine is propounded, in
the shape of aphorisms, after the fashion of the Hindū
philosophers, with a commentary, on each aphorism, com-
bating whatever in any of the three Hindū systems is
opposed to the reception of the Christian doctrine
therein propounded. A systematic exposition of the
dogmas of Christianity seems to furnish the likeliest
means of inviting the discussion of the essential points
of difference,—any points of difference in philosophy
that do not emerge in the course of such an exposition
being, we may reasonably assume, comparatively unimportant to the Christian argument.

SUMMARY OF THE NYĀYA PHILOSOPHY.

The *Nyāya*, as already remarked, offers the General character of the Nyāya system. sensational aspect of Hindū philosophy. In saying this, it is not meant that the *Nyāya* confines itself to sensation, excluding emotion and intellection; nor, that the other two systems ignore the fact of sensation; but that the arrangement of this system of philosophy has a more pointed regard to the fact of the five senses than either of the others has, and treats the external more frankly as a solid reality.

The word *Nyāya* means "propriety or fit- Meaning of the name. ness." The system undertakes to declare the *proper method* of arriving at that knowledge of the truth, the fruit of which, it promises, is the chief end of man. The name is also used, in a more limited application, to denominate the proper method of setting forth an *argument*. This has led to the practice of calling the *Nyāya* the "Hindū Logic,"—a name which suggests a very inadequate conception of the scope of the system.

The *Nyāya* system was delivered by GAU- The Nyāya text-book. TAMA in a set of aphorisms so very concise that they must from the first have been accompanied by a commentary, oral or written. The aphorisms of the several Hindū systems, in fact, appear designed not so much to *communicate* the doctrine of the particular schools as to *aid*, by the briefest possible suggestions, the memory of him to whom the doctrine shall have been *already* communicated. To this end they are in general admirably adapted. The sixty aphorisms, for example, which constitute the first of Gautama's Five Lectures, present a methodical summary of the whole system; while the first aphorism, again, of the sixty, presents a summary

Summary of
the topics. of these sixty. The first aphorism is as follows:—"From knowledge of the truth in regard to evidence, the ascertainable, doubt, motive, example, dogma, confutation, ascertainment, disquisition, controversy, cavil, fallacy, perversion, futility, and occasion for rebuke, there is the attainment of the *summum bonum*."[1]

Beatitude the
result of know-
ledge. In the next aphorism it is declared how knowledge operates mediately in producing this result. "Pain, birth, activity, fault, false notions, —since on the successive departure of these in turn there is the departure of the antecedent one, there is Beatitude."[2] That is to say,—when knowledge of the truth is attained to, false notions depart; on their departure, the fault of concerning one's-self about any external object ceases; thereupon the enlightened sage ceases to *act;* then, there being no actions that call for either reward or punishment, there is no occasion, after his death, for his being born again to receive reward or punishment; then, not being born again, so as to be liable to pain, there is no room for pain;—and the absence of pain is the *Nyāya* conception of the *summum bonum.*

---

[1] प्रमाण्प्रमेयसंश्यप्रयोजनदृष्टान्तसिद्धान्तावयवतर्कनिर्णयवादजल्पवि-तण्डाहेत्वाभासच्छलजातिनिग्रहस्थानानां तत्त्वज्ञानानि:श्रेयसाधिगमः॥१॥

[2] दुःखजन्मप्रवृत्तिदोषमिथ्याज्ञानानामुत्तरोत्तरापाये तदनन्तरापाया दपवर्गः ॥ २ ॥

Well, have we *instruments* adapted to the acquisition of a knowledge of the truth? He tells us:— The means of right knowledge. "Proofs [*i.e.*, instruments of right knowledge], are the senses, the recognition of signs, the recognition of likeness, and speech [or testimony]."[1] As the present work is concerned with those errors only which are opposed to Christian Theism, it would be irrelevant here to discuss, at any length, the question whether the *Nyāya* is justified in asserting, or the other systems in denying, that the determining of something by "the recognition of a likeness," is specifically different from the determining of something by the recognition of a sign; but it may be worth while to explain the nature of the dispute, because it suggests a caution which is practically important. Let the example be the stock one of the *Nyāya* books. "Some one unacquainted with the meaning of the term *Bos Gavaeus* is told by a forester that the *Bos Gavaeus* is an animal like a cow. Going thereafter to the forest, and remembering the purport of what he has been told, he sees an animal like a cow. Thereupon arises the 'cognition from likeness' that this is what is meant by the term *Bos Gavaeus*."[2] Now it has been asked, what is there here different from the recognition of a sign? What is here recognised, is the likeness to a cow, and this is the sign by means of which we infer that the animal is the Bos Gavaeus. The *Naiyā-yika* replies, that there is the following difference. In the

---

[1] प्रत्यचानुमानोपमानशब्दाः प्रमाणानि ॥ ३ ॥

[2] गवयशब्दवाच्यमजानन् कुतश्चिदारण्यकपुरुषान्नोसदृशो गवय इति श्रुत्वा वनं गतो वाक्यार्थं स्मरन् गोसदृश्यपिण्डं पश्यति । तदनन्तरमसौ गवयशब्दवाच्य इत्युपमितिरुत्पद्यते । इति तर्कसंग्रहः ॥

case of knowledge arrived at by means of a sign, we must, he contends, have inductively ascertained that so and so is a sign; and in the present instance there has been no induction.   So much for this disputed

A caution to the missionary. point; and we advert to it in order to caution the missionary not to attribute too great importance to this and similar real or seeming discrepancies between the several systems, when he meets with any such mutually conflicting views.   The dispute is frequently verbal only, as in the present instance, where the dispute turns on the question whether an indicated "likeness" is or is not entitled to be called by the name of sign.   And even where the difference is real, the Hindūs have long ago reconciled all the discrepancies to their own entire satisfaction, so that he who warmly insists upon the existence of the discrepancy gains credit only for being ignorant of the recognised means of harmonious reconcilement.   He is regarded very much as the confident supporter of some stale sceptical objection to Christianity is regarded in a company of orthodox Christians.   Whether the founders of the Hindū systems attributed no more importance to their mutual discrepancies than is attributed to them by their modern followers, may be open to question; but the practical caution here suggested is not the less worthy of attention.   Opportunities, no doubt, may occur, where the discrepancies between the several systems may be urged with effect; and here the missionary must use his discretion, always bearing in mind the general caution not to lay too much stress on what will in most cases practically go for nothing as an argument.

To return to Gautama : if we have instruments for the obtaining of right knowledge, what are the objects in regard to which we have to obtain right knowledge by means of the appropriate instruments? These he enumerates as follows : — "Soul, body, sense, sense-object, knowledge, the mind, activity, fault, transmigration, fruit, pain, and beatitude,—are that regarding which we are to have right knowledge."[1] Here it is to be carefully observed that the soul (*ātman*) is spoken of as an entirely different entity from the mind (*manas*). The neglect of this distinction may bring a debate with a Hindū into inextricable confusion. The English reader who is accustomed to hear the words soul and mind (*anima* and *mens* —ψυχη and φρην) employed interchangeably, must not carry this laxness of phraseology into any Indian dialect, if he desires to be understood, and if he desires to avoid such misconceptions as that of Ritter, who makes the *Naiyāyika* call the soul an *atom*, whereas the *Naiyāyika* calls the soul *all-pervading*, and the *mind* an atom,[2]—or that of Cousin, who makes out the *Sānkhya* to be a materialist, as if he derived *soul* from Nature, whereas the *Sānkhya* only derives the soul's *organs*—external and internal—from something other than soul.[3] In the

Objects regarding which we may have right knowledge.

---

[1] आत्मशरीरेन्द्रियार्थबुद्धिमनःप्रवृत्तिदोषप्रेत्यभावफलदुःखापवर्गास्तु प्रमेयम् ॥ ९ ॥

[2] Of the Soul it is declared—(see our version of the *Tarka-sangraha*, §§ 20, 21)— that it is "different in each body—*all-pervading* and eternal"—जीवः प्रतिशरीरं भिन्नो विभुर्नित्यश्च—; while of the Mind it is declared that "it is in the form of an *atom*, and eternal"—परमाणुरूपं नित्यश्च ॥ Ritter (at p. 376, vol. iv. of his *History of Ancient Philosophy*, as rendered by Mr. Morrison,) assumes that it is a "principle of the *Nyāya*, that the soul is an atom."

[3] M. Cousin (*Cours de l'Hist. de la Philosophie*, vol. ii., p. 125), speaking of the "principles" of the *Sānkhya*, says correctly, "Il y en vingt-cinq." These he

Hindū systems, the soul is the *self,* and the mind is the organ or faculty, which, standing between the self and the deliverances of sense, prevents those deliverances from crowding in pell-mell; just as a minister stands between the monarch and the thousand simultaneous claims upon his attention, and hands up for his consideration one thing at a time. We offer here no opinion on this theory of the Hindūs; we only put the reader on his guard in respect of an established phraseology, the misconception of which has so egregiously misled Ritter and Cousin. What Gautama under-

Soul. stands by soul, he tells us as follows: — "Desire, aversion, volition, pleasure, pain, and knowledge, are that whereby we recognise soul (*ātman*)."[1]

Mind. Of the mind he speaks as follows:—"The sign [whereby we infer the existence] of the mind (*manas*) is the not arising of cognitions [in the soul] simultaneously."[2] Grant that our cognitions are consecutive and not simultaneous. To account for this,

enumerates in a note, giving, as the *Sānkhya* philosophers do, "l'intelligence, bouddhi," as the second in the list; "*manas, mens,*" as the eleventh; and soul, "l'âme," as the twenty-fifth. All of these three, unlike the *Sānkhya* philosophers, he derives from one and the same source; for he says, "voici quel est le principe premier des choses, duquel dérivent tous les autres principes: c'est prakriti ou moula prakriti, la nature, 'la matière eternelle sans formes, sans parties, la cause materielle, universelle, qu'on peut induire de ses effets, qui produit et n'est pas produite.'" Now of this radical Nature, "l'intelligence, bouddhi," as well as the soul's internal organ, "*manas, mens,*" is reckoned by the *Sānkhya* to be a product; but the notion that the *soul* is either identical with, or anywise akin to, this or any other *product,* is positively the one notion which the *Sānkhya* labours to *eradicate.* In the words of the third of the *Sānkhya Kārikās,* "Soul is neither a production nor productive,"— न प्रक्षतिर्न विक्षतिः पुरुष: ॥ That liberation is held by the *Sānkhya* to ensue solely on the *discriminating* of Soul from Nature and the products of Nature, see Aphorism 105, quoted *infra,* p. xxx.

[1] इच्छाद्वेषप्रयत्नसुखदुःखज्ञानान्यात्मनो लिङ्गम् ॥ १० ॥
[2] युगपत् ज्ञानानुत्पत्तिर्मनसो लिङ्गम् ॥ १६ ॥

Dugald Stewart tells us that the mind can attend to only one thought at a time. Gautama, recognising the same fact, but speaking of the *knower* invariably as *soul*, accounts for the fact in question by assuming that there is an *instrument*, or internal organ, termed the *mind*, through which alone can knowledge reach the soul, and which, as it gives admission to only one thought at a time, the *Naiyāyika* infers must be no larger than an atom. The conception of such an atomic inlet to the soul may be illustrated by the case of the eye; inasmuch as while the whole body is presented to the rays reflected from external objects, it is only through a special channel, the organ of vision, that these find entrance so as to cause knowledge. The soul, then, may be practically regarded as corresponding to the thinking principle, and the mind (*manas*) to the faculty of attending to one, and only one, thing at a time; it being further to be kept in remembrance, in case of accidents, that the *Naiyāyika* reckons the mind to be a substance and not a faculty.[1]

In the list of the objects, regarding which   Activity. right knowledge is to be, obtained, the next after mind is activity (*pravritti*). This is defined as "that which originates the [utterances of the] voice, the [cognitions of the] understanding, and the [gestures of the] body."[2] This "activity," we have seen under Aph. 2nd, Gau-

---

[1] To quote the *Tarka-sangraha* :—

तच द्रव्याणि पृथिव्यप्तेजोवाय्वाकाशकालदिगात्ममनांसि नवैव ॥

"The substances (*dravya*) are just nine,—earth (*prithivī*), water (*ap*), light (*tejas*), air (*vāyu*), ether (*ākās'a*), time-(*kāla*), place (*dis'*), soul (*ātman*), and mind (*manas*)."

[2] प्रवृत्तिर्वाग्बुद्धिशरीरारम्भः ॥ १७ ॥

tama regards with an evil eye, as the cause of birth, which is the cause of pain, which it is the *summum bonum* to get permanently rid of.

What the Nyáya reckons a fault. Gautama holds that it is through our own "fault" (*dosha*) that we are active; and he tells us that "faults [or failings] have this characteristic, that they cause activity."[1] These faults are classed under the heads of affection (*rága*), aversion (*dwesha*), and stolidity (*moha*), each of which he regards as a fault or defect, inasmuch as it leads to actions, the recompense of which, whether good or evil, must be received in some birth, or state of mundane existence, to the postponement of the great end of entire emancipation. The immediate obstacle to emancipation, styled "Transmigration" (*pretyabhāva*), he next defines.

Transmigration. "Transmigration means the arising again [and again]."[2] According to the commentator, the word here rendered "transmigration," viz., *pretyabhāva*, is formed out of *pretya*, "having died," and *bhāva*,

---

[1] प्रवर्त्तनालचणा दोषा: ॥ १८ ॥ Mr. Colebrooke appears to have viewed the term which we have rendered *causer* of activity, as if it had signified *caused* by activity; for, with reference to Gautama's definition of "fault" (*dosha*), he says (see his *Essays*, vol. i., p. 289), "From acts proceed faults (*dosha*), including under this designation, passion," etc. It would seem as if Mr. Colebrooke, when giving to his essay a final revision, after having laid it aside for a time, had been struck with the oddness of the expression that "from faults proceed acts," and had reversed it without adverting it to the technical definition of "faults," in the same sentence, as the passions which give *rise* to action. Gautama, the votary of quietism, gives to the passions the name of "faults" with a significance akin to that which the word bore in the remark of Talleyrand on the murder of the Duc D'Enghien,—"ce n'était pas une crime, c'était une *faute:*"—it was a positive *blunder*. The wise man, according to Gautama, is he who avoids the three *blunders* of having a liking for a thing and acting accordingly; or of having a dislike for a thing, and acting accordingly; or of being *stupidly* indifferent, and thereupon acting; instead of being *intelligently* indifferent, and not acting at all.

[2] पुनरुत्पत्ति: प्रेत्यभाव: ॥ १९ ॥

"the becoming [born into the world again]." "As, by the expression 'again,' here *habitualness* is meant to be implied,—there is first a birth, then death, then a birth; thus transmigration, commencing with a birth, ends [only] with [final] emancipation."[1]

After defining pain (*du'kha*) as "that which is characterised by uneasiness,"[2] he declares that "absolute deliverance therefrom is emancipation (*aparvarga*)."[3]

Pain and final emancipation.

Such is, in brief, Gautama's theory of the *summum bonum* and the means of its attainment. His *summum bonum* is absolute deliverance from pain; and this deliverance is to be attained by an abnegation of all action, good or bad. We proceed to review the *Sānkhya* theory.

SUMMARY OF THE SĀNKHYA PHILOSOPHY.

The *Sānkhya*, as already observed, makes a step in advance of the *Nyāya*, towards the ultimate simplification aimed at in the *Vedānta*, by reducing the external from the category of *substance* to that of *quality*. Souls alone are, in the *Sānkhya*, regarded as substances; whatever affects the soul being

General character of the system.

---

[1] प्रेत्य मृत्वा भावो जननं प्रेत्यभावः । तच्च पुनरित्यनेनाभ्यासकथनात् प्रागुत्पत्तिस्ततो मरणं तत उत्पत्तिरिति प्रेत्यभावो जननादिरपवर्गान्तः ॥

Hence Mr. Colebrooke's definition of *pretyabhava* as the "condition of the soul after death" (see his *Essays*, vol. i., p. 290), while it is literally correct, may mislead the reader if he does not bear in mind that this, according to Hindū notions, is the condition of *every man now alive*; for as we are all supposed to have lived and died, one knows not how often, we are each of us always in the condition "after death."

[2] बाधनालचणं दुःखम् ॥ २१ ॥

[3] तद्त्यन्तविमोचो ऽपवर्गः ॥ २२ ॥

ranged under the head of a quality,—1, pleasing; 2, displeasing; or, 3, indifferent. This mode of viewing the universe we have designated the emotional view of things.

The word *Sānkhya* means "numeral, rational, or discriminative." The system promises beati-
Meaning of the name.
tude as the reward of that discrimination which rightly distinguishes between soul and nature. What is here meant by "nature" will be explained presently.

The Sānkhya text-book.
The *Sānkhya* system was delivered by KAPILA in a set of aphorisms no less concise than those of the *Nyāya*. Kapila begins by defining the
The chief end of man.
chief end of man. His first aphorism is as follows:—"Well, the complete cessation of pain, of three kinds, is the complete end of man."[1] By the three kinds of pain are meant—1, diseases and griefs, etc., which are intrinsic, or inherent in the sufferer; 2, injuries from ordinary external things; and, 3, injuries from things supernatural or meteorological. In his 19th aphorism he declares that the bondage (*bandha*) under which the soul (*purusha*) groans, is due to its conjunction with nature (*prakriti*); and this bondage is merely *seeming*, because soul is "ever essentially a pure and free intelligence." His words are,—"But not without the conjunction thereof [*i.e.* of nature] is there the connection of that [*i.e.* of pain] with that [*viz.* with the soul] which is ever essentially a pure and free intelligence."[2] In his 59th aphorism, he says again, of the soul's

---

[1] अथ त्रिविधदुःखात्यन्तनिवृत्तिरत्यन्तपुरुषार्थः ॥ १ ॥

[2] न नित्यशुद्धबुद्धमुक्तस्वभावस्य तद्योगस्तद्योगादृते तु ॥ १९ ॥

bondage,—"It is merely verbal, and not a reality, since it resides in [the soul's organ] the *mind* [and not in the soul or self],"[1] on which the commentator observes,—"That is to say, since bondage, etc., resides only in the mind (*chitta*), all this, as far as concerns the soul (*purusha*), is merely verbal,—*i.e.*, it is 'vox et praeterea nihil,' because it is merely a *reflection*, like the redness of [pellucid] crystal [when a China rose is near it], but not a reality, with no false imputation, like the redness of the China rose itself."[2]

Of nature, which, by its so-much-to-be- Nature, what. deprecated conjunction, makes the soul seem to be in bondage when it really is not, he gives in his 62nd aphorism the following account:—"Nature (*prakriti*) is the state of equipoise of goodness (*sattwa*), passion (*rajas*), and darkness (*tamas*); — from nature [proceeds] intellect (*mahat*), from intellect self-consciousness (*ahankāra*), from self-consciousness the five subtile elements (*tanmātra*) and both sets [external and internal] of organs (*indriya*), and from the subtile elements the gross elements (*sthūla-bhūta*); [then besides there is] soul (*purusha*);—such is the class of twenty-five."[3]

It might be interesting to probe the precise philosophic import of the successive development alleged in

---

[1] वाङ्मात्रं नतु तत्त्वं चित्तस्थिते: ॥ ५१ ॥

[2] बन्धादीनां सर्वेषां चित्त एवावस्थानात्तत्सर्वमुरुषे वाङ्मात्रं शब्दमात्रं स्फटिकलौहित्यवत्प्रतिविम्बमाचलात् नतु तत्त्वमनारोपितं जवालौहित्य-वदित्यर्थ: ॥

[3] सत्त्वरजस्तमसां साम्यावस्था प्रकृति: प्रकृतेर्महान् महतो ऽहङ्कारो ऽहङ्कारात्पञ्च तन्मात्राणि उभयमिन्द्रियं तन्मात्रेभ्य: स्थूलभूतानि पुरुष इति पञ्चविंशतिगण: ॥ ६२ ॥

the foregoing aphorism; but the special aim of the
present treatise (or of this treatise in its present shape)
forbids whatever excursion can be safely dispensed with.

Liberation,
what and
when.
We shall here, therefore, only add, that we
are told, in aphorism 105, that "experience
[whether of pleasure or pain, liberation from both of
which is desiderated], ends with [the discrimination of]
thought [*i.e.* soul, as contradistinguished from nature]";[1]
that a plurality of souls, in opposition to the *Vedânta,* is
asserted in aphorism 150, "From the diverse allotment
of birth, etc., the plurality of souls [is to be inferred]";[2]
and that the paradoxical conception of the soul in bondage, whilst not really in bondage, may be illustrated by
Don Quixote hanging in the dark from the ledge of a
supposed enormous precipice, and bound to hold on for
his life till daybreak, from not knowing that his toes
were within six inches of the ground.

Annihilation
not sought.
It may be proper to observe that the
Sânkhya explicitly repudiates the charge of
craving *annihilation.* In aphorism 47 we are told that,
"In neither way [whether as a means or as an end] is
this [viz., annihilation] the soul's aim."[3]

We next advance to a survey of the *Vedânta* theory.

---

[1] चिद्वसानो भोगः ॥ १०५ ॥ That the word "thought" (*chit*) here means
"soul" (*âtman*) we are told by the commentator—चिदात्मा ॥

[2] जन्मादिव्यवस्थातः पुरुषबहुत्वम् ॥ १५० ॥

[3] अपुरुषार्थत्वमुभयथा ॥ ४७ ॥

SUMMARY OF THE VEDĀNTA SYSTEM.

The Vedānta theory arrives at the limit of *Its great tenet.* simplification, by deciding that nothing really exists besides *one*, and that this one real being is absolutely simple. This one simple being, according to the *Vedānta*, is *knowledge* (*jnāna*),—not the knowledge *of* anything, for this would imply a contradiction to the dogma that nothing exists except knowledge simply. This conception, of the possible nature of knowledge, is quite at variance with the European view, which regards knowledge as the synthesis of subject and object. According to the *Vedanta* there is *no* object, and hence it follows that the term subject is not strictly applicable, any more than is the term substance,[1] to the one reality. Both of these terms, being indicative of a relation, are inapplicable under a theory which, denying duality, does not admit the conditions of a relation. Soul, the one reality, *The one reality, how designated.* is accordingly spoken of in the *Vedānta*, not as a substance (*dravya*) as it is reckoned in the *Nyāya*, but as the *thing*, or, literally, "that which abides" (*vastu*). Let us enquire how this conception may have been arrived at, consistently with the seeming existence of the world.

Suppose that God — omnipresent, omnis- *Possible course of the Vedāntin's speculations.* cient, and omnipotent — exists. Suppose, further, that, at some time or other, God

---

[1] At the opening of the *Vedānta-Sāra*, indeed, the one is spoken of as the substratum of all (*akhilādhāra*); but the existence of aught else being subsequently denied, it remains ultimately the substratum of nothing, or no *sub*-stratum at all.

exists and nothing else does. Suppose, in the next
place, as held long in Europe and still in India, that
nothing is made out of nothing (*ex nihilo nihil fit*); and
suppose, finally, that God wills to make a world. Being
omnipotent, He *can* make it. The dogma "ex nihilo
nihil fit" being, by the hypothesis, an axiom, it follows
that God, being able to make a world, can make it
without making it out of *nothing*. The world so made
must then consist of what previously existed,—*i.e.* of
God. Now what do we understand by a world? Let
it be an aggregate of souls with limited capacities—
and of what these souls (rightly or wrongly) regard
as objects—the special or intermediate causes of various
modes of consciousness. Taking this to be what is
meant by a world, how is God to form it out of Himself? God is omniscient,—and, in virtue of his omnipresence, his omniscience is everywhere. Where is the
room for a *limited* intelligence? Viewing the matter
(if that were strictly possible) *à priori*, one would incline to say "nowhere." But the Vedāntin, before he
had got this length, was too painfully affected by the
conviction, forced upon him, as on the rest of
us, by a consciousness which will take no
denial, that there *are* limited intelligences. "I am
ignorant," he says; and if he is *wrong* in saying so,
then (as a Pandit once remarked to me) his ignorance
is established just as well as if he were right in saying
so. Holding, then, that the soul *is* God, and confronted
with the inevitable fact that the soul does *not* spontaneously *recognize* itself as God, there was nothing for
it but to make the fact itself do duty as its own cause,

Why igno-
rance must be
admitted.

to say that the soul does not know itself to be God, just because it does not know it,—*i.e.* because it is ignorant, —*i.e.* because it is obstructed by ignorance (*ajnāna*).[1]

At this point let us suppose that our speculator stopped, but that a disciple took up the matter and tried to make something more palpably definite out of the indefinite term *ignorance*. Were it not, he argues, for this *ajnāna*, of which my teacher speaks, the soul would know itself to be God, —there would be nothing but God,—there would be no world. It is this *ajnāna*, then, that *makes* the world; and, this being the case, it ought to have a name suggestive of the fact. Let it be called *prakriti*, the name by which the *Sānkhyas* speak of their unconscious maker of worlds.[2] Good, says another; but recollect that this *prakriti*, or "energy," can be nothing else than the power of the All-powerful, for we can admit the independent existence of God alone; so that the *ajnāna* which you have shown to be entitled to the name of *prakriti*, will be even more accurately denoted by the word *sakti*,[3] God's "power," by an exertion of which power alone the fact can be accounted for, that souls which are God *do not know* that they are so. The reasoning is accepted, and the term *sakti* is enrolled among the synonymes of *ajnāna*. Lastly comes the mythologist. You declare, says he, that this world would

How Ignorance may have got its various synonymes.

---

[1] अज्ञान ॥

[2] See the *Sānkhya* Aphorism, B. I. § 127,—त्रिगुणाचेतनत्वादि द्वयोः ॥१२७॥ "Of both [nature, or 'the radical energy,' and her products] the fact that they consist of the three qualities, and that they are *unthinking*, etc. [is the common property]."

[3] शक्ति ॥

not even appear to be real, were it not for *ignorance*. Its apparent reality, then, is an *illusion*; and for the word *ajnāna* you had better substitute the more expressive term *māyā*,[1] " deceit, illusion, jugglery." The addition of this to the list of synonymes, being acquiesced in, the mythologist furnishes his *māyā* with all the requisites of a goddess, and she takes her seat in his pantheon as the wife of *Brahmā* the Creator.

Ignorance, how defined in the Vedānta.   The definition of "ignorance," in the *Vedānta*, requires notice. Ignorance, we are informed, is "a somewhat that is not to be called positively either real or unreal, — [not a mere negation, but] in the shape of an entity, the opponent of knowledge,—consisting of the three fetters."[2] According to the *Naiyāyikas*, *ajnāna* is merely the privation (*abhāva*) of *jnāna*. To exclude such a meaning here it is asserted to be "in the shape of an entity" (*bhāva-rūpa*). The description of it as something "not to be called positively either real or unreal" corresponds with Plato's ὸν καὶ μὴ ὸν, as distinguished from the ὸντως ὸν.[3] The distinction is that of the phenomenal and the real. The universe being held to be the joint result of soul and ignorance, and soul being the only substance, or "substratum of all," it follows that ignorance is equivalent to and identical with the sum total of *qualities*. These, as in the *Sānkhya* system, are held to be three; so that ignorance, as we have just seen, is spoken of as "con-

---

[1] माया ॥

[2] अज्ञानन्तु सदसद्भ्यामनिर्वचनीयं चिगुणात्मकं भावरूपं ज्ञानविरोधि यत्किञ्चिदिति वदन्ति ॥

[3] See Sir Wm. Hamilton's note on Reid's works, p. 262.

sisting of the three qualities" (*trigunatmaka*), or, as it may be also rendered, "consisting of the three *fetters*," the word for "quality" (viz., *guna*), meaning originally a "fetter," and these two senses, in Hindū philosophy, being closely related.[1] Let us see what can have led to the division of quality into three.

The one reality—the universal substratum—being veiled by the garb of the phenomenal world, certain marked distinctions of character among the phenomena present themselves. We have phenomena of pure cognition, of lively emotion, and, finally, of inertness, or, in Shakspere's phrase, "cold obstruction." To one or other of these three heads every phenomenon may, with a little ingenuity, be referred. The three heads are named respectively, in Sanskrit, *sattwa*, *rajas*, and *tamas*.[2] According to the commentators, the first of the qualities, whilst endlessly subdivisible into calmness, complacency, patience, rejoicing, etc., consists summarily of *happiness*. The second, on the other hand, consists summarily of *pain*. To these categories belong almost all the sensations and thoughts of thinking beings;—scarcely any feeling, viewed strictly, being one of sheer *indifference*. This *indifference*, the third of the qualities, is exemplified in

[margin note: Why Ignorance is held to consist of three qualities.]

---

[1] See the *Sānkhya Pravachana Bhāshya* on Aphorism 62, Bk I., viz. :—

अत्र शास्त्रे श्रुत्यादौच गुणशब्दः पुरुषोपकरणत्वात्पुरुषप्रयोजनसम्बन्धकत्विगुणात्म-कमहदादिरज्जुनिर्मातृत्वाच्च प्रयुज्यते ॥ "In this [*Sānkhya*] system, and in Scripture, etc., the word 'quality' (*guna*) is employed [as the name of the three things under discussion], because they are subservient to soul [and hold a secondary rank in the scale of being], and because they form the *cords* [which the word *guna* also signifies], viz., understanding, etc., which consist of the three [so-called] qualities, and which *bind*, as if it were a [cow or other] brute, the soul."

[2] सत्त्व । रजस् । तमस् ॥

its highest potency in such things as stocks and stones, where soul, the substratum of these as of all else, is altogether "immersed in matter," or obfuscated by the quality of *darkness*, as the word *tamas*, the name of the quality, literally signifies. In its lower potencies this third of the qualities exemplifies itself in sloth, drowsiness, etc.

These three qualities, separately or commingled, more or less obscure the soul, which is held to be simple *knowledge—jñāna*; and as the aggregate of them is the opposite of soul, or, in other words, *not*-soul, the aggregate, as we have seen, takes the name of *a-jñāna*, *i.e. not*-knowledge, or "ignorance." The soul is often spoken The operation of the qualities illustrated. of as a *light*. Now, suppose a lamp to be enclosed in a lamp-shade; the glass may be either so pure that the light passes through scarcely diminished; or it may be stained, so that the light is tinged and partly dimmed; or the lamp-shade may be of opaque materials, so that the light within is altogether obstructed. These three cases may perhaps illustrate the supposed operation of the three qualities, as well as account for the names by which they are spoken of as "purity," "foulness," and "darkness" (*sattwa, rajas,* and *tamas*).

"Ignorance," according to the *Vedānta*, has two *powers*; that by which it *envelopes* soul, giving rise to the conceit of personality or conscious individuality, and that by which it *projects* the phantasmagoria of a world which the individual regards as external to himself.[1] Soul thus invested is what the universe consists of.

---

[1] अस्त्यज्ञानस्यावरणविक्षेपनामकं शक्तिद्वयमस्ति ॥

The supposed root of all evil—the belief that aught besides the "one" exists—is to be got rid of, *Means of emancipation, according to the Vedānta.* we are told, by a right understanding of the great sentence, "That art thou," *i.e.,* "Thou—whosoever thou art—art the one." When this dictum has been rightly understood and accepted, the accepter of it, changing the "thou" to the first person, reflects thus—"*I* am the one." This is so far well; but he must finally get rid of the habit of making even *himself* an *object* of thought. There must be *no* object. What was previously the *subject* must now remain alone,—an entity, a thought, a joy; but these three being one only—the existent joy-thought.[1]

Let us now contrast the scheme of Christian revelation with these three Hindū theories of man and of the universe.

[1] See our "Lecture on the *Vedānta,* embracing the text of the *Vedānta Sāra*" (Allahabad, 1851), §§ 95-152.

CHRISTIANITY

CONTRASTED WITH

HINDŪ PHILOSOPHY.

BOOK I.

A PARTIAL EXPOSITION OF CHRISTIAN DOCTRINE.

MAY God, the giver of all good, the Saviour of those who believe on Him, accept this my humble effort in His service; and may the hearers of it, those skilled in the *Vedānta*, the *Sānkhya*, and the *Nyāya*, with discriminating judgment examine it candidly.[1]

In the first place the writer states the subject of the proposed work.

स देव: सर्वकल्याणदाता भक्तजनाविता । अनुगृह्णातु सेवेति प्रणतस्य.मम श्रमम् ॥ श्रोतारश्चापि वेदान्तसाङ्ख्यायविशारदा: । परीच- न्नामिदं बुद्ध्या विवेकिन्या वि- मत्सरा: ॥

तचादौ चिकीर्षितस्य ग्रन्थ- स्य विषयमाह ।

---

[1] As an argument can be satisfactorily addressed only to one whose sentiments are definitely known, what follows in Sanskrit is addressed, we may remark, to the Vedāntin who knows and values the *Nyāya* and the *Sānkhya* as introductory to the *Vedānta*. The question here is not what do those need to be told who know nothing, but what do those need to be told who know just what Hindūism can tell.

APHORISM I.

The inquiry what. Now the inquiry regards the means of the attainment of the chief end of man.

अथ परमपुरुषार्थप्राप्त्युपायजिज्ञासा ॥ १ ॥

(1) Next he states the definition of the chief end of man.

। १ । अथ परमपुरुषार्थस्य लचणमाच ।

APHORISM II.

Man's chief end. Man's chief end is to glorify God, and enjoy Him for ever.

देवमाचात्म्यवर्द्धनमनन्तं तत्सान्निध्यसुखाखादनचेति द्वयं परमपुरुषार्थः ॥ २ ॥

(1) What is God, will be stated in the fifth Aphorism. If it be said that it is impossible to glorify God because man cannot add in the slightest degree to the glory of God, we reply:—Not so,—because by glorifying God we mean the acknowledging His perfections, and behaving suitably to them, by trusting, loving, and obeying Him.

। १ । देवस्य लचणं पञ्चमसूचे वच्च्यते । ननु देवमाचात्म्यवर्द्धनं न सम्भवति देवमचात्मे खेग्रतो ऽप्याधिकस्य पुरुषेण विधातुमशक्यलादिति चेन्न । तन्माचात्म्यवर्द्धनस्य तदीयगुणपूर्त्तिंखीकारः अङ्ग्या भक्यानुवृत्त्याच तङ्गुणानुरूपाचरणमिति द्वयरूपलात् ।

(2) To enjoy God [to experience the joy of His pre-

। २ । तत्सान्निध्यसुखाखा-

sence] is to be the object of His special favour here and hereafter.

(3) But the *Nyāya* [Bk. I., § 22] says that the chief end of man is the absolute cessation of pain; and the *Sānkhya* [Bk. I., § 1] says that it is entire liberation from all the three kinds of pain : why, abandoning that simpler view, is this new definition made ? If you say this, then take this in reply :—Since such a *summum bonum*, implying nothing more than a state of nonenity, and unconnected with any sort of moral action, might satisfy beasts indeed [such as tortoises or dormice], but not men, therefore ought a different definition of the chief end of man, *e.g.* as above laid down, to be accepted.

(4) But then, it may be said, the Vedāntins say that, all pain having surceased on the final intuition of deity, the chief end of man consists in the soul's then spontaneous manifestation of the joy which is its

दनच्चेदामुम्भिन् लोके विभ्रि-
ष्टतत्त्वापाभागित्वम् ।

। ३ । ननु दुःखात्यन्तविमो-
चोऽपवर्ग दति न्यायविदः त-
थाचिविधदुःखात्यन्तनिट्टृत्ति-
रात्यन्तपुरुषार्थं दति साङ्खा
ब्राहुः किमिति तद्दर्शनं वि-
हायाभिनवमेतत् तस्य लचणं
कियत दति चेत् ताद्दृश्ते हि
परमपुरुषार्थः केवलं श्रून्या-
वस्थात्मकलाद् धर्माधर्माधि-
काराननुरूपक्रियाजातविरहि-
तो ऽत्यन्तालसान् पश्रूनेव
प्रीणयेन्तु मनुष्यानिति पूर्वो-
क्तमेव परमपुरुषार्थलचणं ग्रा-
ह्यमिति गृहाण ।

। ४ । ननु चरमब्रह्मसाचा-
त्कारेण सर्वदुःखोपशान्तौ
जीवस्य स्त एव सस्तरूपान-
न्दाविष्कारो ब्रह्मणि लयश्च
परमपुरुषार्थं दति वेदान्तिनो
वदन्ति तदनादृत्य किं तत

own essence, and in its mergence in deity. Why then, disregarding this, need anything higher than this be sought? If you say this, then hearken :—Since there is no evidence that there is such a chief end of man as is imagined by the Vedāntins, the chief end of man had to be enquired after, and it is that which was stated before. Moreover, the opinion of the Vedāntins shall be subjected to examination in the concluding section of Book II.

(5) But then, it may be asked, where is the evidence of this, too, which you have asserted, viz., that man's chief end is to glorify God and enjoy Him for ever? We reply: Say not so; because the evidence of this is the plain argument that, if there is an omnipotent Ruler of all, then the supposition that man's chief end can be irrespective of His favour, would be incongruous.

(6) Well, granting that

उक्तष्टं ष्टग्यत इति चेत् ष्टूष्ट वेदान्त्यभिमते परमपुरुषार्थे मानाभावादुक्तस्वरूप: परम- पुरुषार्थो ष्टग्यते । अपिचेदं वेदान्तिमतं दितीयाध्याय- स्यान्तिमप्रकरणे परीचिष्यते ।

। ५ । ननु देवमाहात्म्यवद्ध- नमनन्तं तत्स्वान्निष्ठसुखास्वा- दनचेत्यनयो: परमपुरुषार्थ- लं यदुक्तं तचापि किं मानमि- ति चेन्न तचानुमानखैव प्रमा- णलात् तथाहि यदि तावत् सर्वशक्तिर्जगन्नियामक: कश्चि- दस्ति तर्हि तस्य प्रसादमनपे- च्यैव पुरुषाणां परमपुरुषार्थ- सिद्धिकल्पनात्यन्तमसङ्गतैव स्यादिति ।

। ६ । अथ स्वीक्रियतां सर्व-

there *is* an omnipotent Ruler, still what evidence is there that there exist any means of obtaining His favour? With an eye to this, we declare as follows :—

शक्तिनियामकस्तथापि केषा-
श्चित् तत्प्रसादप्राप्युपायानां
सत्वे किं मानमित्याकाङ्क्षा-
यामाह ।

APHORISM III.

The rule for Man's direction to his chief end. The word of God, which is contained in the Scriptures of the Old and New Testament, is the only rule to direct us how we may glorify and enjoy Him.

पूर्वोत्तरसंविद्ग्रन्थस्थानि दे-
वस्य वचांस्येव केवलं तन्मा-
हात्म्यवर्द्धनानन्ततत्सान्निध्य-
सुखास्वादनयोरितिकर्त्तव्य-
ताबोधकानि ॥ ३ ॥

(1) If it be asked how the sentences which stand in the Scriptures of the Old and New Testament are the word of God, we reply that they are so because they were composed by the makers of the books under the influence of God's power. And, in respect of this, the operation of God's power is in three ways: to explain,—1, God sometimes suggested to the writers the words as well as the matter; 2, and sometimes the matter

। १ । ननु पूर्वोत्तरसंविद्-
ग्रन्थस्थानां वाक्यानां देवोक्तत्वं
कथमिति चेत् देवशक्तिव्यापा-
रद्वारा तेषां ग्रन्थकारैर्निबन्ध-
नात् । तच्च देवशक्तिव्यापा-
रस्त्रेधा तथाहि कदाचित् दे-
वो निबन्धृभ्यो ऽर्थमिव शब्द-
मप्युपदिदेश । कदाचित्त्वर्थ-
मेव सच निबन्धकारैर्यथेच्छं
वाक्यैरुपनिबद्धः । कदाचिच्च
कस्यचिदुपलब्धार्थस्य निबन्धने
प्रसक्तेभ्यो विस्मरणादिदोषे-

only, which was put into language by the writers according to their own genius; 3, and at other times He guarded the writers from errors of memory, etc., to which they might have been liable in narrating a matter with which they had been previously acquainted.

(2) If it be asked how a communication could be made without words, then hearken: We do not now undertake to explain this; but that there actually are means of revelation such as it is impossible to explain to others who are debarred from knowing through such means, we cite an example to show. Our illustration is as follows:—In a certain village, the whole of the inhabitants were blind from their birth, and one of them obtained his sight by means of a surgical operation. His companions having learned that he was able to describe what was going on at a great distance even better than they themselves

भ्यो निबन्धॄणां वारणमकरो-
दिति ।

।२। ननु कथं शब्दं विनैवा-
र्थोपदेश इति चेच्छृणु। न वय-
मेतदिदानीमुपपादयामः प-
रन्तु तादृशा अथपूर्वज्ञानो-
पाया: सन्ति यांस्तज्ज्ञान्श्रा-
नरहितेभ्यो ऽन्येभ्यः प्रतिपाद-
यितुं न शक्नोतीत्येतद्दर्शनाय
दृष्टान्तं दर्शयामः । यथा ।
कस्मिंश्चिद् ग्रामे सर्व एव पुरु-
षा जन्मनान्धा आसन्। तेषुच
केनचिद् वैद्योपचारवशाद्
दृष्टिरासादिता। अथात्यन्त-
समीपे ऽपि जायमानानां का-
र्याणां यावद् वर्णनं वयं कर्त्तुं
शक्नुमस्ततो ऽप्यतिसमीचीनम-
तिदूरस्थानामपि कार्याणां
वर्णनं कर्त्तुमेष शक्नोतीति

could tell what was going on close beside them, desired him to say by what means it was that this knowledge reached him. He endeavoured to declare it to them, but he found his endeavours useless. They could not in any way understand how a knowledge of the shape of objects not within reach of his hand could enter by the front of his head; but that such knowledge really did belong to the man, those who candidly investigated the truth of his words became assured. The application of the illustration to the matter illustrated is obvious.

ज्ञात्वा तस्य सहचारा: केनोपायेन भवानिदं ज्ञानं प्राप्नोति कथयेति तं प्रार्थयामासु:। स च तेषां समाधानाय प्रायतत स्वप्रयत्नांश्च व्यर्थानपश्यत् यतो हस्तेनालभ्यानामपि विषयाणामाकारस्य ज्ञानं शिर:प्राग्भागावच्छेदेन जायत इति बोद्धुं ते कथमपि नाश्नुवन् परन्तु ये मत्सररहिता: सन्तस्तदीयवचनस्य तत्त्वं विचारयामासुस्ते तादृशं ज्ञानं तस्मिन् पुरुषे वस्तुतो वर्त्तत इति निश्चिता अभवन्निति। अस्य च दृष्टान्तस्य दार्ष्टान्तिके योजनं स्पष्टम्

(3) If it be asked : But what proof is there that the words contained in the Old and New Testament declare the truth? —then listen. The evidence of it is of two kinds, external and internal. First, the truthfulness of the Old Testament is proved by the testimony of Jesus Christ, the Son of God,

।३। ननु पूर्वोत्तरसंविद्ग्रन्थस्थानां वचसां यथार्थाभिधायकत्वे किं मानमिति चेच्छृणु। द्विविधं हि तत्र मानं वाह्याभ्यन्तरञ्चेति। तत्र प्रथमं यथा। पूर्वसंविद्ग्रन्थस्य तत्त्वार्थाभिधायित्वं मनुष्यशरीरेणावतीर्णस्य देवपुत्रस्य देवाद्-

incarnate in human form, and one with God. That Jesus Christ possessed the character just stated, is proved by the words of the New Testament. That the New Testament declares what is true, is proved by the testimony of the disciples of Jesus, who could not have been mistaken, and who could have had no reason for asserting what was not true. This point will be discussed more fully in Book II. The second [the internal evidence] is the tendency of the Scriptures of the Old and New Testament to the glorifying of God and to the promoting the happiness of mortals, — the mutual consistency of all their parts, etc. This also there will be frequent occasion to advert to.

(4) If it be said: But, though the Scriptures of the Old and New Testament be not inconsistent among themselves, yet they cannot declare the truth, inasmuch as they are inconsistent with the *Veda*,

भिन्नस्य स्रष्टुस्य वचनात् सि-
ध्यति । स्रष्टृोक्तविधलं त्त-
त्तरसंविद्ग्रन्थवचनात् सिध्य-
ति । उत्तरसंविद्ग्रन्थस्य यथा-
र्थाभिधायकलं लप्रमाणवक्तृ-
ले कारणरहितानां निर्भ्रमा-
णाच्च स्रष्टशिष्याणां वचनैः
सिद्धम्। एषच विषयो विस्त-
रेण द्वितीयाध्याये विवेचयि-
ष्यते। द्वितीयं यथा। पूर्वोत्त-
रसंविद्ग्रन्थवचनानां देवमा-
हात्म्यवर्द्धनानुकूललंमर्त्यंजा-
तिकल्याणट्ट्ह्यानुकूललं सर्वे-
ष्वंशेषु परस्पराविरोधश्चेत्या-
दि । इदमपि बङ्कधा सप्रसङ्कं
निरूपयिष्यते ।

। ४ । ननु पूर्वोत्तरसंविद्ग्र-
न्यस्थवचनानांपरस्पराविरो-
धे ऽपि वेदविरोधादेव तत्त्वा-
र्थविधायकलं न सम्भवतीति
चेन्न । उक्तयुक्त्या तेषां तत्त्वा-
र्थाभिधायकलसिद्धौ तद्विरो-

we reply: Not so; because, their truthfulness having been established by the foregoing reasoning, it is of the Vedas themselves, in consequence of this inconsistency, that the authoritativeness is disproved. The nugatory pretension to authority on the part of the Veda will be disposed of in Book II.

धाद् वेदानामेव प्रामाण्या-सिद्धे: । दूयञ्च निरर्थिका वेद्प्रामाण्दुराशा द्वितीया-ध्याये निवारचिष्यते ।

(5) Next we state what matters are principally declared in the Scriptures of the Old and New Testament.

। ५। अथ पूर्वोत्तरसंविद्व्यस्थानां वचसां प्राधान्येना-भिधेयमर्थमाच ।

APHORISM IV.

What the Scriptures principally teach. The Scriptures principally teach what man is to believe concerning God, and what duty God requires of man.

यादृशं देवस्य रूपं मर्त्येण अद्वेयं यादृशानि वा मनुष्यो-चितानि कार्याणि देवो ऽपे-चते नदुभयं पूर्वोत्तरसंविद्व्या अभिद्धति ॥ ४ ॥

(1) We now state what is declared in Scripture concerning the nature of God.

। १। अथ यादृशं देवस्य रूपं तचोक्तं तदाच ।

APHORISM V.

What we are to believe concerning God. God is a spirit [a certain non-material substance], infinite, eter-

देवो नामानादिनिधनो निर्विकारै: सत्ताज्ञानशक्ति-

nal, and unchangeable in His being, wisdom, power, holiness, justice, goodness, and truth.

(1) But then, if it be argued that such is the nature of God, why say that it is by the Scriptures of the Old and New Testament that such a character of God is made known, seeing that God is declared by the Veda also to be a spirit, from everlasting to everlasting, and unchangeable? To this we reply: True. Whether it be that this which is declared in the Vedas was derived from primitive tradition, or from the power of conscience placed by God in the human heart, either way we welcome it. But where are God's justice, goodness, and truth, declared in the Vedas? Nay, rather these characteristics are in the Veda denied to be possible in God. For example, to whom should the God (*Brahm*) of the *Vedānta*, if just, be just, since there is none besides himself? For the same reason,

पाविच्रन्यायिलसाधुलसत्यव-
क्तृलादिभिर्गुणैर्युक्तस्राभौति-
कट्र व्यविग्रेष: ॥ ५ ॥

। २ । ननु यद्येताद्दृशमेव
देवस्र स्खरूपमभिमतं तर्हि
किमर्थमिदमुच्यते पूर्वोत्तर-
संविद्भ्न्याभ्यामेवैवंविधं देवस्र
स्खरूपं प्रतिपाद्यत द्रति वेदे-
नाप्यनाद्यनन्ताविकरात्मरूप-
स्र देवस्र प्रतिपादनादिति
चेत्सत्यम्। यदेतद् वेदेषु
वर्णितं तत्तावत्पूर्वपूर्वसम्ब-
दायप्राप्तमस्खथवा देवेन म-
त्यैमाचस्र ह्द्ये निहिताया
उचितानुचितविवेचनश्क्तेर्यो-
गेन प्राप्तमस्तु उभयथापि वयं
तमर्थमाद्रियामहे । परन्तु
वेदेषु देवस्र न्यायिलसाधुल-
सत्यवक्तृलानि क प्रतिपादिता-
नि सन्ति। प्रत्युत ते धर्मा देवे
प्रतिषिद्धा: । तथाच वेदान्त-
गोचरं ब्रह्म न्यायि भवत्कं
प्रति न्यायि स्यात्स्खातिरिक्त-
स्र कस्याप्यभावात्। अत एव

to whom should he be good or true? Nay, rather, since he is the sole being in existence, it must be himself whom he deludes by the phantasmagoria of a false creation.

(2) That God is infinite, eternal, and unchangeable, it is unnecessary to demonstrate to the Vedāntin. As for the assertion by the author of the *Sānkhya* [in his Aph. 93 of Bk. I.], that the fact of there being a " Lord" (*iswara*) is unproved,—the import of this is explained by the commentators to be, that it is not intended, by the expression "For a Lord is unproved," to *deny* a Lord, but that the author of the *Sānkhya* denies that he is bound to show the consistency of certain of his own statements with other statements which, he says, are "unproved,"—and so, until his opponent shall have proved them, he is under no obligation to take them into consideration.

(3) Again, as for what the

तत् साधु सत्यवक्ता वा कं प्रति स्यात्। प्रत्युत तदद्वितीयत्वात् खं प्रति मिथ्याभूतसृष्टिप्रदर्शनेनात्मवञ्चकमेव तत्।

।२। तच देवस्थानाद्यनन्ता- विकारित्वानां साधनं वेदा- न्तिनां पुरतो नावश्यकम्। यत्तु साङ्ख्याचार्य ईश्वरासिद्धे- रित्याह तस्य तात्पर्यं तस्यैव टीकाकारैरेवमुपवर्णितं य- दीश्वरासिद्धेरित्यनेन नेश्वर- निषेधो ऽभिप्रेत आचार्यस्था- पितसिद्धविषयकवाक्यैः केषा- ञ्चिदाक्यानां विरोधपरिहा- रावश्यकत्वं तथा यावत् परो न साधयति तावत् तद्विचा- रानावश्यकत्वच्च साङ्ख्याचार्या निषेधतीति।

।३। यत् पुनः साङ्ख्या आ-

Sānkhyas say, that if there be any primal energy, competent to produce the world, then let it be called Nature, or the chief one; but, in that case, the supposition of an all-directing Lord is superfluous. We reply: Not so; because there is a plain contradiction in holding that a primal energy, competent to the production of the world, labours for soul's end, and is at the same time unintelligent, — inasmuch as the working towards an end is proof of intelligence. This shall be set forth diffusively in Book III.

(4) The followers of the *Nyāya* [see the *Siddhānta Muktāvali*, p. 2], in demonstration of the being of a God, say that "such productions as a water-jar are produced by a maker, and so also are the vegetable sprouts and the earth, etc.; and to make these is not possible for such as we are; hence the existence of the Lord, as the Maker of these, is demonstrated."

ङ्ग: यदि जगज्जननानुकूला प्रधानशक्ति: कापि वर्तते तर्हि तस्या: प्रकृतिरिति प्रधानमिति वा व्यवहार: क्रियतां परन्तु तथा सति सर्वनियामके श्वराभ्युपगमो निरर्थक इति । तन्न । जगज्जननानुकूलप्रधानशक्ते: पुरुषार्थप्रवृत्तिशीलतायाः जडतायाश्च खीक्रियमाणायाः स्फुटं विरोधात् । प्रवृत्तेश्चैतन्यलिङ्गत्वात् । एतच्च तृतीये ऽध्याये विस्तरेण वच्यते ।

। ४ । नैयायिकाश्चीश्वरसत्वसाधनायेदमाङ्ग: यथा घटादिकार्यं कर्तृजन्यं तथा चित्यङ्कुरादिकमपि । नच तत्कर्त्वमस्मदादीनां सम्भवति अतस्तत्कर्तृत्वेनेश्वरसिद्धिरिति ।

(5) But, it may be objected, that the assertion that God is a spiritual substance cannot be true ; because what is spiritual is without parts, whereas in the Scriptures of the Old and New Testament there is mention of God's eyes, hands, and other bodily parts. But we reply : Not so ; because there the expressions, "eyes," etc., are figurative, the word "eyes" signifying knowledge, "hands" signifying power, and so on.

। ५। नन्वभौतिकद्रव्यविशे-
षो देव इत्युक्तं तन्न सम्भवति
अभौतिकलस्य निरवयवलरू-
पलात् पूर्वोत्तरसंविद्धन्ययो-
स्च देवस्य चचुर्हस्तादिशरीरा-
वयवानामुक्तलादिति । तन्न ।
तच चचुरादिनिर्देशस्य गौण-
लात् । तथाहि चचु: पदं
ज्ञानबोधाय हस्तपदं शक्ति-
बोधायेत्यादि ।

(6) It being thus settled, then, that God exists, we deny that there are more gods than one. For—

। ६। अथैवं देवस्य सिद्धौ
तदनेकलं प्रतिषेधति ।

APHORISM VI.

The unity of God. There is but one God, the living and true God.

चेतन: सत्यस्च देव एक एव
॥ ६ ॥

(1) We say "living," in order to exclude idols ; and "true," in order to exclude imaginary gods.

। १। चेतनलं मूर्तीनां व्या-
वृत्तये। सत्यलं काल्पनिकानां
व्यावृत्तये ।

(2) If it be said that there is no proof that there is but

। २। नन्वेताद्टश्येश्वरप-
दाभिधेयस्य देवस्यैकले न कि-

one such God as is here designated "the Lord," we reply: Not so; because both
reasoning and Scripture furnish proof of this. The reasoning is this, that God is one,
because a unity of design runs
through all created things.

(3) Now, in order to ob-
viate the doubt how we
are justified in saying that
only one God is declared in
Scripture, when, in the New
Testament, three persons are
spoken of under the name of
God, we declare as follows:—

द्विन्मानमिति चेन्न श्रनुमा-
नागमयोस्त्व प्रमाणत्वात् ।
तथाच प्रयोग: देव एक: त-
त्सृष्टानां सर्वेषां पदार्थ।ना-
मेकफलपर्यवसायित्वादिति ।

। ३ । ननूत्तरसंविद्वन्थे त्रय:
पुरुषा देवपदेन व्यवद्रियन्ते
तथाच कथमुच्यते एक एव
देव श्रागमेन प्रतिपाद्यत इति
ग्रङ्कां निरसितुमाह ।

APHORISM VII.

The Trinity in Unity.   There are three persons in the Godhead, the Fa-
ther, and the Son, and the Holy
Ghost, and these three are one
God, the same in substance,
equal in power and glory.

(1) This dogma will be discussed in the Fourth Book.

(2) Having thus far de-
scribed the nature of God, we
proceed to describe the nature
of what is other than He.

पिता पुच: पविचात्मेति च-
यो देवत्वविशिष्टा अभिन्नाश्र-
न्यूनानतिरिक्तशक्तिमाहात्म्या-
दिका: सन्ति ॥ ७ ॥

। १ । एष सिद्धान्तश्चतुर्थे
ऽध्याये विचारयिष्यते ।

। २ । अथैवं देवस्वरूपनिरू-
पणं परिसमाप्य तदितरपदा-
र्थस्वरूपं निरूपयति ।

APHORISM VIII.

Creation. , God made all things of nothing, by his mere word, in the space of six days, and all very good.

(1) But how is it possible that God " made all things of nothing?" We retort: How should it not be possible? To explain,—We ask you in turn, how does fire burn fuel? If you answer, from the nature of things,—then we rejoin that it is the same in the case before us [—God makes things out of nothing " from the nature of things"]. If you ask, how can this or that thing be produced without the aggregate of its concurrent causes? we reply, that the doubt would be a fitting one if we were speaking of *men's* works; for we do not assert that a potter can make a jar without a lump of clay, or a weaver a web without yarn, and so on: but this doubt is inapplicable to

देवः शब्दमात्रेणषड्भिर्दिनैः
सर्वाणि वस्त्वन्यसत उत्पाद-
यत् तानिच सर्वशः साधून्येव
॥ ८ ॥

। ८ । ननु कथं सम्भवति
सर्वाणि वस्त्वन्यसत उत्पाद-
यदिति । न कथं सम्भवति । त-
द्याचि त्वमेवं प्रतिप्रष्ट्यः क-
थमग्निरिन्धनानां दाहं करो-
तीति । स्वभावादिति चेत् प्र-
कृते ऽपि तुल्यम् । विनैव
तत्तत्पदार्थोपादानकारण -
कलापं कथं तत्तत्पदार्थो-
त्पत्तिरिति चेत् युज्येतैषा
शङ्का यदि मनुष्यकर्तृकसृष्टे-
रेष प्रक्रमः स्यात् नहि वयं
कुलालकुविन्दादीनां विनैव
मृत्पिण्डतन्त्वादिकं घटपटा-
द्युत्पादनसामर्थ्यं प्रतिपादया-
मः । प्रक्रान्ते सर्वलोकातीत-
सामर्थ्यशालिनि परमेश्वरे तु
नैषा शङ्का युक्ता । यदिचास्म-

the case in question, of the Supreme Lord possessed of power beyond that of all creatures. And if we suppose, from the example of the like of us, that God's power of creation also is dependent on an aggregate of concurrent causes, then we ought to suppose, from the example of the child's walking with the support of the nurse's finger [see the *Raghuvansa*, canto iii., v. 25], that your power also of walking [—grown-up person as you are—] is dependent on the support of a nurse's finger.

(2) And if you say that the world could not have arisen from nothing, because what exists must have been without beginning, on the rule that nothing comes of nothing ["ex nihilo nihil fit"],—then we reply: Not so; for there is no proof that there is any such absolute rule, and an unsupported allegation deserves to be met only by an unsupported [or blank] negative. Moreover, were the case as you say,

दादिदृष्टान्तेनेश्वरस्थाप्युपा -
दानकारणकलापपराधीन -
सर्ज्जनसामर्थ्यवत्तं कल्प्यते त-
र्हि धात्रीकरशाखावलम्बेनो-
च्चलन्तं बालं दृष्टान्तमादाय
यूनामपि धात्रीकरशाखाव-
लम्बपराधीनोच्चलनसामर्थ्य -
वत्तं कल्प्येत ।

। २ । यदि च सत एवोत्प-
त्तिर्नासत इति नियमाद् यद्-
दुत्पन्नं तदनादेवेति नासतो
जगदुत्पत्तिसम्भव इति चेन्न ।
तथाविधे नियमे मानाभा-
वात् । निर्हेतुकस्यचाचेपस्य
निर्हेतुकेनैव नेत्यनेन निरास-
योग्यत्वात्। अपिचैवं सति पु-
रुषाणां च्वणं जायमानसुख-
दुःखसाचात्कारो ऽनादिर-
तस्मानन्तः स्यात् । नान्तः

then the feeling, whether of pleasure or of pain, which at any moment arises in the mind of a man, must have existed from eternity, and as such must be imperishable. If it be rejoined that what we assert is the arising not merely of real changes of the mind, but the arising also of substances, we reply: Say not so; for that makes no difference :—if you yourself admit that mental states, not previously existing, do arise, how should this be wrong in the case of substances ?

करणपरिणामानां सतामेवो-त्यक्तिरुच्यते ऽपितु द्रव्याणा-मिति चेन्न विशेषाभावात्,य-दि तावच्चित्तवृत्तीनामसती-नामुत्पक्तिरिष्यते किमपराद्धं द्रव्यै: ।

(3) But still, it may be said, it is impossible that God should have made all things out of nothing, because the souls of men, etc., are without beginning. To this we reply: Not so. To explain:—That the ground of all is the One Self-existent we are both agreed. Such being the case, there remains the consideration—whence has come the existence of anything apart from Him ?—and this is entirely hidden with

। ३ । ननु तथापि सर्वाणि वस्त्वन्यसत उत्पादयदिति न सम्भवति जीवात्मनामनादि-त्वादिति चेन्न। तथाहि। सर्वे-षां मूलभूत: कश्चित्,स्वयंभू-रस्तीति तावन्निर्विवादमाव-योः । एवं सति तस्मादतिरि-क्तस्य कस्यापि सत्त्वं कस्मादा-यातमिति चिन्तावशिष्यते । तच्चेदं सर्वथा देवगुह्यं यत्रोप-पादनंस स्वयंभूरेवकर्त्तुं शक्नो-

God, and can be explained by the Self-existent alone, and by none other. But this is agreed, alike by those who accept the authority of the Vedas and by those who accept the authority of the Bible, that there is so much of difference between the existence of the Self-existent and the existence of the human soul, that rules are required for the guidance of men,—otherwise what need of the Vedas? what need of the Bible? In the Bible there is no discussion as to how the human soul is numerically different from God; but rules are laid down for human guidance, clearly on the understanding that the difference is a fact. If, therefore, the Bible be acknowledged to be the Word of God, to say that the human soul is not numerically different from the Lord would be to make God a liar. And it must not be said that the difference between God and the soul is illusory and not real, because such illusoriness is in-

ति नान्यः । इदन्तु वेदप्रामा-
ण्याभ्युपगन्तृभिः पूर्वोत्तरसं-
विद्वन्थप्रामाण्याभ्युपगन्तृभिश्च
तुल्यमेव स्वीक्रियते यत् स्वय-
म्भुसत्तातो जीवसत्ताया द-
यान् विश्रेषो यज्जीवानां प्रवृ-
त्तये केषाञ्चिन्नियमानामपे-
चा वर्तत इति । अन्यथा हि किं
वेदैः किं वा पूर्वोत्तरसंविद्वन्था-
भ्यां प्रयोजनम् । पूर्वोत्तरसं-
विद्वन्थयोर्हि न जीवेश्वरभेदक-
यभावो विचार्यते किन्तु तयो-
र्भेदं सिद्धवन्निर्दिश्य जीवप्रवृ-
त्तिनियमा अभिधीयन्ते । यदि
तु पूर्वोत्तरसंविद्वन्थयोरीश्वर-
प्रणीतलं स्वीकृत्यापि ताभ्यां
प्रतिपादितो जीवेश्वरव्यक्तिभे-
दो नाभ्युपेयते तर्हीश्वरस्यास-
त्यवक्तृलमेव स्वीकृतं स्यात् ।
नच जीवेश्वरयोर्भेदो मायि-
को नतु तात्त्विक इति वाचम्
प्रत्यच्चसिद्धस्य मायिकलायो-
गादिति ।

consistent with the facts of consciousness.

So much, in our elucidation of the Christian religion, for the First Book, that devoted to the exposition of the dogmas about which we wish to speak.

इति ष्ष्टधर्मकौमुद्यां वि-
वचितसिद्धान्तोद्देशो नाम
प्रथमो ऽध्याय: ॥

BOOK II.

THE EVIDENCES OF CHRISTIANITY.

Now we commence a second Book in order to establish what was treated under the 3rd Aphorism of the preceding Book as if already established, that the Scriptures of the Old and New Testament are the Word of God. It was there stated [Aph. III. 3] that the authority of the contents of the Old Testament is established by force of the declarations of Christ conveyed in the New Testament, and that the authority of the declarations of Christ is established by the testimony of His disciples. And all this is founded on historical inference, so that by those can it be clearly understood who, by

अथ पूर्वाध्याये तृतीयसूत्रे सिद्धवन्निर्दिष्टं पूर्वोत्तरसंविद्- न्ययोरीश्वरोक्तत्वं व्यवस्थापयि- तुं द्वितीयाध्यायमारभते । त- च्चोत्तरसंविद्ग्रन्थस्थऋष्टवचनब- लेन पूर्वसंविद्ग्रन्थस्थस्य प्रामाण्यं ऋष्टवचनस्यत् तच्छिष्यवचन- बलात् प्रामाण्यं सिद्धमीत्यभि- हितं तच्च सर्वमैतिहासिकानु- मानमूलकमतो ये विवेचनानु- कूलेन धीशक्तिसंस्कारेण प्रमा- णतत्त्वविवेचननिपुनास्तैः स- ष्टवेद्यमत इतिहासपरिचयात् ऋष्टमतस्येश्वरादायतत्वविष- ये या: साधिका युक्तयो ऽवग- म्यन्ते ता वक्तुमुपक्रमते ।

the appropriate culture of their mental faculties, have become skilled in discriminating the reality [from the semblance] of evidence. We therefore proceed to state what valid arguments, in respect of the fact that the Christian religion came from God, are derivable from the stores of history.

APHORISM I.

Miracles the credentials of a religion.

A religion attested by miracles is from God, and the Christian religion is attested by miracles, therefore it is from God.

यद्धन्मतमद्भुतचरितोपपन्नं तदीश्वरादायातं खृष्टमत- ञ्चाद्भुतचरितोपपन्नमतखदी- श्वरादायातम्॥ १॥

(1) The miracles performed by Christ, in order to establish the fact that he was sent by God, are such as these:—His giving, by a word merely, eyes to the blind and life to the dead; and His Himself rising again alive on the third day after he had been put to death.

। १। खखेश्वरप्रेरितलं द्रढ- यितुं खृष्टेन कृतान्यद्भुतचरि- तानि तावदिमानि तथाचि वचनमाचेणान्धेभ्यो नयनदा- नं मृतेभ्यो जीवनदानं खस्य वधानन्तरं द्वतीयदिनेपुनर्जी- विलोत्यानमित्यादीनि ।

(2) But, it may be asked: Granting that miracles displayed could be so only through

। २। ननु प्रदर्शितान्यद्भुत- चरितानि केवलमीश्वरशक्त्येव

the power of God,—still what
proof is there of this that
such were performed by
Christ ? To this question we
reply—

भवितुमर्हन्तीत्यस्तु परन्तु ता-
नि खृष्टेन कृतानीत्यत्र किं
मानमित्याकाङ्क्षायामाह ।

APHORISM II.

The Christian
miracles worthy
of credit.

Miracles attested
by such evidence as
exists in attestation of the
Christian miracles, are to be
believed.

खृष्टकृताद्भुतचरितोपपाद-
कप्रमाणजातीयप्रमाणैरूपप -
न्नान्यद्भुतचरितानि श्रद्धेया-
नि ॥ २ ॥

(1) "Attested by evidence,"
etc. The import is this, that
the proof which should set at
rest this question is this,
that many men, professing
themselves to be original witnesses of the miracles performed by Christ, voluntarily
underwent, as long as they
lived, toil and danger and
suffering, in attestation of what
they had witnessed, and solely
through belief in what they
reported. But no such sufferings were ever undergone, in
the case of any other supposed
miracles, by men alleging
themselves to be original wit-

। २ । प्रमाणैरित्यादि । अयं
भावः । इदमेवेह जिज्ञासानि-
वर्त्तकं मानमस्ति यद् बहवः
पुरुषा आत्मनः खृष्टकृताद्भुत-
चरितप्रथमसाक्षितां प्रतिपा-
दयन्तः केवलं दृष्टवृत्तान्तो-
पपादनार्थं तद्वृत्तान्तविश्वा-
सादेव यावज्जीवं श्रमभयदुः-
खानि स्वेच्छयैव सेहिरे इति ।
अद्भुतलाभिमतचरितान्तर -
विषयेतु तत्प्रथमसाक्षितामा-
त्मनः कथयद्भिः पुरुषैः कथ्य-
मानवृत्तान्तोपपादनार्थं त-
द्वृत्तान्तविश्वासादेवंविधानि

nesses thereof, in attestation of what they narrated, and through belief in the narrative: this also is a proof which should set the question at rest.

(2) But if the voluntary undergoing of sufferings entitles persons to confidence, then whatever is asserted by the Indian ascetics, who voluntarily undergo the sharpest sufferings, ought also to be accepted. If this be urged, we reply: Not so; for we do not say that the mere voluntary undergoing of sufferings produces a title to confidence, but only that the endurance of suffering, inflicted by others, and endured with no view to any fruit beyond the establishing of a particular occurrence, does so. But the sufferings of the Indian ascetics are self-inflicted, and are not undergone in attestation of any particular occurrence. That is to say, these ascetics undergo sufferings, seeking, in some cases, the gratification of

दुःखानि न सोढानीत्येतदेव जिज्ञासानिवर्त्तकं मानम्।

।२। ननु यदि खेच्छया दुःखभारसहनमेव पुरुषाणां विश्वासयोग्यतासम्पादकं तर्हि भारतवर्षीया खेच्छयैव तीच्णतमान् क्लेशान् सहमानास्तपखिनो ऽपि यद्यद् वदन्ति तदपि खीकार्यमिति चेन्न। नहि वयं केवलं खेच्छया दुःखभारसहनमात्रं विश्वासयोग्यतासम्पादकं ब्रूमो ऽपितु टत्तविश्रेषोपपादनव्यतिरिक्तफलाभिसन्धिरहितं परक्तृतपीडासहनमेव तथा। भारतवर्षीयतपखिनां दुःखानि तु खयं कृतानि नच टत्तविश्रे-षोपपादनार्थमनुभूतानि तथाचि ते कदाचिदाभिमानिकानि फलान्यनुसन्धाय खश-रीरसुखमनादृत्य प्रेचकाणां सरोमाञ्चविस्मयमधिकमि -

vanity, disregarding bodily ease and desiring more the rapturous admiration of the spectators ; and, in other cases, hoping for supramundane glory and enjoyment which they imagine is thus to be obtained in another birth. In the first case no motive is established besides vanity ; and there needs no proof of this vanity, for the vanity of these is equally clear with that of the silly women who undergo the pain of tattooing and the boring of their noses for the reception of a nose-jewel. And in the second case there is established their belief merely in the assurances of those who inculcate that present sufferings are the causes of future enjoyment, but not likewise the veracity of those who thus inculcate.

(3) But the circumstances of the sufferings voluntarily undergone by the first believers in Christ were quite different from the foregoing.

च्चन्तः कदाचिच्च जन्मान्तर-
प्राप्यलेनाभिमते लोकोत्तर-
प्रभावप्रमोदादौ श्रद्धाना
दुःखानि सहन्ते । तत्र प्रथम-
पचे मूर्खतातिरिक्तः को ऽपि
हेतुर्न सिद्ध्यति मूर्खतासिद्धौ च
न हेलपेचा उत्तुङ्खितपचलेखं
नासाभरणधारणोपयोगि -
नासावेधश्च सहमानानां मू-
र्खस्त्रीणां साम्येन स्फुटमेव ते-
षां मौर्ख्यसिद्धेः । द्वितीयेच
पचे वर्त्तमानि दुःखानि भा-
विसुखकारणानीत्युपदेशका-
रिपुरुषवचने तेषां विश्वास-
मात्रं सिद्ध्यति नतु तादृशो-
पदेशकारिपुरुषवचनप्रामा -
ण्यमपि ।

।६। परन्त्वादौः रृष्टभक्तैः स्वे-
च्छया सोढानां दुःखानां रृत्तं
पूर्वस्मादत्यन्तविलचणमस्ति ।
यदि चैतेष्वपि दिनेषु कश्चित्

And if in the present day any believer in Christ, when called upon to abjure his religion, should prefer undergoing death or other sufferings, then the sincerity of his profession of Christianity is what would be thereby proved : but sufferings were undergone by the first believers in Christ, in attestation of events which they had themselves beheld, by their giving attestation whereof the world was enraged against them, and in respect of which they were under no delusion ; whilst, on the alternative of their being deceivers; they could reap no fruit besides the anger of God for having obstinately borne testimony to a wilful lie. And by merely refraining from bearing such testimony, they might have remained quietly, clear of the sufferings which they underwent. Would men in such circumstances assert that they had seen what they never saw ? would they declare what they had no know-

ख़ृष्टभक्तः ख़मतच्युतिप्रसङ्गे ख़ेच्छया मरणादिदुःखानि सचेत्_तर्हि तेन कर्मणा तद्ीयख़ृष्टधर्माङ्गीकारख़ निष्कपटत्वं सिद्ध्यति । आद्यख़ृष्टभक्तैस्तु प्रत्यचीकृततादृगृत्ताल्तविग्रेषोपपादनाय दुःखान्यनुभूतानि यत्साच्छ्यदानात्_ तेभ्यो जगच्चुक्रोध यद्विषयेच तेषां भ्रमो नासीत्_येचासत्यलपच्चे बुद्धिपूर्वकानृतसाच्छ्यग्रहप्रयुक्तपरमेश्वरीयकोपाद्न्यत्_ फलं नोद्पाद्यिष्यन् । केवलञ्च तादृग्रसाच्छ्यदानपरिवर्जनमाचादेवानुभूतसकलदुःखपरिवर्जनपूर्वकं तूष्णीं स्थिता अभविष्यन् । किं लोका एवंविधविषये यं वृत्ताल्तं कदापि नापश्यंस्तमपि दृष्टं ब्रूयुः । अविज्ञातमेव किमपि कथयेयुः । धर्मोपदेश्रार्थंच्चानृतभाषणे प्रवृत्ता भवेयुः । अपिच न केवलं ख़ृष्टस्य वञ्चकतां यावत्_तादृग्रवञ्चकताफलभूतं तद्धर्ममपि दृष्ट्वा ता-

ledge of? and employ themselves in telling lies in order
to teach virtue? Further,
not only having seen Christ
to be an impostor, but having
seen also the result of such
imposture in his being put to
death, how could they have
persisted in bringing upon
themselves, for nothing and
with a full knowledge of the
consequences, enmity, con-
tumely, contempt, danger, and
death, by obstinately carrying
out such an imposture? It is
impossible.

(4) Now, in regard to the
doubt as to what proof there
is that sufferings *were* undergone, in the way just mentioned, by the first promoters
of Christianity, we observe—

दृष्टवच्चकलानुष्ठानायहानि-
ष्फले बुद्धिपूर्वकेच देषमान-
भङ्गानादरभयम्टत्युखीकारे
कतायहा: कथं स्यु: । नह्वेवं
सम्भवति ।

। ४ । अथाच्ैे: ष्टष्टभक्तिप्र-
वर्त्तकै: पूर्वोक्तरीत्या दु:खानि
सोढानील्यच किं मानमिल्या-
यङ्कायामाच ।

APHORISM III.

Sufferings of the first Christian martyrs. That sufferings
should be undergone
by the attesters of the miracles
of Christ was likely, and moreover that they were established
by cumulative evidence.

ष्टष्टकताङ्घुतचरितसाचि-
भिर्दु:खानि सोढानीति सम्भ-
वति अपिच खतन्त्वानेकप्रमा-
णमङ्गावादेतत्सिद्ध्यति ॥ ३ ॥

(1) That is to say, it is likely that they underwent sufferings, because they were promulgators of a religion distasteful both to the Jews and to the rest of the world. For the Jewish people, misconceiving the import of the Word of God in the Old Testament, looked for a Redeemer from temporal bondage, and not from the spiritual bondage of sin; while the Gentiles resented the Christian scheme of salvation because of its requiring the entire abandonment of man's natural pride. Further, that the Christians did suffer, is established by the testimony of profane writers of good authority. Again, the writings of the Christians themselves furnish evidence to the same effect. And these arguments are mutually independent, as each separately goes to establish the probability of the one common conclusion that the first followers of Christ underwent sufferings.

(2) Now, to the question

। २ । तथाहि ते दुःखमनु-
भूतवन्तो यह्नदीयतदन्यजन-
समूहृदयद्वेष्यमतप्रचारकत्वा-
दिति सम्भवति । यह्नदीया हि
जनाः प्रत्नसंविद्वन्थस्थेश्वरवच-
नस्यार्थमन्यथा पश्यन्तो लौ-
किकादेव बन्धान्मोचनकारि-
णं कञ्चन प्रतीचाच्छिक्रिरे नतु
पापकृतादलौकिकबन्धात् ।
तदन्यजनास्तु खृष्टनिर्दिष्टं मु-
क्तिप्रकारं मनुष्यजातीयगर्वा-
त्यन्तपरिहारकत्वादनिष्टं मे-
निरे । अपिच खृष्टभक्तैः कृतं
दुःखसहनं तदन्यजनानां प्रा-
माणिकग्रन्थकाराणां वचनैः
सिध्यति । किञ्चैतद्विषयप्रमा-
णानि खृष्टभक्तवचनान्यपि स-
न्ति । इमानिच प्रमाणानि
खतन्त्राणि । आद्यखृष्टभक्तै-
र्दुःखानि सोढानीत्येवंविध-
समाननिगमनसम्भवसाधक -
त्वात् ।

। २ । अथाद्भुतचरितान्तरं

whether no other miracle has been established by such evidence, we reply—

नैवंविधप्रमाणसिद्धमित्याह ।

APHORISM IV.

Unlikelihood that the matters so attested should be false. It is improbable that any false story should have been adopted by witnesses of this kind.

असत्यकथानामेवंविधसा-
च्छ्यनुष्ठीतलं न सम्भवति ॥ ४ ॥

(1) "Is improbable," etc. For no *false* story of miracles ever *has been* adopted by witnesses of this kind; and, further, no other miraculous story *whatever* has been seen to be adopted by such witnesses. Such is the import.

। १ । न सम्भवतीति । नच्छ्-
तचरितविषयिण्या असत्य-
कथायाः कदापितथाविधसा-
च्छ्यनुष्ठीतलं दृष्टं नवान्या
काचिदथ्छ्तचरितकथा त-
थाविधसाच्छ्यनुष्ठीता दृश्य-
ते ऽपीति भावः ।

(2) If you say, but were not the miracles of Kṛishṇa, such as his lifting up the mountain of Govardhana, attested by witnesses such as attested the miracles of Christ? We reply: Not so. For, even supposing them to be true, we require you to tell us, by what persons, professing to have witnessed them, was even the slightest suffering undergone

। २ । ननु कृष्टक्तानाद्भुत-
चरितानामिव क्रष्णक्तानामपि गोवर्धनोद्धरणादीनां
तादृग्साच्छ्यनुष्ठीतलमस्ती-
ति चेन्न । तेषां हि सत्यत्वपत्ते
ऽपि तत्साचितामात्मनः कथ-
यद्भिः कैस्तद्विषयकविश्वासप-
रीचाक्षेशो लेशेनाप्यनुभूत
इति वक्तव्यम् ।

in testimony of their belief of them ?

(3) But, it may be said, the Vedas are themselves proof [*i.e.* causal of right knowledge], for they are divine ; and therefore there is no need of another proof to corroborate their authority, just as there is no need of a lamp in order to see the sun.   We clear up this doubt as follows :—

। ३ । ननु वेदाः स्वत एव प्रमाणमपौरुषेयत्वात् । अतस्व तत्प्रामाण्यसमर्थनाय न प्रमाणान्तरापेचा सूर्यदर्शने दीपापेचावदित्याशङ्कां समाधत्ते ।

APHORISM V.

No evidence of the veracity of the Veda producible.   In claiming for the Veda that it is self-evidently an authority, it is acknowledged in so many words that no evidence of its being an authority is producible.

वेदस्य स्वतप्रामाण्यस्वीकारे तत्प्रामाण्ये प्रमाणाभावः कण्ठोक्तः ॥ ५ ॥

(1) Be it so ;—but, it may be said, it suffices to establish the authority of the Veda that it is in harmony with all demonstration.   In the Bible, on the other hand, we are told that the world was produced out of nothing ; while great sages among the moderns—such as Sir William Hamilton—seem to adhere to the tenet

। १ । स्यादेतत् । वेदस्य प्रामाण्ये तदीयमुपपत्त्यविरुद्धत्वमेव साधकम् । पूर्वोत्तरसंविद्वन्धयोरसतो जगदुत्पत्तिः श्रूयते तच्च नवीना हमिल्ट-नाख्यप्रभृतयः सुपण्डिता विप्रतिपन्नाः सन्तः शक्तस्य श्रकार्यकरणादिति प्रथमाध्यायीयाष्टादशोत्तरशततमकापि-

laid down in the 118th Aphorism of Book I. of the *Sānkhya*, viz.: "Because that
which is possible is made out
of that which is competent to
the making of it."

लसूचसिद्धान्तमेवाङ्गीकुर्दन्ती-
ति दृश्यते ।

[For the convenience of the English reader, we
cite here the remarks, above referred to, of Sir William
Hamilton, at p. 585 of his *Discussions*.

"When aware of a new appearance, we are *unable*
to conceive that therein has originated any new existence, and are, therefore, *constrained* to think that what
now appears to us under a new form, had previously
an existence under others. These *others* (for they are
always plural) are called its cause; and a cause (or
more properly causes) we cannot but suppose, for a
cause is simply everything without which the effect
would not result, and all such concurring, the effect
cannot but result. We are utterly unable to *construe
it in thought* as possible, that the complement of existence has been either increased or diminished. We
cannot conceive either, on the one hand, nothing becoming something, or, on the other, something becoming
nothing. When God is said to create the universe out
of nothing, we think this, by supposing, that He evolves
the universe out of Himself; and, in like manner, we
conceive annihilation only by conceiving the Creator
to withdraw his creation from actuality into power.

"'Nil posse creari
De Nihilo, neque quod genitu 'st ad Nil revocari.'
"'——— Gigni
De Nihilo Nihil, in Nihilum Nil posse reverti.'

"—— these lines of Lucretius and Persius enounce a physical axiom of antiquity, which, when interpreted by the doctrine of the conditioned, is itself at once recalled to harmony with revealed truth, and expressing in its purest form the conditions of human thought, expresses also implicitly the whole intellectual phenomenon of causality.

" *b.* The mind is thus compelled to recognize an absolute identity of existence in the effect and in the complement of its causes, between the *causatum* and the *causa.* We think the causes .to contain all that is contained in the effect, the effect to contain nothing but what is contained in the causes. Each is the sum of the other. *Omnia mutantur, nihil interit,* is what we think, what we must think; nor can the change itself be thought without a cause. Our judgment of causality simply is: We necessarily deny in thought, that the object which we apprehend as beginning to be, really so begins; but, on the contrary, affirm, as we must, the identity of its present sum of being, with the sum of its past existence. And here, it is not requisite for us to know under what form, under what combination this *quantum* previously existed; in other words, it is unnecessary for us to recognize the particular causes of this particular effect. A discovery of the determinate antecedents into which a determinate consequent may be refunded, is merely contingent,— merely the result of experience; but the judgment, that every event should have its causes, is necessary, and imposed on us, as a condition of our human intelligence itself. This necessity of so thinking is the

only phenomenon to be explained." And he adds (at
p. 591), "We cannot know, we cannot think a thing,
except under the attribute of *existence;* we cannot know
or think a thing to exist, except in *time;* and we cannot
know or think a thing to exist in time, and think it
absolutely to commence."]

(2) Again, Bishop Berke-
ley has brought forward co-
gent arguments to prove that
the "matter"[1] which [you
say] is alleged in the Bible
to have been brought from
non-existence into existence,
neither exists nor could possibly exist.

(3) In like manner Sir William Jones, who was versed
in the scriptures of the Hindūs
as well as in those of the
Christians, appears to hold the
tenet of Kapila above cited.

।२। तथा बर्क्लीनामको ऽप्य-
सतः सकाशात् परमेश्वरो-
त्यादितलेन पूर्वोत्तरसंविध्-
न्ययोः प्रतिपादितानामना-
त्मद्रव्याणामसत्त्वमसम्भावित-
सत्ताकलञ्च साधयितुं प्रबला-
नि प्रमाणान्युपन्यस्तवान् ।

। ६ । तथा विलियम् जो-
न्साख्यो ऽपि खृष्टीयधर्मग्रन्था-
नामिव भारतवर्षीयधर्मग्रन्था-
नामपि विचारकः पूर्वोक्तमेव
कपिलसिद्धान्तं स्वीकरोतीति
दृश्यत इति ।

[Sir William Jones, at p. 367, vol. i. of his works,
remarks that "the inextricable difficulty attending the
vulgar notion of *material substances,* concerning which

"' We know this only, that we nothing know,'

induced many of the wisest among the ancients, and
some of the most enlightened among the moderns, to

---

[1] See the question of "Matter," as regards the philosophical terminology of the
East and of the West, discussed in Appendix, Note A.

believe that the whole creation was rather an *energy*
than a *work*, by which the Infinite Being, who is present at all times, in all places, exhibits to the minds
of His creatures a set of perceptions, like a wonderful
picture or piece of music, always varied yet always
uniform ; so that all bodies and their qualities exist
indeed to every wise and useful purpose, but exist only
as far as they are *perceived*, a theory no less pious than
sublime, and as different from any principle of atheism
as the brightest sunshine differs from the blackest mid-
night."]

(4) Why then am I bound
to believe what Christians
themselves acknowledge to be
impossible, and to abandon
my belief in the Veda, which
harmonizes with the evidence
which commends itself to me,
and the matter of which [as
in the instances just cited]
is accepted even by Christians ? To clear up this *primâ
facie* view, we remark as follows.

। ४ । तथाच यं विषयं खृ-
ष्टीया एव खयमसम्भाव्यं मन्य-
न्ते स मया किमिति खीकर्त्त-
व्यः किमितिच मदभिमतप्र-
माणाविरुद्धे खृष्टीयजनैरपि
खीकृतविषये वेदे न विश्वसनी-
यमिति पूर्वपचं समाधत्ते ।

APHORISM VI.

The Veda, how
the result of
speculation, not
of revelation.　　It is not likely
that the Veda should
have been revealed by God,
because, apart from trifles, it

वेदखेश्वरप्रणीतलं न सम्भव-
ति । ईश्वरवचनसाहाय्यमन्त-
रा विचारकबुद्धिगम्यानां वि-

reveals only such things as यथाणां कतिपयचुद्रवस्तुनाङ्ग the speculative intellect is disposed to arrive at without the aid of God's word.

प्रकाशकत्वात् ॥ ६ ॥

[I say "apart from trifles," because that to which I refer especially is the great tenet that only One exists, and that nothing but One ever really existed or will exist or could exist. To this *conception*, if not to this belief, every one, we think, must come, who, studying the mystery of being—by the bare light of his own reason—determinedly analyses and takes account of every thought and every term in the chain of his speculation. I can articulate the term *creation*, and I may appear to attach a distinct idea to the term when I say that it means "making out of nothing," which I do hold it to mean ; but is it possible for me to conceive that what is so made has in it a principle of existence which would sustain it for an instant if the creative force were withdrawn? I am *not* able to conceive this. I believe that, by a confusion of mind—or confusion of words—people may persuade themselves that they have a conception of it (as a child may imagine that it has a clear conception of a *round square*); but I find in my inmost thoughts that I have *not*. Were there a withdrawal of the support of the One, I cannot conceive otherwise than that all *that appears* must collapse—as the electro-magnet drops the load that it sustained the instant that it is disconnected from the source of its magnetic power. Can we call such a thing a *magnet*—a *real* magnet? No ; it only appears to be one through the influx of an adventitious power. The illustration is an imperfect one;—as what illustration, of the conception here spoken of, but must be?

Now, while the speculative reason, fearlessly followed, brings us inevitably to the brink of that precipice of Pantheism over which the Vedāntin would have us cast ourselves, *here*, I say, is a worthy occasion for the intervention of a benevolent Providence, if a benevolent Providence there be; and here, accordingly, a benevolent Providence *has* interposed].

(1) The import is this. Had the tenets, that the Real is but One,—that sin, misery, etc., are all illusion,—that Man himself is God, and so forth, been true, there would be no need of a divine revelation to teach them, inasmuch as these facts might have been ascertained by the unassisted intellect. But, though in Him, the Almighty, we live and move and have our being, our destiny is at His disposal; and so, to set at rest such enquiries as this, viz., what that destiny, alternatively, must be, and what are the conditions by which that destiny is to be determined, a revelation was needed, and it has been given by the Most High.

। १ । अयं भावः । एकमेव सत्यं । पापदुःखादिकं सर्वं मिथ्या । जीव एवेश्वर इत्यादि-सिद्धान्तानां सत्यत्वे तज्ज्ञान ईश्वरोक्त्यपेचा नास्ति तद्सद्-कृतयापि बुद्ध्योक्तसिद्धान्तनि-श्चयस्य शक्यत्वात् । परन्तु तस्य सर्वशक्तेरन्तर्जीवन्तस्व-रन्तः सत्तावन्तो ऽपि वयं तदिच्छाधीनभवितव्यताका : स्मः । तथाच कतरास्माकं भ-वितव्यता वर्त्तते केच त उपा-याः सन्ति चैर्भवितव्यता नि-श्चीयेतेत्येवमादिजिज्ञासानि - वृत्तये ईश्वरोक्तिरपचिता द-त्ताच सा भगवता सर्वोत्कृष्टे-नेति ।

[Now, with regard to the declaration above quoted, of Sir William Hamilton, that creation, as usually defined, is unthinkable, we have to observe further, that "unthinkable" is not synonymous with "impossible." As Sir William Hamilton remarks (at p. 596), "there is no ground for inferring a certain fact to be impossible, merely from *our inability to conceive it possible*." Those, then, who prefer the ordinary explanation of the term creation, are not bound to surrender their view simply on the ground of our inability to conceive the possibility of such a thing. But, on the other hand, a Christian is just as little under any obligation to adopt that view; and a missionary among the Hindūs will give himself a great deal of needless trouble if he insist on inculcating, as an essential element of Christianity, a questionable metaphysical dogma which he himself, in all probability, has only taken up by rote. St. Augustine wisely remarks, that, "the opinions of philosophers should never be proposed as dogmas of faith, or rejected as contrary to faith, when it is not certain that they are so." He draws this general conclusion from the more special case of questions of natural philosophy. "A Christian," he says, "should beware how he speaks on questions of natural philosophy as if they were doctrines of Holy Scripture; for an infidel who should hear him deliver his absurdities could not avoid laughing. Thus the Christian would be confused, and the infidel but little edified; for the infidel would conclude that our authors really entertained these extravagant opinions, and therefore he would despise them, to his own eternal ruin."

Moreover, those who, like the Pandits, can really brace

their minds to metaphysical speculation, are not to be overborne by those more lazy minds which cannot. Dr. Whewell somewhere acutely observes that when a disputant professes that he will have nothing to do with metaphysics, you may safely expect to hear him propound some excessively bad metaphysics of his own, for which he arrogates an immunity from discussion. Now I have no sympathy with those (bad and most dogmatic of all metaphysicians) who profess to despise metaphysics, but great sympathy with those who would deprecate the raising of obstructions to mutual good understanding on the ground of points in metaphysical theory which are absolutely indifferent as regards practical results. The thinker is not to be overridden by the talker, who insists that there is " matter" (by which he means he knows not what), because, forsooth, *language* implies its existence. Language implies that there is redness in the rose, though no thoughtful person in Europe now believes that colour or any other secondary quality exists, as such, apart from a percipient mind. The *Idola Fori*, the fictions of the Market-place, are not entitled to the implicit deference in general so arrogantly claimed for them by the indolent and impatient, who, while, justly enough, professing that they have no turn for metaphysics, might advisably abstain from intermeddling where a turn for metaphysics (and perhaps even more than this) is indispensable for usefulness.]

(2) Now, to show how the foregoing considerations affect the matter in hand, we assert that—

। २ । अथ पूर्वोक्तं विचारं प्रकृते योजयन्नाह ।

APHORISM VII.

Granting to the Vedāntin that nothing *of itself* exists besides the One, it neither follows that a man *is* the One, nor that a man's endless course of existence depends upon himself alone.

तस्मादेकस्मादन्यस्य सत्ता खतन्त्रा नास्तीति वेदान्तिम- ताभ्युपगमे ऽपि जीवस्तस्माद- भिन्न इति जीवस्यानन्तः सं- सारः खमाचाधीन इति वा न सिद्धति ॥ ७ ॥

[Since we here use the expression " exists *of itself*," it is fitting that we should consider what is meant by saying that something " exists " in a different sense of the word from that in which something else exists. To quote the words of Berkeley (*Principles of Human Knowledge*, § 89), " Nothing seems of more importance towards erecting a firm system of sound and real knowledge, which may be proof against the assaults of scepticism, than to lay the beginning in a distinct explication of what is meant by *thing, reality, existence;* for in vain shall we dispute concerning the real existence of things, or pretend to any knowledge thereof, so long as we have not fixed the meaning of those words."

Now, according to the *Vedānta*,[1] "Existence or being (*sattwa*) is of three kinds,—1, Being, in its highest sense (*pāramārthika*); 2, such as has to be dealt with (*vyāvahārika*); and, 3, merely seeming (*prātibhāsika*).[2]

---

[1] We quote from the *Vedānta-paribhāshā*, Chapter II.
[2] सत्त्व ॥ पारमार्थिक ॥ व्यावहारिक ॥ प्रातिभासिक ॥

Of these, being, in its highest sense, belongs to God (*i.e.* soul or spirit); being, such as has to be dealt with, belongs to the ether [or space], etc.; and merely seeming being, belongs to the [merely seeming] silver, which is [in fact] mother-o'-pearl [mistaken for silver by a beholder]." The first of these is equivalent to substantial or independent existence, the second to phenomenal or dependent existence, and the third to deceptive appearance. Let us compare this with the views of Berkeley. In regard to the first kind of existence, Berkeley declares, " From what has been said, it follows there is not any other substance than *spirit*, or that which perceives."[1]   Here we have independent existence. But such an existence as this, Berkeley concurs with the Vedāntists in denying to the objects perceived. To these (whose " esse " he holds to be " percipi ") while he denies " an existence independent of a substance,"[2] contending that it is either a direct contradiction, or else nothing at all, to speak of " the absolute existence of sensible objects in themselves, or without the mind;"[3] yet he does not deny a *real* existence. He says, " I can as well doubt of my own being, as of those things which I actually perceive by sense, it being a manifest contradiction that any sensible object should be immediately perceived by sight or touch, and at the same time have no existence in nature, since the very existence of an unthinking being consists in *being perceived.*[4] The third degree of existence,

---

[1] *Principles of Human Knowledge*, § vii.   [2] *Ibid*, § xci.
[3] *Ibid*, § xxiv. It must be remembered that mind and spirit, in Berkeley's language, mean the same thing. This is not the case with मनस् (*manas*) and आत्मन् (*ātman*) in Sanskrit. See *ante*, p. 23.   [4] *Ibid*, § lxxxviii.

inferior to this, he assigns to dreams and creatures of the imagination; for, in comparison with these, he says, "The ideas of sense are allowed to have *more reality* in them, that is, to be more strong, orderly, and coherent;"[1] and these, being impressed upon the mind "according to certain rules or laws of nature, speak themselves the effects of a mind more powerful and wise than human spirits."[2]

While Berkeley and the Vedāntists, then, agree in holding that existence differs in its degrees, and agree also in allowing the first degree—viz., that of independent or substantial existence—to spirit alone; they differ—apparently at least—in their application of the term *real*. In examining this part of the question, therefore, we may expect to come upon some difference of opinion, such as shall imply, on one side or the other, an error requiring to be combated. But before proceeding to investigate this, let us take account of what has been ascertained. We have seen that the Vedāntins, in allowing the rank of substantial existence to spirit alone, hold the opinion which one of the most pious and thoughtful of Christian bishops advocated, not as merely harmless, but as a grand bulwark of the truth against the assaults of a debasing materialism. Verily, there seems to be anything but an obligation upon us to insist that the Vedāntin should give up this philosophical belief, and accept at our hands, as something indispensable to his further progress, "an unknown quiddity with an absolute existence," the term designating which, Berkeley adds,

---

[1] *Principles of Human Knowledge,* § xxxiii.   [2] *Ibid,* § xxxvi.

"should be never missed in common talk. And in philosophical discourses (he goes on to say) it seems the best way to leave it quite out, since there is not, perhaps, any one thing that hath more favoured and strengthened the depraved bent of the mind towards atheism, than the use of that general confused term."[1]

With regard to the third degree of existence—that belonging to what presents itself in dreams, etc.—there is no occasion for our here remarking more than this, that the missionary is not likely to quarrel with the Vedāntin for calling such things, in general, illusions rather than realities. What we are more particularly concerned about is the *second* degree of existence, which some of the Vedāntins *professedly*, and the others too generally *in fact*, degrade to the level of the third. The second and third degrees are in effect reduced to much the same level by the employment of the term *vastu* to denote spirit, and, on the other hand, its contradictory—*a-vastu*—to denote all else. Now the word *vastu* means a "thing," and since *a-vastu*, therefore, means "*not* a thing," the Vedāntins are disposed to treat whatever comes under the name as being (in the familiar sense of the word) no *thing*,—or *unreal*. They are, in fact, not disinclined to own the impeachment, against which Berkeley has in his own case so repeatedly protested,

[1] Third Dialogue, between Hylas and Philonous. We beg leave to remind the reader that we are not here professing ourselves a follower of Berkeley, nor urging any one to adopt his views. We are simply concerned to show which of the Vedānta tenets, by being Berkeleian, are not in any way anti-Christian, and not therefore the points against which it were wise to direct our efforts. Hence we are at present under no engagement to satisfy the reader in regard to all the difficulties which Berkeley's theory may, at first sight, appear to give occasion for. More objections than were likely to have occurred to any single objector, Berkeley himself has anticipated and replied to. His treatises are open to all, and are not voluminous.

of holding that the phenomenal universe is delusive, *because* phenomenal and dependent. The Vedāntins—as philosophers—(for at present we are viewing them as speculative ontologists and not as assertors of a revelation)—would seem to have been duped by the word *thing* and its kindred term *real*. They chose to restrict the name of *thing* to spirit, and then jumped to the conclusion that all else must be *nothing*, or nothing of any consequence.

Waiving here the question of revelation, which does not fall within the present section of our argument, we would recommend, therefore, that, in reasoning with a Vedāntin on his philosophical belief, he should be left in the undisturbed enjoyment of the opinion that there is no independent entity besides spirit,—that opinion being one which need not prevent his becoming as good a Christian as Bishop Berkeley. We should also leave him to think, for the present, as he may choose in regard to dreams or waking misapprehensions; but we should press him with the unreasonableness of holding that the phenomena of waking existence are beneath the notice of the wise, because, forsooth, they are not entitled to the name of *vastu*—the name of *substance* or *thing*. If phenomena have an existence "that must be dealt with" (*vyāvahārika*), their importance will depend upon our relation to them; and if it so happen that our relation to them is to be *eternal*, it is idle to disparage their immense importance by dubbing them "insubstantial." Whether their relation to us *is* to be eternal, and what relation our spirits bear to that Great Spirit whom we agree with the Vedāntins in holding to be the sole independently

existent—the Self-existent—are questions to be answered
only by a revelation. Confining ourselves, for the present, to the consideration of ontological theories and terminology, we proceed
to inquire what is the Vedāntic conception of the relation
of the phenomenal to the real. The Vedāntists are sometimes charged with holding that the phenomenal *is* the
real,—in other words, with material Pantheism. At the
same time they are charged with the wildest extravagance, of an opposite description, in declaring that the
Supreme is *devoid of qualities*, or, in Sanskrit, *nir-guṇa*.
With regard to the relation of the real and the phenomenal, no point appears to have occasioned more perplexity to the European assailants of Vedāntism than
the employment of this term *nir-guṇa*, so frequently connected in the Vedāntic writings with the name of the
Supreme (*Brahm*). We find, for example, a zealous
writer against Vedāntism declaring that, "In any sense,
within the reach of human understanding, he (*Brahm*)
is *nothing*. For the mind of man can form no notion of
matter or spirit apart from its properties or attributes."
And the same writer calls upon his readers to admire
the extravagant notion that *Brahm* exists "without
intellect, without intelligence, without even the consciousness of his own existence!" Now, the reply to
all this is, that the word *nir-guṇa* is a technical term, and
must be understood in its technical acceptation. It
means "devoid of whatever is meant by the term *guṇa*,"
and the term *guṇa* is employed (as already explained at
pp. xxxiv. xxxvi.) to denote whatever is phenomenal.
In denying that anything phenomenal belongs constitu-

6

tively to the Supreme Being, the Vedāntin speaks very
much like Bishop Berkeley, and like other good Christians whom Milton's epic has not educated into a semi-
conscious Anthropomorphism. Berkeley expresses himself as follows :—" We, who are limited and dependent
spirits, are liable to impressions of sense, the effects of
an external agent, which, being produced against our
wills, are sometimes painful and uneasy. But God,
whom no external being can affect, who perceives nothing by sense as we do, whose will is absolute and
independent, causing all things, and liable to be thwarted
or resisted by nothing ; it is evident such a being as this
can suffer nothing, nor be affected by any painful sensation, or indeed any sensation at all. We are chained to
a body ; that is to say, our perceptions are connected
with corporeal motions. By the law of our nature we
are affected upon every alteration in the nervous parts of
our sensible body ; which sensible body, rightly considered, is nothing but a complexion of such qualities,"[1]
and so on. The Vedāntin, in like manner, denying that
such " qualities" belong to the Supreme, declares, " We
ought not to ascribe to Almighty God properties, attributes, or modes of being, which are the peculiar characteristics of humanity, such as the faculty of vision,"[2]
etc. In short, the Vedāntin denies that the Supreme
either has or requires either senses or bodily organs ;
and, holding that organs of sense or motion are made up
of what he calls *guṇa*, as we Europeans in general say
they are made up of what we prefer to call *matter*, he

---

[1] Berkeley's Third Dialogue.

[2] The *Tattwa-bodhinī Patrikā*—the Calcutta organ of the modern Vedāntins—
p. 113.

asserts that the Supreme is *nir-guṇa*, in very much the sense that we Europeans assert that God is *immaterial.* We say, guardedly, "in very much the sense," and not simply "in the sense," because the term *guṇa* denotes strictly, not the *imperceptible* quiddity "matter," but what Berkeley calls *the sensible*, or the sum of the objects of sense. Theologically, the Vedāntin, asserting that the Deity is *nir-guṇa*, and the Christian, asserting that God is *immaterial*, are asserting the very same fact in terms of separate theories,—just as two chemists might make each the same assertion in regard to some individual specimen, while the one spoke of it as destitute of chlorine, and the other spoke of it as destitute of oxymuriatic acid.

To say that "the mind of man can form no notion of matter or spirit apart from its properties or attributes," is therefore no *reductio ad absurdum* of the Vedāntic dogma that nothing of what is technically called *guṇa* enters into the essence of God. Take away everything of what is comprised under the name of *guṇa*,—that is to say, take away everything that is perceived through the organs of sense, and take away every sense-organ, and take away all human feelings or mental processes, such as alarm, delighted surprise, recollection, computation, deduction,—take away all this, and there remains to the Vedāntin, not a mere empty substratum, but the One Reality, consisting of existence, thought, and joy, in their identity as an ever-existing joy-thought. This, whatever else we may think of it, is something very different from a substratum evacuated to nonentity. *We* are accustomed to regard eternal existence, wisdom, and blessedness, as *attributes* of God. The Vedāntin, on the other hand, instead of regarding these as attributes of God, regards them, in their eternal identity, as God himself.[1] Instead of holding, as they have been so often accused of holding, that God has no attributes in *our* sense of the term, they hold, in fact, that He is *all* attribute,—sheer existence, sheer thought, sheer joy, "as a lump of salt is wholly of uniform taste within and without." So far is the conception of *Brahm* from being reduced to that of a non-entity by the Vedāntic tenet of his being *nir-guna*, that, according to one of Vyāsa's aphorisms, as rendered by Mr. Colebrooke (*Essays*, p. 352), "Every attribute of a first cause (omniscience, omnipotence, etc.), exists in *Brahme*, who is devoid of qualities." It is rather strange that the occurrence of this passage in Mr. Colebrooke's well-known essay should not have sufficed to awaken a suspicion that the term "devoid of qualities," must be employed in a sense other than that of an empty substratum—a non-entity. The Vedāntin, seeing no occasion for any such vehicle of the joy-thought, never postulated any such. The empty substratum, the "nothing," which they are fancied to place in the room of the Supreme, is precisely what, as a nothing, does not enter into their conception of the Supreme at all. It will readily occur to the reader that the Hindū conception of *thought*, as the ultimate ground of all, independently of any substratum beyond it, anticipates, in its own way, Hume's extreme development of Locke.

---

[1] Compare St. John's expression, "God is love." I do not suggest a parallelism, for the Vedāntic enunciation is meant literally. See *ante*. p. xxxvii.

The misconception to which we have now been adverting, furnishing, as it has done, seeming ground for a charge which has been reiterated against the Vedāntins under all the varied forms of remonstrance, taunt, anathema, and virtuous indignation, has, we fear, done much harm. It has done much to confirm the modern Vedāntin in his opinion that his European assailants are incompetent to appreciate his system, and in his belief that the creed pressed upon his acceptance by such assailants cannot have any solid claims on his attention. If it be asked why the Vedāntin could not explain so simple a matter as this misconception to the person who blamed him unjustly, we reply, that the asker had better reflect what intense confusion of mind has been again and again occasioned, in every part of the world, by a mutual misunderstanding of a term when the two parties were not aware that they really misunderstood one another. People are always too apt to fancy that it is in regard to some *opinion* that they differ, when they only differ in regard to *the employment of a term.*

Reverting to the charge of extravagance in the notion that *Brahm* exists " without intellect, without intelligence, without even the consciousness of his own existence," it may be well to repeat here what the Vedāntin means by the terms thus rendered. By intellect (or mind) he means an internal organ which, in concert with the senses, brings the human soul into cognitive relation with the external. This, of course, he denies to *Brahm*, who, as Berkeley says of God, " perceives nothing by sense as we do." By intelligence, again, the Vedāntin means the conceptions of an intellect, as just defined, which, of course, cannot be present where an intellect, as just defined, is not. Finally, by consciousness, he means the individualizing of one's-self by the thought of "ego," thereby implying an existent "non ego;" and with reference to *what* is the *One* sole existent thus to individualize Himself? The denial of *Brahm's* "consciousness" in *this* sense, does not imply unconsciousness in the sense in which *we* employ the term. It merely implies that the one—who is not three as consisting of existence, thought, and joy,—is an existence, which existence is in the shape of thought only, and that thought an ever existent joy, which never really abandons (however much it may *seem* to abandon) its absolute unity by shaping itself into the complex thought that "*I* am blessedness." The practically important mistake of the Vedāntin, as we have argued in the aphorism, is his assuming that what *seems* is of no consequence.

But, it may be asked, is not this system—view it as you will — one of Pantheism? We admit that it is; but we would recommend that it be borne in mind that there is, as urged by Sir William Jones (see *ante*, p. 32), a great difference between the Pantheism which, in—or rather across—all that it sees, sees God alone, and the Pantheism (more properly called Atheism) which, beyond what it sees, acknowledges no God. The condemnation due to the grovelling system last mentioned, it were idly mischievous cruelty to hurl against the Vedāntin. The man who believes that his spirit is in the same category with his digestion, that his soul is a function of his brain, as the secretion of bile is a function of his liver, let us not, in common justice, insult the Vedāntin by mentioning in the same breath with him. If the Vedāntin be a Pantheist, he must be one of the other order, — a spirit of a far higher mood, erring though he be. Let us be cautious, too, lest we condemn him on a charge which he repudiates. Two expressions, familiar in the *Vedānta*, are usually cited in contending that the Vedāntin confounds the Creator with the creature, viz., the Vedic text, "All this· is God," and the illustration of the spider spinning its web from its own body. The passage in the *Vedānta-sāra*, where the illustration of the spider occurs, we render as follows :—" Thought [*i.e.* Deity] located in *ajnana* [*i.e.* in the aggregate of the phenomenal], which has the two powers [of obscuring the light and of projecting its own shadow[1]], is, in virtue of itself, the efficient cause, and, in virtue of what it is located in, the substantial cause ; as the spider is in itself the efficient, and in virtue of its *body* [—which body is not the agent, but the locus of the agent—] the substantial cause, as regards that product [which we call] its threads."[2] Now, as no one charges the man who says that the spider made its web from its own stores, with saying that the web is the spider, so we think that no one is justified in deciding that the Vedāntin says "The world is God," on the allegation that the Vedāntin virtually does say,

[1] See *ante*, p. xxxvi.
[2] शक्तिद्वयवद्ज्ञानोपहितं चैतन्यं स्वप्रधानतया निमित्तं स्वोपाधिप्रधा-नतयोपादानञ्च भवति । यथा लूता तत्कार्यं प्रति स्वप्रधानतया निमित्तं शरीरप्रधानतयोपादानञ्च भवति ॥

"God made the world out of stores of His own."
What were those stores? They are, in the creed of
the Vedāntin, just what amount to the sense of the
word *power*, the word *śakti*, the recognised synonyme
for the aggregate of the phenomenal, for the *ajñāna*,
—*i.e.* for that which is *not* God.[1]

But the reader will be ready to exclaim, how can
we be said to be unfair in assuming that the Vedāntin
says "The world is God," when there is no dispute
that a *Vedanta* text declares, "All this is God?" We
reply, that there is a distinction between "the world"
and "all this," which, however wire-drawn it may
seem, yet requires to be recognized. "The world" is
the display of the phenomenal. It is not *this*, as we
have shown from the *Vedānta-sāra*, that the Vedāntin
regards as God. But when he looks on the phenomenal,
the Vedāntist feels that an unchangeable reality must
underlie this changeable; he recognizes, through the
phenomenal veil, the one reality; and if he exclaims,
"*All* is God," is the exclamation necessarily profane?
Understood as we have put it, the phenomenal being
ignored as a reality, we think it is not. He only says,
"All that is *real* in this visible is the God who is
invisible." I have discussed this again and again with
learned Hindūs, and I here state my conviction that
those who condemn the Vedāntins as Pantheists on
this particular ground, would in like manner condemn
St. Paul, if—not recognized as St. Paul—he were to
reappear, declaring explicitly what was implied in his
asserting of God that in Him "we live and move and
have our being."   See *ante*, p. xxxiii.

In making these remarks, we have been regarding the system under its philosophical aspect, and we have therefore sought our data in the systematic treatises of the school. But there is in Bengal a modern sect of Vedāntists—to our mind not the least interesting among the followers of the Vedas — who deny the authority of the systematic treatises, and allow of no appeal except to the Vedāntic portion of the *Veda* itself. We cannot reasonably dispute their right to take up this position. The claim is not other than that which Protestants asserted at the Reformation,— the privilege of having Scripture as their rule of faith and not uninspired dictation. The removal of the contest from the *champ-clos* of the systematic treatises to the wide and diversified region of the *Upanishads*, is, indeed, inconvenient for those who would rather meet their man than hunt him. But the challenger cannot claim the choosing of the ground, and the missionary who heartily seeks the conversion of these men will seek it vainly if he shirk the task, however irksome, of exploring the field where alone the Vedāntists of modern Bengal will consent to be found. He must try to take accurate account of the *Upanishads ;* that is to say, he must not content himself with picking out a few of the passages which are most open to ridicule, but he must endeavour candidly to understand what it is, in these treatises, that *satisfies* the modern thinkers of Bengal. The study, if entered upon in a mocking spirit, might at least as profitably not be entered upon at all.

In the aphorism on which we have been commenting, we affirm that, even granting that nothing *of itself* exists besides the One, it neither follows that a man is the One, nor that a man's eternal destiny depends upon himself alone.

(1) But [the Hindū may ask] if the identity of the human soul and the divine soul be denied, then of what nature do you hold the human soul to be? In regard to this doubt we declare as follows.

। १। ननु यदि जीवात्मपर-मात्मनोस्तादात्म्यं निषिध्यते तर्हिं जीवस्य स्वरूपं कीदृग्भंस्री-क्रियत इत्याकाङ्क्षायामाह।

APHORISM VIII.

The eternity of human souls, of what kind.   Human souls, though created, will have no end.

जीवात्मनां सादित्वे ऽप्यन-न्तत्व सम्भवति ॥ ८ ॥

(1) If it be said that in that case there is a contradiction to a necessary rule, viz., that whatever had a beginning must have an end, we reply: Not so; because there is no proof that such is the necessary rule, and because the blank assertion of it can be set aside by a blank denial, and because, as in the 45th Aphorism of Book I. of the *Sankhya Pravachana*, so here

। १। अथैवं सति सादिभा-वमाचस्य विनाश्रित्वमिति नि-यमविरोध इति चेन्न। तादृ-श्रनियमे मानाभावात्। उ-क्तिमात्रेच तस्मिन्नुक्तिमात्रेनि-षेधस्य सम्भवात्। साङ्ख्यप्रवच-नप्रथमाध्याये ऽपवादमाच-मबुद्धानामिति पञ्चचत्वारि-ंश्रत्तमसूचवदिहापि वक्तुं श्र-क्यत्वात्। अपिच य ईश्र स्व-

too we may say, this [—that nothing can be endless which had a beginning—] is, "a mere denial on the part of unintelligent persons." Further, God, who is able to sustain for one moment those whom he has created, can with equal ease sustain them during an eternity. The question only remains, whether or not He chooses to do so. To this we reply, that, in the book which we hold to be the revelation of the will of God, we are informed of the promise of God that He will sustain the human soul in existence through eternity. But the doubt is not to be entertained whether there be any proof that that book reveals the will of God, for we have already discussed the establishment of the authority of that book by the argument from miracles, and by the testimony of competent persons who underwent suffering in this world solely for the purpose of attesting those miracles.

यमुत्पादितान् क्षणं रचितुं स-
मर्थः स तथैवानायासेनान-
न्तकाले रचितुं समर्थ एवेति।
केवलन्तु स एवमिच्छति नवे-
ति चिन्तावग्रिह्यते तच्च ब्रूमः
तथाह्रीश्वरेच्छाप्रकाशनपर -
लेनाभिमते ग्रन्थे पूर्वोक्तसार्व-
कालिकजीवरचणविषयिणी
परमेश्वरस्य प्रतिज्ञा श्रूयत
इति। तस्य ग्रन्थस्येश्वरेच्छाप्र-
काशनपरले किं मानमिति तु
न शङ्कम्। अद्भुतचरितलिङ्ग-
कानुमानेन तादृशाद्भुतचरि-
तसाचिल्वमाचार्यं लौकिक-
दुःखं सोढवतामाप्तपुरुषाणां
वचनेनच तद्ग्रन्थप्रामाण्यसिद्धे-
रस्माभिः पूर्वं विचरितत्वात्।

(2) Now we bring forward another proof that the Christian religion is from God.

। २ । अथ खृष्टीयधर्मस्येश्वरोक्तत्वे प्रमाणान्तरमुपन्यस्यति ।

APHORISM IX.

Evidence of Christianity furnished by prophecy. The Christian religion is established by the evidence of prophecy.

भविष्यदुक्तिरूपप्रमाणेन खृष्टीयधर्मः सुव्यवस्थापितो भवति ॥ ८ ॥

(1) If you say, but if prophecy be a sign of authority, then why should not those lists of kings, which were drawn up in the *Purāṇas* before those kings came into existence, be worthy of our belief? We reply: Not so; because we see there nothing to determine whether these lists of kings were drawn up before the kings came into existence, or whether they were interpolated in the *Purāṇas* afterwards.

। १ । ननु यदि भविष्यदुक्तिः प्रामाण्यलिङ्गं तर्हि तत्तद्राजोत्पत्तेः पूर्वमेव पुराणेषूपनिबद्धा राजवंशावली किमिति न विश्वासपात्रं भवेदिति चेन्न सा राजवंशावली तत्तद्राजोत्पत्तेः पूर्वमुपन्यस्ताथ वा तत उत्तरं पुराणेषु प्रक्षिप्तेत्यत्र विनिगमकादर्शनात् ।

(2) Now we state what peculiarly distinguishes the Christian miracles [from the miracles of the *Purāṇas*].

। २ । अथ खृष्टशास्त्रीयभविष्यदुक्तिभ्यो ऽसाधारणं भेदकमाह ।

APHORISM X.

That the pro-
phecies were
really such.
The prophecies which establish Christianity were made before the advent of Christ, because they are found in the sacred books of the Jews, who are up to this day the enemies of Christ.

(1) That is to say,—the prophecies regarding the Messiah, to be found in the Old Testament, the Scripture of the Jews, represent the Anointed One under the seemingly irreconcileáble characters of a conqueror and a sufferer. But the Jews, eager for deliverance from the tyranny of strange governors, looked only for a Messiah who should cause the overthrow of their enemies. When Christ came on earth, to suffer, and to conquer sin, death, and hell, then the Jews denied that this was the Christ's office;—to this day they look for a temporal deliverer. Yet when the matter is con-

खृष्टधर्मसाधका भविष्यदु-
क्तयः खृष्टोत्पत्तेः पूर्वं सञ्जाता
अद्यापि खृष्टं द्विषतां यहूदी-
यानां धर्मग्रन्थेषूपलभ्यमान-
त्वात्॥ १० ॥

। १ । तथाहि मूर्धाभिषिक्तं
विषयाक्रत्य यहूदीयधर्मग्र-
न्थरूपे पूर्वंसंविद्बन्ध उपलभ्य-
माना भविष्यदुक्तयो व्यक्तं वि-
रुद्धाभ्यां विजयिलदुःखिल्ला-
भ्यामुपलचितं खृष्टं प्रतिपाद्-
यन्ति यहूदीयास्तु परराज-
बलात्कारादात्मनो मुक्तिं
कामयमानाः कञ्चन केवलं
श्रुचुपराजयकारिणं मूर्धाभि-
षिक्तं प्रतीचाच्चक्रिरे । यदा
खृष्टो दुःखीभवितुं पापमृ-
त्युनरकान् पराजेतुञ्च भुवमा-
जगाम तदा यहूदीयास्तस्य
तमधिकारं निषिषिधुः तेद्या-
द्यापि कञ्चन लौकिकं रचकं
प्रतीचन्ते । परन्तु विचार्यमा-

sidered, it appears clearly
that the prophecies do not in
every respect consist with a
merely triumphant and temporal deliverer; but they find
in every respect their fulfilment in the history of Christ.

(2) The veracity of the
Jewish Scriptures, of which
we possess volumes transcribed
several hundred years ago, as
well as translations into hundreds of languages—so that,
even if an invention, yet, like
the Vedas, with their[volumin-
ous and various]commentaries,
they could not be supposed to
be a recent invention—is cor-
roborated by fresh evidence,
through the discovery of cities
[such as Nineveh] which had
disappeared under the sands
of the desert, exactly where
the Scriptures describe them
to have stood in all their
pomp, and where the prophets
declared that they would become an uninhabited waste.
And the predictions in regard
to the Jews themselves fur-

ऐ स्फुटमेतत् प्रतीयते यद्
भविष्यदुक्तय: केवलं प्रतापवि-
जयशालिनि लौकिके रचके
न सर्वरूपै: संवादं प्राप्नुवन्ति
ख्रृष्टचरितेतु ता: सर्वरूपै:
पूर्णतां प्राप्नुवन्ति ।

। २ । कतिपयवर्षसहस्रेभ्य:
पूर्वं लिखितानां पुस्तकानां
तथा भाषासहस्रेष्ववतरणा-
नाद्याद्यायुपलम्भात् कल्पित-
त्वादे ऽपि वेदवदेव खटी-
काभि: सहार्वाचीनकल्पितत्वे-
न शक्तितुमश्क्यानां यह्रदी-
यधर्मग्रन्थानां साधुत्वमारण्य-
कवालुकानिचयपिधानाद्दृ-
ष्यभावं गतानां नगरीणां य-
चैव तासां सर्वोत्कर्षस्थितिर्ध-
र्मग्रन्थैर्वर्णिता यच्च भविष्य-
दादिनो भाविनं निर्मानुषा-
रण्यभावमवदंस्तचैव खल उ-
पलभ्यादाधुनिकप्रमाणेनापि
सिद्धम् । यह्रदीयजातिविष-
यिणस्च भविष्यदुक्तयस्तद्ग्रन्थ-
साधुत्वे प्रमाणान्तरम् । अ-

nish further proof of the veracity of the book. The existence of this people up to the present time, throughout all nations, and yet commingling with none, is a standing miracle.

(3) If it be said that the prophecies are no evidence, because they are of obscure and doubtful meaning, we reply : Not so; because the obscurity of their meaning may have been designed to baffle attempts at their fictitious fulfilment. " No prophecy is of private interpretation," for all the prophecies are severally explained through the manifestation, on the fulfilment of the matter, that each really was a prophecy.

(4) Now, it were fruitless to bring forward evidence that a particular book contains a revelation of the will of God, if evidence have not been shown that there *is* a God; so we have to consider whether there be a God. According to the teaching of the

द्यापि कयापि जात्या सङ्कर-
मप्राप्य सर्वदेशेषु वर्तमानाया
ऋथा जातेः सत्यमथाधुनिक-
मद्भुतचरितमेव।

। ३। ननु भविष्यदुक्तयो ऽप्र-
सिद्धमन्दिग्धार्थत्वान्न प्रमाण-
मिति चेन्न क्वचिमतदर्थानुष्ठा-
नप्रयत्नवारणार्थं तदर्थगोप-
नमुद्दिश्य सन्दिग्धार्थताकर-
णसम्भवात्। नच कापि भवि-
ष्यदुक्तिः खतः स्पष्टार्था तद-
र्थमिद्धैव तदीयभविष्यदुक्तित्व-
प्रकटनद्वारा सर्वासां भविष्य-
दुक्तीनां व्याख्यातत्वात्।

। ४। अथेश्वरसत्त्वे प्रमाण-
प्रदर्शनमन्तरा ग्रन्थविशेषस्थे-
श्वरेच्छाप्रकाशकत्वे प्रमाणप्र-
दर्शनं निष्फलमितीश्वरसत्त्वं
चिन्त्यते। किं तावदीश्वरसत्त्वे
मानं। तत्र वेदान्तनयानुसा-
रेणेश्वरेच्छैव वस्तुतो नास्ति

Vedānta, there is really no will of God; for if by the word God, is meant *Brahm,* then *that* consists of knowledge only, and is what is meant by the word *Veda* itself. And the *Veda* cannot be the *revealer* of the will of God, else we should find a duality; whereas, according to the creed of the Vedāntin, there is no distinction between the Veda and the Lord.

(5) Again, according to the *Sānkhya* creed, there is no need of acknowledging a Lord, since everything is accounted for by Nature, the unintelligent maker of worlds. In reply to these opinions of the *Vedānta* and the *Sānkhya* we have this to say,—that if it be not agreed that there exists anything besides *Brahm,* then there is no foundation for the employment of arguments, either affirmative or negative. If there is any real Vedāntin in the world, then to argue with him would be like arguing with a child or a

यदि हि ब्रह्मेश्वरशब्देनाभिप्रे-
तं तर्हि तद् विज्ञानमाचरूपं
वेदपदस्याप्येतदेव प्रतिपा-
द्यम् । नच वेद ईश्वरेच्छाप्र-
काशक इति सम्भवति द्वैताप-
त्ते: । वेदेश्वरयोर्वेदान्तिमते
भेदाभावात् ।

। ५ । किञ्च साङ्ख्यमतानुसा-
रेणेश्वरखीकारे प्रयोजनं ना-
स्ति अचेतनया जगत्कर्चा प्र-
कृत्यैवोपपत्ते: । अनयोर्वेदा-
न्तसाङ्ख्यमतयो: प्रथम इदम-
भिधीयते तथाहि ब्रह्मसत्ता-
तिरिक्तसत्ताया अनभ्युपगमे
सर्वेषां साधनबाधनव्यवहारा-
णां निरालम्बनतापत्ति: ।
यदि हि कश्चिदास्तविको वे-
दान्ती जगति स्यात् तर्हि तेन
सम्भाषणं बालोन्मत्तादिस-
म्भाषणतुल्यं स्यात् । तदुक्तं
साङ्ख्यप्रवचनप्रथमाध्यायषष्टिं-

madman. In the words of the 26th Aphorism, Book I., of the *Sānkhya Pravachana*, "There is no acceptance of the inconsistent; else we come to the level of children, madmen, and the like."

(6) We commence, then, a separate Book, in order to establish that the Creator of the world is intelligent: a point acknowledged by the *Naiyāyika*, but denied by the *Sānkhya* Institute, which is the vestibule of the *Vedānta*.[1]

ग्रतिसूचे नायौक्तिकस्य सङ्ग्रहो ऽन्यथा बालोन्मत्तादिसमत्वमिति ।

। ६ । अथ जगत्कर्तुर्बुद्धिपूर्वकारित्वं नैयायिकानां सम्मतं वेदान्तिमतपूर्वभूमिकाभूते साङ्ख्यशास्त्रे प्रतिषिद्धं व्यवस्थापयितुमध्यायान्तरमारभते ।

---

[1] See p xviii.

BOOK III.

NATURAL THEOLOGY.

Now, following out the argument already cited as current among the *Naiyāyikas*, viz., that the earth, with its sprouts, etc., had a Maker, because it is a product, and it could not be made by the like of us; so that one different from us, a God, must be its Maker,—we first set forth the principle on which the argument is based.

तच्च चित्यङ्कुरादिकं कर्तृजन्यं कार्यत्वात् नच तत्कर्तृत्वमस्मदादीनां सम्भवतीति तत्कर्तृत्वेनास्मदादिविलचणेश्वर-सिद्धिरित्यनुमानं नैयायिकसम्प्रदायमनुसृत्य पूर्वमुपन्यसं तस्य मूलभूतं नियममादौ निरूपयति ।

APHORISM I.

Evidence of a Designer. It is settled that the Cause of the world operates intelligently, because we see means adapted to the production of ends.

तत्तत्कार्यौत्पत्तिनियतत -त्तत्कारणदर्शनाज्जगत्कारणं बुद्धिपूर्वकारि सिद्ध्यति ॥ १ ॥

(1) Now, in opposition to the *Sānkhyas*, who say that the world is not made by one operating intelligently, because Nature alone may, unconsciously and spontaneously, construct the world, just as the milk spontaneously and unconsciously becomes developed in the udder of the cow for the sake of the calf, we declare as follows :—

। १। अथ प्रकृतिरेवाबुद्धि-
पूर्वकं स्वातन्त्र्येण जगदुत्पाद-
यिष्यति यथा गोरूधसि चीर-
मबुद्धिपूर्वकं स्वातन्त्र्येण वत्सा-
र्थं प्रवर्त्तते उतो जगन्न बुद्धि-
पूर्वकारिनिर्मितमिति वदतः
साङ्खान् प्रत्याह ।

APHORISM II.

The Sānkhya theory of unintelligent design redargued. [We reject the argument of the *Sankhya*] because the illustration is not a fact; for it is quite impossible that the milk should exert itself spontaneously for the sake of the calf.

(1) In explanation, let this story be heard by the attentive :—A certain king's son, observing that, always at the time of his hunger's becoming sharp, a variety of food, brought by the hands of his immediate attendants, is set before him, fancied that *cooked*

दृष्टान्तासिद्धेः चीरस्य व-
त्सार्थं स्वतः प्रवृत्त्यत्यन्तास-
म्भवात् ॥ २ ॥

। २। तथाह्यवहितैरेषा क-
था श्रूयताम्। कश्चिद्राजस्-
नुर्नित्यं बुभुचोत्तेजनसमये वि-
विधमन्नं सन्निहितपरिजनक-
रोपनीतमुपसीदतीत्युपलभ्य
पक्कमन्न मदर्थं स्वत एव प्र-
वर्त्तेत इति मेने तथैव घृष्टखतां

food developes itself spontane-
ously for my sake, and he expressed himself to this effect
before his attendants. But
they, having smiled to one
another, instructed him as follows :—"Prince ! this food is
the result of arrangements established by the will of the
king, thy father ; for nothing
unintelligent, such as a jar or
a web, is ever seen to exert
itself spontaneously." Just
so, too, in the case in hand,
does a melancholy smile come
over the face of the wise when
they hear the *Sānkhyas* fool-
ishly saying, as if in emula-
tion of this king's son, that
the preparation of the calf's
food is independent of intelligence, and spontaneous, instead of being effected by a
Divine Foreseer for the accomplishment of a proposed end.

(2) But [the *Sānkhya* may
say] the soul is itself Divine :
so that, claiming the services
of Nature, it is competent to
create the world ; and though
it be in the bonds of Ignorance,

पुरतो जगादच तेत्त परस्परं
स्मितमवलोक्य तं निबोध-
यामासुः । ननु कुमार तव
तातस्य नृपतेरीच्छया विहिता-
नां नियमानां फलमिदमन्नं
नच्चेतनं घटपटादि स्वतः
प्रवर्त्तमानं दृष्टमिति । तथैव
प्रकृते ऽपि वत्सभच्छ्योत्पत्तिर-
बुद्धिपूर्विका स्वतन्त्राच नत्तु
दिव्येनानागतद्रद्रोद्दिष्टफल-
सिद्धये क्रतेति बालिष्ठाद्
राजसूनुवत् स्वयमुत्प्रेच्छ
ब्रुवतः साङ्ख्यान् ष्टण्वतां विदु-
षां मुखे सविषादो द्दास उज्ज-
सति ।

। २ । अथ जीवः स्वयमीश्वर
एवातः प्रकृतिमधिष्ठाय जग-
त् स्रष्टुं समर्थः । तथाचाज्ञा-
नवश्स्थापि स्वीयैश्वर्यज्ञान-
मात्रोपदेशाद् भवितुमर्हति

it may recognise its divinity through instruction by a fit person, as was the case with the king's son [in the story given under Aph. I., Bk. IV., of the *Sānkhya Pravachana*], as follows:—"A certain king's son, in consequence of his being born under the star of the tenth [and unlucky] portion [of the twenty-seven portions into which the ecliptic is divided by astrologers], having been expelled from his city, and reared by a certain forester, remains under the impression that 'I am a forester.' Having learned that he was alive, a certain minister informed him, 'Thou art not a forester : thou art a king's son.' Just as he, immediately, having abandoned the impression of his being an outcast, falls back on his royal condition, saying. 'I am a king;' so too it [the soul], in consequence of the instruction of some kind person, to the effect that 'Thou, who didst originate from the First Soul, which

राजपुत्रवत् । तथाहि कश्चि-
द्राजपुत्रो गण्डर्चंजन्मना पु-
रान्निसारितः शबरेण केन-
चित् पोषितो ऽहं शबर इत्य-
भिमन्यमान आस्ते तं जीवन्तं
ज्ञात्वा कश्चिदमात्यः प्रबो-
धयति न त्वं शबरो राजपुत्रो
ऽसीति । स यथा झटित्येव चा-
ण्डालाभिमानं त्यक्ता तात्त्वि-
कं राजभावमेवावलम्बते रा-
जाहमस्मीति । एवमेवादिपु-
रुषात् परिपूर्णचिन्मात्रेण-
भिव्यक्तादुत्पन्नस्त्वं तथांश इ-
ति कारुणिकोपदेशात् प्रकृ-
त्यभिमानं त्यक्ता ब्रह्मपुत्रत्वा-
दहमपि ब्रह्मैव नतु तद्वि-
लक्षणः संसारीत्येवं स्व-
रूपमेवावलम्बत इति निध्र-
योजनं जीवव्यतिरिक्तेश्वर-
क्ल्पनमिति चेत् । अन्नोच्यते ।
तादृशकथामात्रेण कस्यचि-
दर्थस्याखिद्धेः दृष्टान्तदार्ष्टा-
न्तिकयोः प्रमाणाभावसाम्या-
त् । यदि राजपुत्रो राजपुत्र-
त्वेनाभिमत इति तस्य राजपु-

manifests itself merely as pure
Thought, art thyself a portion
thereof,' having abandoned the
impression of Nature [or of
being something material and
phenomenal], falls back upon
its own character, saying,
' Since I am the son of the
Deity, I am myself Deity, and
not something mundane and
different therefrom.' And so
it is needless to postulate any
deity besides the soul." If
you say all this, I reply : [Not
so], for such a story proves
nothing, the illustration and
the thing illustrated being
alike groundless. For that
prince was a prince by con-
vention—princehood [indepen-
dently of the consent of others]
being a fiction. In like manner the fruits of soul's works
are dependent on the will of
Another; not dependent on its
own fancies as to its inherent
divinity. And that Will on
which soul's treatment is dependent cannot be that of a Nature which is [devoid of will,
being] devoid of intelligence.

चलमल्लीकमेव । तथैव जीवस्य
कर्मफलानि परकीयेच्छाधी-
नानि नतु खीयखाभाविकैश्व-
र्यकल्पनाधीनानि । साच जी-
वस्य कर्मफलनियामिकेच्छा
ज्ञानशून्यायाः प्रकृतेर्न सम्भ-
वति ।

(3) To make this matter clear, we cite the doctrine of the *Naiyāyikas* [Gautama, Bk. I., Aph. X.], to the effect that effort [or volition, *pra-yatna*], as it is a property of soul only, is therefore evidence of it, in opposition to the decision of the *Sānkhyas* [Kapila, Bk. III., Aph. 59], to the effect that "Though she be unintelligent, yet Nature acts, as is the case with milk."

। ३ । अथैनं विषयं स्पष्टी-कर्त्तुं प्रयत्नस्यात्ममात्रधर्मत-यात्मलिङ्गत्मेवेति नैयायिक-मतमचेतनले ऽपि चीरवच्चे ष्टितं प्रधानस्त्रेति साङ्ख्यसिद्धा-न्तविरुद्धमुपन्यस्यति ।

APHORISM III.

The criterion of the intelligent.

Desire, aversion, *effort*, enjoyment, suffering, and thought, are the mark of soul.

(1) And each of these severally is to be understood to be a mark. And thus it is rightly declared by the *Naiyāyikas* that the doctrine of an unintelligent Nature's working with a view to a special end, is untenable because self-contradictory.

(2) But [it may be said]

इच्छाद्वेषप्रयत्नसुखदुः ख-ज्ञानान्यात्मनो लिङ्गम् ॥ ३ ॥

। १ । एतेषाञ्च प्रत्येकं लिङ्ग-ता बोध्या । एवञ्चाचेतने प्र-धाने फलविश्रेषोद्द्र्यकप्रवृ-त्तिविधानं व्याघातान्न सम्भ-वतीति नैयायिकोक्तं सम्यक् ।

। २ । अथ प्रमाणान्तरविरो-

though this may be held inconsistent with other evidence,
yet that Nature does work
unconsciously with a view to
a special end can be gathered
from the *Veda*. This *primâ
facie* view we repel [in the
words of Vijnāna Bhikshu,
commenting on Aphorism 9,
Book I. of the *Sánkhya*].

घे ऽपि प्रक्कतेरबुद्धिपूर्वकं फ-
लविग्रेषोद्धेष्वकप्रवृत्तिर्वेदा -
दधिगन्तुं यक्केति पूर्वपचं नि-
रस्यति ।

APHORISM IV.

The self-con-
tradictory not
receivable on
any authority.   [This cannot be],
" for it is an esta-
blished maxim that not even
the *Veda* can make one see
sense in what is absurd."

बाधितमर्थं वेदो ऽपि न
बोधयतीति न्यायात् ॥ ४ ॥

(1) Well, it has been laid
down [in Aph. 1 of this Bk.
III.] that, through our seeing
the adaptation of means to
ends, it is demonstrated that
there is an intelligent Maker
of the world. We proceed to
show how it is that His intelligence [or designingness] is
thus proved by our seeing in
the case before us the employment of means adapted to ends.
To explain [in words adapted

। १ । अथ तत्तत्कार्योत्पत्ते-
स्तत्कारणनियतलदर्शनात्
कश्चिज्जगतो बुद्धिपूर्वकारी
कर्त्ता सिद्ध्यतीत्युक्तं तच कार्यो-
द्धेष्वककारणप्रयोगदर्शनेन
तस्य बुद्धिपूर्वकत्वसिद्धिप्रकारः
प्रदर्श्यते । तथाहि । यत् कि-
मपि प्रयोजनं स्फुटं सिद्धं प-
श्यन्नीश्वरवादी नियतमेवं वि-
चारयति यदि तावदहमिदं

from those of Lord Brougham's Discourse, p. 32] :— A theologian, on seeing any purpose manifestly accomplished, always reflects as follows:— "If I myself desired to perform this operation, and were acquainted with the laws on which its performance depends, should I accomplish it by any other means than the means here seen to be employed for its accomplishment? If not, then it is clear that some intelligent agent, possessing a knowledge of what is required to be done for the production of this result, has employed those means in producing the result."

(2) Having thus shown the scientific ground of the decision that the employment of means with a view to an end presupposes intelligence, now desiring to set forth a narrative illustration to exemplify the ground thereof popularly, we state the illustration in an aphorism.

कार्य्यं खयं कर्त्तुमिच्छेयं तदु-
त्पत्त्यावश्यकेतिकर्त्तव्यतानिय-
मांश्व जानीयां तच्चंच तदुत्प-
त्तिप्रयोजकतया परिदृश्य-
मानानुपायान् विहायोपा-
यान्तरेणैतत् कुर्य्यां नवेति ।
नो चेत् । कश्विद्बुद्धिपूर्व्वका-
रीतत्त्कार्य्यप्रयोजकेतिकर्त्तं-
व्यताज्ञानवानेतानुपायानेत-
त्कार्य्योत्पत्तौ योजितवानिति
सिध्यति ।

। २ । एवं कार्य्यादृश्यकका-
रणप्रयोगस्य बुद्धिपूर्व्वकत्व-
सिद्धेः श्रास्त्रीयं खलं प्रदर्श्य
लौकिकं तत्त्खलं वक्तुं सेतिद्दा-
सदृष्टान्तं कथयिष्यन् दृष्टान्तं
सूचयति ।

APHORISM V.

As a boat.

(1) And the narrative re-
garding the boat is this, *e.g.*,
When a man of the woods,
having arrived at the bank of
a river, beholds the branch of
a tree carried down by the
stream, then perchance he
reasons thus: "This tree, the
bank having been undermined
by the stream, having fallen
into the current, and having
been stripped of all its leaves
by friction with the bottom,
is borne along by the water:"
and further than this he does
not reflect upon the case. But
when he perceives a boat,
deserted by its crew by reason
of a squall, floating on the
water, and, after coming towards him, stranded on the
bank, then, having his curiosity excited, he considers that
structure.   "This structure,
which, by reason of its having
a hollow form, is buoyant like

नौवत्॥ ५ ॥

। १ । नौप्रधानक इतिहा-
सख्ायं यथा यदा कश्चिदा-
रण्यको नदीतीरं प्राप्य जल-
पूरेण नीयमानां वृचशाखा-
मवलोकयति तदा नूनमेष
वृचो जलपूरोत्खाते तीरे प्र-
वाहे निपत्य तलदेश घर्षणवि-
गलितपचजालो जलेन नी-
यत इति तर्कयति नचेतो
ऽधिकं तं विषयं विचारयति ।
परन्तु यदा स काश्चिन्नावं वा-
त्यातिश्रयवशात् पोतवाहवि-
रहितां जले तरन्तीं खाभिमु-
खमागत्य तीरे लग्नामुपलभ-
ते तदा जातजिज्ञासस्तं संघा-
तं विचारयति य एष संघातो
रिक्ताकारतथा रिक्कघटवत्
स्रवमानो दृश्यते तस्याधो-
भागो ऽन्योन्यसंश्लेषितकाष्ठफ-
लकैर्घटितो ऽस्ति येनायमति-

a hollow jar, has its lower portion composed of planks joined together, so that being very light it may float. And staves are arranged on both sides, moveable and with flattened ends, so that these if put in motion would cause this [vessel] also to move. And places for sitting are seen, convenient for the persons who are to pull the propellant staves. And staves are fitted inside, at such a distance from the seats as is exactly proportioned to the measure of an ordinary man, so that the rowers, by resting their feet firmly against these, may without hindrance apply their strength." From all this, without going into the question of the sails, the mast, the-rudder, etc., even the man of the woods decides with certainty that — "Therefore this structure was evidently made by some one intelligently, with the design of accomplishing such an end as this."

लघुभूत्वा तरेत् । दण्डाश्च त-
था सुचलास्तनूकृताग्राः पा-
र्श्वद्वये घटिताः सन्ति यथा ते
चाल्यमाना इममपि चालये-
युः । उपवेश्नस्थानानिच स-
मीचीनानि चालकदण्डचेप-
कारिपुरुषाणां कृते कृतानि
दृश्यन्ते । अभ्यन्तरदण्डास्था-
सनेभ्यः सामान्यपुरुषप्रमाण-
मित एवावान्तरे निर्मिताः
सन्ति यावता चेपणीपुरुषास्ते-
षु पादौ दृढमवष्टभ्य निघ्न-
निबन्धं खबलप्रयोगं कुर्युरिति
ततो जवनिकाकूपककेनि-
पातकादिकमविचार्यँवारण-
को ऽपि तस्मादेव संघातः
स्फुटं केनचिदेवंविधफलनिघ्न-
त्युद्देश्येन बुद्धिपूर्वं कृतो ऽस्तीति
निश्चिनोति ।

(2) So, pray, in the composition of the bodily parts of plants and animals, is not the extraordinariness of the employment of means adapted to ends even more striking than the extraordinariness which belongs to the above-described composition of parts in a boat? Or, in the way shown in the *Muktāvali* [as cited in Bk. I., Aph. V., § 4], is not this earth with its vegetable growths, etc., distinguished above artificial things by endless distinctions, so that here there must be a pre-eminent Lord, possessing supramundane knowledge and power, who makes use of means with a view to ends? Let not this be regarded by the intelligent as a superfluous repetition.

(3) But then, if it be said, Granting that there is a God, of the character above stated, still, how can it be proved that there is a Trinity of Persons in that One God, as asserted in Bk. I., Aph. VII., we reply: This, like the other mys-

। २ । तथैव किं स्थावरजङ्ग-
मशरीरावयवसंस्थाने तत्त-
त्कार्यौद्देश्यकतत्तत्कारणप्र -
योगवैजात्यं न प्रदर्शितनौका-
वयवसंस्थानगततद्वैजात्याद -
धिकविस्मयावहं किं वा चित्य-
ङ्कुरादिकं क्वचिमपदार्थेभ्यो
मुक्तावलीप्रदर्शितरीत्यानन्त-
विश्रेषैर्न विशिष्यते येन लोको-
त्तरज्ञानक्रतिमान् कार्यौद्दे-
श्यककारणप्रयोगकर्त्ता परमे-
श्वरो ऽस्तीति वचनं विदुषां
पुरतः पुनरुक्तं न स्यात् ।

। ३ । ननु भवतु परमेश्वरो
नाम कश्चिदुक्तप्रकारकः परन्तु
तस्यैकस्यापि व्यक्तित्रयं प्रथमा-
ध्याये प्रदर्शितं कथमुपपद्यत
इति चेदुच्यते द्वष्टमतीयरह-
स्यान्तरवदस्यापि विचारः क-

teries of the Christian religion, is matter for consideration. Now, therefore, although the mind of man is incompetent to clear up the several mysteries of this religion, we commence a Fourth Book for the purpose of discussing, briefly and to the best of our judgment, the Christian mysteries.

न्तव्यः । अथ मनुष्यबुद्धा तन्म-तस्वसकलरहस्योपपत्तेरग्रक्य-ले ऽपि यथामति संचेपतः रू-ष्टमतरहस्व विवेकार्थं चतुर्थं-माध्यायमारभते ।

BOOK IV.

OF THE MYSTERIOUS POINTS IN CHRISTIANITY.

Now, beginning to speak of the mysteries of the Christian religion, we first state, as follows, the doctrine of the divine Trinity.

अथ ख्रृष्टमतरहस्यं निर्वक्तु-
मारभमानः पारमेश्वरचैह्-
ष्यसिद्धान्तमादौ सूचयति ।

APHORISM I.

Mystery of the Trinity in Unity. In the Scripture we are told that the Father is God, so also is the Son, and so also the Holy Ghost, and further that there is but one God; but we are not told how this is to be explained.

ख्रृष्टीयधर्मशास्त्रे श्रूयते ई-
श्वरः पिता स एव पुचः स ए-
वच पविचात्मेति तथेश्वर एक
एवेत्यपि परन्तु तदुपपत्तिर्न
श्रूयते ॥ १ ॥

(1) If the *Vedāntin* throws out the doubt—how is this possible,—to be in the shape of three, and yet one? this is our first reply. If the truth

। १ । अथ कथमेतत् सम्भवति
चिरूपत्वैकत्वेति वेदान्ती शङ्के-
त चेत् तच प्रथममुत्तरमुच्यते
यदि तावत् पूर्वोक्तयुक्तिभिः

of the Christian Scriptures has
been established by the preceding arguments, and if these
contain statements which inform us of a unity in trinity,
then, though it be not stated
in the Scripture how this is
to be explained, yet these
statements must be in *some*
way reconcileable.

(2) Our second answer is
this. If it be hard to conceive
how the One God subsists in
Three Persons, it is as hard to
conceive how the One Eternal
Spirit has produced human
thinking souls personally distinct from Himself ;—yet this
distinct personality is proved
by the separate self-consciousness of souls severally.

(3) Our third answer is this.
If the *Vedāntins* say that it is
the One Sole Spirit which is
manifested in the form of all
human souls, then what stum-
bling-block is there in the way
of their acceptance of the doctrine of the Divine Trinity?
For if the one doctrine have
been accepted by them on the

खृष्टीयधर्मशास्त्रस्य प्रामाण्यं
सिद्धं तद्घटकलञ्च त्रैरूप्ये ऽऐ-
कताबोधकवाक्यानां तर्हि त-
दुपपत्तेर्धर्मग्रन्थे ऽनुक्तले ऽपि
तानि कथमपि समाधेयान्येव।

।२। द्वितीयं द्वत्तरं यदि
ह्येक एवेश्वरस्त्रिरूप इति दु-
र्ज्ञेयं तर्ह्यनादिरात्मा स्वाति-
रिक्तान् व्यक्तिभेदवतो ज्ञाना-
श्रयान् जीवान् ससर्जेत्यपि दु-
र्बोधमेव व्यक्तिभेदश्च जीवाना-
महंप्रत्ययवैजात्यात सिद्धः।

।३। त्रतीयञ्चोत्तरं यदि
तावद्वेदान्तिन एकमेवात्मानं
सर्वजीवरूपेण दृश्यमानं वद-
न्ति तर्हि पारमेश्वरत्रैरूप्यसि-
द्धान्तस्य स्वीकारे किं बाधकं।
यदि हि वेदं प्रमाणं मत्वा तै-
रेकः पक्षः स्वीकृतस्तर्हि खृष्टी-
यधर्मग्रन्थः प्रमाणं नत्तु वेद

authority of the *Veda*, then they ought to be prepared to accept the other doctrine, since it has been already proved that the Christian Scripture, and not the *Veda*, is the true authority.

(4) Further, it is not necessary to hold that whatever transcends our comprehension involves a contradiction. The prophetic description of Christ, as a sufferer and yet triumphant, as the humblest and yet the highest, etc., was matter of mystery until explained by the events of His life.

(5) Now, in order to set aside the doubt that a mystery is neither matter of proof nor of disproof, but that one must just remain silent in regard to it,—intending to suggest that proof and disproof cannot both be inapplicable, because of the rule [known as that of " Excluded Middle "], that there can be no alternative besides being and not being,—we propound that rule as an aphorism.

द्वयस्य पूर्वं प्रसाधितत्वादपर-पक्षस्वीकारे ऽपि तैः सज्जीभ-वितव्यम् ।

।४। किञ्च यद्यद् दुज्ञेयं तत्तद् बाधितमिति स्वीकर्त्तुमनावश्यकं यतः स्पृष्टविषयिका दुःखभा-गपि विजयी नक्षतमो ऽपि म-हत्तम इत्याद्या भविष्यदुक्ति-र्यावत् तदीयवृत्तान्तेन न व्याख्याता तावद् रहस्यार्थैवा-सीत् ।

। ५ । अथ रहस्यवस्तु न सा-ध्यते बाध्यते वा किन्तु तद्विषये तूष्णीं स्थीयत इति शङ्कां नि-राकर्त्तुं भावाभावयोरन्यप्र-कारासम्भवनियमात् साधन-बाधनोभयनिवृत्तिर्न सम्भवती ति सूचयत्तं नियमं सूचयति ।

APHORISM II.

The Rule of Excluded Middle. An assertion must either be true, or else its contradictory ; there is no other way, because there is no way besides being and not being.[1]

(1) To illustrate :—[as Sir William Hamilton remarks, at p. 529 of his Discussions, "We find. that there are contradictory opposites, one of which, by the rule of Excluded Middle, must be true, but neither of which can by us be positively thought as possible." For example, as he observes at p. 581], Time cannot be conceived by the mind either on the one hand as absolutely commencing or absolutely terminating, or, on the other, as without beginning or end. Yet time *must* be either of the one nature or the other [—though neither alternative can be positively

साधनं वा सम्वेद्गाधनं वा
नतु प्रकारान्तरं भावाभाव-
योरन्यप्रकारासम्भवात् ॥ २ ॥

। २ । तथाहि । कालस्तावत्
सादिप्रध्वंसिलेन वानाद्यन्त-
लेन वा मनसा न ग्रह्णीतं श्-
क्यस्तथापि कालो ऽन्यतररू-
पोऽवश्यं स्यात् । तथावर्त्तमा-
नकालो ऽपि यथा यथा वि-
चार्यते तथा तथा दैर्घ्यपिण्ड-
विस्ताराद्दिभावधर्मानुपलभ्भा-

---

[1] Stated by Mr. Thomson (*Laws of Thought*, p. 280), thus :—" Either a given judgment must be true, or its contradictory ; there is no middle course."

thought, our conception of
time as without beginning and
end being not positive but
negative, whilst a conception
of it as absolutely beginning
or ending cannot be formed at
all]. So again [as Sir William
adds], time present, when we
meditate on it, ceases to present an object for meditation,
as if vanishing into nonentity,
since we discern in it no positive character whatever, of
length, quantity, protension,
etc. And for this reason, in
Bk. II. of the *Nyāya*, Section
VI., " On the sifting of time
present," having stated, as the
primâ facie view, the unreasonableness, as aforesaid, of
time present, and then deciding that although the nature
of time present be inconceivable by the mind, yet time
present is inferrible from perception [of the objective or
subjective], inasmuch as without that [time present, in
which, and not elsewhere, any
perception has place], perception would be impossible,

दभाववत् तिरोभूयविचारा-
गोचरो भवति । अत एवान्वी-
चिक्यां दितीयाध्याये षष्ठे वर्त्त-
मानपरीचाप्रकरणे पूर्वोक्तां
वर्त्तमानकालग्रहणानुपपत्तिं
पूर्वपचलेनोद्ग्राव्य वर्त्तमानका-
लस्य मनसा स्वरूपग्रहणास-
म्भवे ऽपि प्रत्यचरूपकार्येण व-
र्त्तमानकालो ऽनुमीयते तेन
विना प्रत्यचासम्भवादिति स-
माद्धानो गौतमो वर्त्तमा-
नाभावे सर्वाग्रहणं प्रत्यचानु-
पपत्तेरिति साधु सूचयामास ।
तथाच वर्त्तमानकालविषये
भावाभावरूपतायाा अग्राह्यले
ऽपि न भावाभावविलचणसि-
द्धिः किन्तु कार्येण कारणस्य
भावरूपतासाधनमेव सम्भव-
ति भावाभावयोरन्यप्रकारा-
सम्भवादिति ।

Gautama has well declared in his aphorism [42 of Bk. II.], that "were there no present, there would be no cognition of anything, because perception [together with inference, and all else that is based on perception], would be impossible." And thus, although as regards time present, it be impossible to conceive it either as being or not being, yet this does not establish anything distinct alike from what is and what is not; but, what is proved by an effect, is just the existence of the cause, since, besides a thing's either being or not being, there can be no other alternative, [and it is not the *non-existence* of a cause that is deducible from an effect].

(2) Now, intimating that this rule does not help us to *explain* a mystery, we declare as follows :—

। २ । अथायं नियमो रह-स्यनिर्वेचनविषये ऽकिञ्चित्कर इति सूचयन् सूचयति ।

APHORISM III.

Mystery ex-
plicable were
no mystery. By explaining things which we acknowledge to be mysteries, we should contradict our acknowledgment of their being mysteries.

(1) For instance, such illustrations, adduced in explanation of the mysterious doctrine of the Divine Trinity, as that of the triangle consisting of three lines mutually combined, or of Chaitra Maitra and Vishṇudatta, rendered of one mind by friendship, are to be eschewed by acute reasoners, because the momentary light thrown thereby on such doctrines is immediately swallowed up in the glaring spuriousness of such illustration, resulting from its utter inapplicability to the case of what is sought to be illustrated.

(2) Now, in order to describe the peculiarities set forth in the Christian Scrip-

रहस्यत्वेनाभिमतानां वस्तु-
नां निर्वचने रहस्यत्वव्याघातः
॥ ३ ॥

। १ । तथाहि । पारमेश्वर-
त्रैरूप्यसिद्धान्तरूपस्य रहस्यस्य
निर्वचनायोपन्यस्ताः परस्पर-
संयुक्तरेखात्रयघटितत्रिकोण-
वत् सख्येकीकृतमनस्कचैत्रमै-
त्रविष्णुदत्तादिव्यक्तित्रयवदि-
त्यादयो दृष्टान्ताः सूक्ष्मवि-
चारकैर्हेयाः । तैरित्यादितस्य
तादृश्यसिद्धान्तविषयकस्य च-
णिकप्रकाशस्य तादृशदृष्टा-
न्तगतेन स्पष्टेन दार्ष्टान्तिकस्य-
लाद्त्यन्तवैधर्म्यप्रयुक्तदृष्टा -
न्ताभासत्वेन कवलीकरणात् ।

। २ । अथ पारमेश्वररूपपन्च-
यान्तर्गतद्वितीयपुरुषस्य रुष्टी-

ture as pertaining to the Second Person in the Divine Trinity, we state as follows :—

यधर्मग्न्थे वर्णितान् विग्नेषान् वक्तुं सूचयति ।

APHORISM IV.

Mystery of the Incarnation.

The Word was made flesh.

स ग्रब्दो मांसं बभूव ॥ ४ ॥

(1) "Was made flesh," that is to say, the Lord became incarnate as the Son.

। १ । मांसं बभूवेति । ई्श्वर: पुचरूपेणावतीर्णं इत्यर्थः ।

(2) Here the dissentient Hindu is to be admonished with arguments similar to the arguments stated when establishing the Divine Trinity; for he, acknowledging many incarnations of the Lord, can find no absurdity in acknowledging the incarnation of Christ; but the only question open to him is, which Scriptures are they by force of the authority of which the incarnation of the Lord is to be acknowledged? And to the question *how* an incarnation could take place? the counter-question—how are our souls linked to our bodies? —is a sufficient reply;—for,

। २ । अच विप्रतिपन्नो भारतवर्षीयः पारमेश्वरचैरूप्योपपादकोक्तयुक्तितुल्याभिर्युक्तिभिर्बोधनीयः स्वयमनेकान्,- श्वरावतारानभ्युपगच्छतस्तस्य रृष्टावतारस्वीकारे बाधकाभावात् केवलं तु कः पुनः स ग्रन्थो यत्प्रामाण्यबलादीश्वरस्यावतारः स्वीकर्त्तव्य इति प्रश्नस्तं प्रति सावकाग्रः । अवतारकथमावप्रश्नेचास्मदादिग्रीरात्मसंयोगकथमावप्रतिप्रश्न एवोत्तरं तद्ज्ञाने ऽपि प्रकृतविषयस्य कथमपि बाधाभावात् ।

although we are ignorant of that, this in no way invalidates the fact in question.

(3) Now, to consider the purpose of the Incarnation, we declare as follows.—

। ३ । अथेश्वरावतारप्रयो-
जनं विचारयितुं छृचयति ।

APHORISM V.

Mystery of the Atonement. The Lord became incarnate as the Son, to make atonement for the sins of men.

(1) If it be asked, how could atonement be made through the acting thus? we reply: Everywhere, even in the *Veda*, etc., it is seen to be the natural conviction of mankind that sin requires atonement. If it be agreed that this universal tendency of man's mind is a just one, then the question remains, what kind of sacrifice is to be offered to the Deity for the removal of sin? Now, whatever offering we can present, in the shape of goats or bulls or the like, all this already belongs to God, and is only lent by Him to us for a few years; and thus these

लोकपातकप्रायश्चित्तायेश्व-
रो ऽवततार पुत्ररूपेण ॥ ५ ॥

। १ । अथ कथमेवं कर्णेन
प्रायश्चित्तं स्यादिति चेदुच्यते ।
पातकं खनिष्टत्तये प्रायश्चि-
त्तमपेचत इति तावद् वेदा-
दिष्वपि सर्वेच मनुजानां मति:
खाभाविकी दृश्यते । सेयं सा-
र्वलौकिकी मनस: प्रवृत्तिर् -
चिताखीति यदि खीक्रियते
तर्हि पापनिवृत्तये कीदृश्रो
बलिर्भगवते समर्पणीय इति
चिन्तावशिष्यते । तच्च यत्
किमपि छागवृषभादिरूपमु-
पायनं तस्मै दातुमस्माभि:
शक्यते तत् सर्वं पूर्वसिद्धमेव
भगवत: खं कतिपयवत्सरपर्य-

offerings can have no efficiency except through God's favour; and so we are informed, in the Law, what sacrifices God gave the Israelites to understand would obtain His favour. A sacrifice, effectual in itself for the removal of sin, can therefore be provided by God alone; and such a sacrifice, we learn from Scripture, was provided through the Incarnation. How God is satisfied even with such a sacrifice is a mystery, and consequently not to be explained; since an explanation would involve self-stultification [on the part of him who should offer explanation of what, in calling it a mystery, he declares to be inexplicable]. But what behoves *us* is merely to appropriate to ourselves the benefits arising from such an atonement.

(2) If it be said that the benefit of an atonement thus prepared by God for the removal of the sins of mankind must be common to all men, since there is no distinction,

न्तमेवच तेनास्मद्रोचरीक्षतं तथाचैते बलयो निष्फला एव च्चते भगवदनुग्रहात्। तथाच तत्तद्वलेरनुग्राह्यत्वमिषरालि- येभ्य उक्तं भगवतेति श्रूयते प्राचीनधर्मश्राखे। अतश्च खा- तन्त्रेण पापनिष्टत्त्यनुक्रूलो ब- लिर्दातुं भगवतैव श्रक्यते स एवचावतारद्वारेण दत्त दृति धर्मश्राखादवगम्यते। भगवां- खयाविधेनापि बलिना कथं तुव्यतीति तु रच्छमिति तद्- निर्वचनीयमेव निर्वचने खतो व्याघातात्। केवलं तु तादृ- श्रप्रायश्चित्तजन्यफलखीकारो ऽस्माकमुचितः।

।२। नन्नेवं लोकपातकनि- टत्तये भगवता कृतस्य प्राय- श्चित्तस्य फलं सर्वपुरुषसाधा- रणं स्यादविश्रेषादिति चेन्न

we reply: Not so, because Faith is the means of appropriating the benefit.

(3) But then, it may be said, according to the text, that "Faith without works is dead," good works must be co-operative in the production of the benefit through faith; and so how can faith alone be the determining cause of the benefit? We reply: Faith alone is the means of appropriating the benefit of the atonement; but good works are an invariable effect of faith, and are evidence of their own cause. In whatever person these [good works] are not found, there is in him no real faith, but only a semblance of faith. And thus there is no conflict between the two declarations [of St. Paul and of St. James] that men are justified by faith, and that faith without works is dead.

(4) Now, it may be asked, how can man, without free-will, be amenable to question as to transgression of duty,

फलोत्पत्तौ श्रद्धाया हेतु-
त्वात् ।

। ३ । ननु निष्क्रिया श्रद्धा
म्रतेत्यागमवचनाच्छ्रद्धया फ-
लोत्पत्तौ   धर्माचरणरूपा
क्रिया सहचारिणी तथाच
कथं श्रद्धा फलनियामिकेति
चेन्न । तादृग्प्रायश्चित्तफ-
लप्राप्तौ केवला श्रद्धा हेतुः
धर्माचरणन्तु श्रद्धाया अव्य-
भिचारि कार्यं खकारणानु-
मापकञ्च तथाच धर्माचरणं
यस्मिन्पुरुषे नोपलभ्यते त-
स्मिन्वास्तविकी श्रद्धा ना-
स्ति किन्तु श्रद्धाभासमाचमि-
त्यञ्च जनाः श्रद्धया घृद्धा
इत्यस्य निष्क्रिया श्रद्धा म्रते-
त्यस्य चागमवचनयोर्न विरो-
धः ।

। ४ । अथ पुरुषः खतन्त्रेच्छ-
तां विनाकथंकर्मश्रद्धयोर्विषये
खाधिकारातिक्रमहेतुप्रश्ना -

whether in the matter of faith or works? And how can freedom of the will, in the shape of non-dependence on a previous cause, consist with the doctrine already laid down [in the commentary on Aph. V. of Bk. II.], of the impossibility of conceiving an uncaused origination? For, on the alternative of freedom, the will must be in the shape of a cause which is not an effect [and this, according to your doctrine, is inconceivable]; and if it *be* an effect, then there is an end of its [independence or] freedom. To remove this doubt, we reply [following Sir Wm. Hamilton at p. 597 of his *Discourses*].

र्ष्: कथं चेच्छायाः कारणा-
न्तरानपेचलरूपं खातन्त्र्यं पू-
र्वोक्तेन कारणरहितोत्पत्ति-
ज्ञानासम्भवसिद्धान्तेन न विरु-
द्धते । खातन्त्र्यपचे चेच्छया का-
र्यानात्मककारणरूपया भा-
व्यं कार्यात्मकले खातन्त्र्यचते-
रिति शङ्कां निरसितुं सूचय
ति ।

APHORISM VI.

The freedom of the will. How freedom of the will is possible in man or God, it is impossible speculatively to understand; but, practically, the fact that our will is free is established by the conscious-

खतन्त्वेच्छता जीवानां पर-
मेश्वरख्यच कथं जानेति ता-
वत्परमार्थतो ऽत्यन्तदुर्ज्ञेयं
व्यवहारतश्चास्माकं खतन्त्वे-
च्छता खाधिकारातिक्रमचे-

ness of [our moral accountability, or] our deserving to
be asked the reason of our
violation of duty.

(1) In accordance with the
indication already given [un-
der Aph. II. of this Bk. IV.],
that things which are inconceivable, may yet be possible,
there is not, on the theory of
freedom, an assumption of
more things inconceivable than
those the assumption of which
is necessary on the alternative
theory of necessity.   Such being the case, the consciousness
of our moral accountability
falls into [and turns] the scale
[in favour] of the theory of
freedom.   On this point a certain sage [Sir Wm. Hamilton,
at p. 597 of his *Discussions*],
says, More things inconceivable are not necessitated on
the scheme of freedom than
on the scheme of necessity.
To explain.   The scheme of
fatalism is pressed on our acceptance by the dread of the
inconceivability of a phenomenon's originating without a

तुप्रश्नार्हतांविषयकात्मप्रत्य -
चेष्वैव सिद्धा ॥ ६ ॥

। १ । दुर्ज्ञेयान्यपि वस्तूनि
संभवन्तीति प्रतिपादितदिशा
स्वातन्त्र्यपचे तावद्धोऽधिका-
नां दुर्ज्ञेयपदार्थानां कल्पनं
नास्ति यावतां पारतन्त्र्यपचे
कल्पनमावश्यकम्। एवं स्थिते
स्वाधिकारातिक्रमहेतुप्रश्ना -
र्हतांविषयकात्मसाचात्कार:
स्वातन्त्र्यपचतुलायां पतति ।
अत्र कश्चित् पण्डित आह ।
पारतन्त्र्यपचावश्यकदुर्ज्ञेयप -
दार्थेभ्योऽधिका दुर्ज्ञेयपदा-
र्था: स्वातन्त्र्यपचे नावश्यका: ।
तथाहि । निष्कारणककार्यो-
त्पत्तिदुर्ज्ञेयताभयादेव पारत-
न्त्र्यपचोऽङ्गीकर्तव्यस्तादृग्वे-
चोत्पत्ति: स्वातन्त्र्यपचाङ्गीका-
रमूलं पारतन्त्र्यपचेऽपि च तु-
ल्यैवानादिकार्यकारणधारा-
दुर्ज्ञेयता सैवचानादिधारा
पारतन्त्र्यपचाङ्गीकारमूलम्

cause, and it is just such origination that is the basis of the acceptance of the doctrine of liberty; while on the scheme of fatality also there is an exactly equal inconceivability of a beginningless series of causes and effects, which [assumed] beginningless series is the basis of the acceptance of the doctrine of fatality. And these two schemes, of liberty and necessity, are thus determined to be theoretically balanced; but, practically, the doctrine of freedom is the most correct, because, without freedom, the consciousness of moral accountability could not be justified. If men are accountable for transgression of duty, it is quite clear that they must be free to perform their duty

तौचेमौ खातन्त्र्यपारतन्त्र्यप-
क्षौ विचारे समतुलाविष्टता-
विव सिद्धौ तथापि खातन्त्र्य-
पच एव व्यवहारे साधीयान्
खातन्त्र्यं विना खाधिकाराति-
क्रमहेतुप्रसाद्धंताविषयकात्म-
प्रत्यचानुपपत्तेः । यदि हि
जीवाः खाधिकारातिक्रमहे-
तुप्रसाद्धाखद्धिखाधिकार्नि-
वेद्वणे खतन्त्रा इति खष्टमेव ।

[The words of Sir Wm. Hamilton, rendered in our Sanskrit version as above, are as follows :—"The scheme of freedom is not more inconceivable than the scheme of necessity. For while fatalism is a recoil from the more obtrusive inconceivability of an absolute commencement, on the fact of which commencement the doctrine of liberty proceeds; the fatalist is shown to overlook the equal, but less obtrusive, inconceivability of an infinite non-commencement, on the assertion of which non-commencement his own doctrine of necessity must ultimately rest. As equally unthinkable, the two counter, the two one-sided, schemes are thus theoretically balanced. But, practically, our consciousness of the moral law, which, without a moral liberty in man, would be a mendacious imperative, gives a decisive preponderance to the doctrine of freedom over the doctrine of fate. We are free in act if we are accountable for our actions."]

(2) But whence is the existence, permitted by God, in this world, of suffering which causes all this perplexity, and why are we involved in this suffering? We state in an aphorism the Christian avoidance of this question, as preferable to the Hindū attempt to get rid of it by the theory of Transmigration.

। २ । अथ कुतो ऽस्मिन् ज-
गति व्याकुलताहेतोर्दुःखस्य
सत्त्वं भगवतो ऽनुमतं कुतस्मा-
कं तादृग्दुःखाट्टत्त्वमच
भारतवर्षीयाणां जन्मान्तर -
सिद्धान्तेन परिहारात् स-
मीचीनं खष्टीयमतखं परि-
हारं सूचयति ।

APHORISM VII.

Abortive attempt of Hindūism to clear up the mystery of evil. The permitted existence of evil, since, as we hold, it is a mystery, is inexplicable. The attempt of the Hindūs to stave off the said inexplicability, by the assumption of the infinite

दुःखसत्त्वानुमतिरस्मन्मते
रहस्यत्वादनिर्वाच्या । जन्म-
धाराया अनादित्वस्वीकारेण
भारतवर्षीयाणामुक्तानुपप -
त्तिपरिहारो न कथमपि वि-
षयनिर्वचनचमः ॥ ७ ॥

non-commencement of the series of births, is in no way adequate to the explaining of the case.

(1) "By the assumption of the infinite non-commencement of the series of births," etc. [To borrow the reasoning of Paley, *Nat. Theol.* chap. ii., in reference to another case, in support of which the same futile attempt at explanation is made.] If, by going further and further back, there were diminution of the unaccountableness, then, by going back indefinitely, even the surcease of the unaccountableness were possible. This method of accounting is applicable only in such a case as that where, accordingly as we suppose the number to be greater and greater [of the terms, here] of the things to be explained [viz., the cases of evil] and the explainers [*e.g.*, the repeated births], there is continually an approach towards a limit. *There*, by supposing the number of

। १ । जन्मधाराया अना-
दिलक्षीकारेणेति । यदि ता-
वत् पूर्वपूर्वानुसरणेनानुपपत्त्य-
पचयः स्यात् तर्ह्यनन्तपूर्वपूर्वा-
नुसरणेनानुपपत्तिनिवृत्तिरपि
सम्भवति । स एष उपपादनप्र-
कारस्तादृश एव स्थले सम्भव-
ति यत्रोपपाद्योपपादकयोर-
धिकाधिकसङ्ख्याकल्पने क्रमे-
णावधिसमीपप्राप्तिर्भवति त-
त्रैवचोपपाद्योपपादकयोर -
नन्तसङ्ख्याकल्पने ऽवधिप्रा-
प्तिः सम्भवति । यत्तु नैवम-
वधिसमीपप्राप्त्याशा तत्रोप-
पाद्योपपादकयोरधिकाधि -
कसङ्ख्याकल्पनमकिञ्चित्करम् ।
एतच्च परिच्छिन्नापरिच्छिन्न-
त्वाद्यप्रकृतधर्मैर्विलक्षणयोर -
पि श्रेष्ठोऽसुखमेव । तथाहि
यथा परिच्छिन्नसङ्ख्याककट -
कघटिता श्रृङ्खला नात्मानं

terms to be infinite, the attainment of the limit is conceivable. But where there is no tendency to approach a limit, nothing is effected by supposing the number of terms to be greater and greater. And this applies alike to one series or another, though they should differ in properties other than the one in question, such as being finite or infinite, etc. To explain,— as a chain consisting of a finite number of links cannot support itself, so exactly is it with one consisting of an infinite number of links. And of this we are assured (though it has never been tried, since that would be impossible), because there is absolutely no approach towards the limit of self-support, though we suppose the number of links, beginning with ten, to be a hundred, a thousand, and so on. And it is the same with all chains, however they may differ in other respects than the one in question [viz., incapacity

धर्नुं चमा तथैवापरिच्छिन्न-
सङ्ख्याककटकघटितापि । ए-
तच्चाश्रक्रलादपरीचितमपि
सिद्धम्। कटकसङ्ख्याया दश-
सङ्ख्यामारभ्य श्रतसहस्रादिष-
ङ्ख्याकल्पने ऽपि स्तनन्त्वधार-
करूपावधिसामीप्याप्राप्यभा -
वात्। एतच्च दीर्घ्यव्यक्तिपरि-
च्छिन्नलाद्यप्रकृतधर्मैर्विलच -
णास्वपि श्रृङ्खलासु तुल्यम्।

of self-support], such as length,
numerical difference, finite-
ness, and so on.

[The words of Paley are as follows :—" If the difficulty were diminished the further we went back, by
going back *indefinitely* we might exhaust it. And this
is the only case to which this sort of reasoning applies.
Where there is a tendency, or, as we increase the number of terms, a continual approach, towards a limit,
there, by supposing the number of terms to be what
is called infinite, we may conceive the limit to be
attained ; but where there is no such limit or approach,
nothing is effected by lengthening the series. There
is no difference as to the point in question (whatever
there may be as to many points) between one series
and another ; between a series which is finite, and a
series which is infinite. A chain composed of an infinite number of links can no more support itself than
a chain composed of a finite number of links. And
of this we are assured (though we never *can* have
tried the experiment), because, by increasing the number of links, from ten for instance to a hundred, from
a hundred to a thousand, etc., we make not the smallest
approach, we observe not the smallest tendency, towards
self-support. There is no difference in this respect (yet
there may be a great difference in several respects)
between a chain of a greater or less length, between
one chain and another, between one that is finite and
one that is infinite."]

(2) And thus it is impos-
sible, by the theory of trans-

। २ । तथाच चाभिरापद्भि-
र्वृंतो ऽयं पुरुषो ऽस्मिन् ज-

migration, to account for the variety of evils encompassed with which a man is born into this world, or to explain how an infant, which never exerted free will at all, comes to experience sufferings. As a chain does not become competent to support itself through indefinite addition of links, just as incompetent is the theory of transmigration to account for the diversity of condition in the case of human souls.

गति ज्ञातस्त्रासां वैजात्यस्त चेतुनिर्वचनं खतन्त्वेच्छाकर-णप्रूत्यो ऽपि शिश्रुदुःखा-न्यनुभवतीत्येतद्धेतुनिर्वचनञ्च जन्मान्तरसिद्धान्तेन न सभव-ति । यथाच्चनन्तानन्तकटक-योजने ऽपि श्टङ्खला कदा-प्यात्मानं धर्त्तुं न चमा तथैव जन्मान्तरवादो जीवावस्थावे-षम्यमुपपाद्यितुं न चमः ।

(3) But, it may be said, such a book, professing to clear up doubts, can be no *revelation* of the will of God, because, since there is no clearing up of the question how the existence of evil is permitted by the Deity, there is really no proof that we have here a revelation of God's will.   To meet this doubt, we propound an aphorism.

। ३ । ननु दुःखस्य सत्तं कि-मित्यनुमतं भगवतेति प्रश्न-स्थानिर्वचनीयतया समाधा-नपरे ग्रन्थ ईश्वरेच्छाप्रकाश-नपरत्वं प्रमाणाभावात्र सभ-वतीति शङ्कां निरसितुं सूच-यति ।

APHORISM VIII.

Mystery not distinctive of Christianity. If you reject Christianity, then you must reject the world of sense also, since else your decisions are inconsistent.

(1) Now, that by such difficulties as the Christian religion is beset by, in respect of the permitted existence of evil, this world also, which has the same author, is beset, — that there are not more difficulties in regard to the Christian religion than there are in regard to the world itself, we commence a Fifth Book on purpose to show.

यदि ख्रष्टीयधर्मो नाभ्युपे-
यते तर्हि प्रत्यचसिद्धं जगदपि
नाभ्युपेतव्यमन्यथा खवचनवि-
रोधात्॥ ८ ॥

। १ । अथ दुःखसत्त्वानुम-
निविषयकयादृशानुपपत्नि -
भिः ख्रष्टधर्मो बाध्यते तादृ-
शीभिरेव समानकर्तृको ऽयं
प्रपञ्चो ऽपि बाधितुं शक्यते
जगद्बाधकानुपपत्तिभ्यो ऽधि-
का अनुपपत्तयः ख्रष्टधर्मे न
सन्तीति संचेपतो वक्तुं पञ्चम-
माध्यायमारभते ॥

BOOK V.

THE ANALOGY OF RELIGION TO THE CONSTITUTION
AND COURSE OF NATURE.

Now, beginning an exposition of the analogy of the Scriptural arrangement to that of the mundane system of cause and effect, we first propound as an aphorism the quintessence of the doctrine of an ancient sage [Origen].

अथ धर्मशास्त्रीयव्यवस्था-
या: सांसारिककार्यकारण-
भावानुरूपतां प्रदर्शयितुमा-
रभमाण श्रादौ कस्यचित् प्रा-
चीनपण्डितस्य मतसारांशं सू-
चयति ।

APHORISM I.

Origen's statement of the argument. The man who believes that the Scriptures were given by the Creator of the world, is not disturbed even when he sees the same sort of difficulties in the world and in the Scriptures.

य: पुमान् धर्मग्रन्थानां ज-
गत्कर्त्रा प्रणीतत्वं स्वीकरोति
सोऽस्मिन् जगति धर्मग्रन्थेषुच
समानानि रहस्यानि पश्यन्न-
पि न व्याकुलितो भवति ॥१॥

(1) "Of the same sort," etc. To the same effect another sage [Bishop Butler] says,—If by such difficulties as these it is proved impossible that the Scriptures should have been given by God, then, by the very same difficulties, it would be also proved impossible that the world should have been made by God. But the arguments for their being both alike the work of God have been already exhibited [in Books II. and III.]

। १ । समानामीति । एतदेवाभिप्रेत्यान्यो ऽपि पण्डित आच यदि तावदेवंविधे रचख्येर्धर्मग्रन्थानां परमेश्वरप्रणीतलं बाध्यते तर्हि ताभिरेव रच्ख्येजंगतो ऽपि परमेश्वरकृतलं बाध्येत विग्रेषाभावात् । तदुभयस्य भगवत्कर्तृत्वेतु युक्तयः पूर्वं प्रदर्शिताः ।

[Origen's words, as given by Butler, are these :— "He who believes the Scripture to have proceeded from Him who is the author of nature, may well expect to find the same sort of difficulties in it as are found in the constitution of nature." Hence, adds Butler, "He who denies the Scripture to have been from God, upon account of these difficulties, may, for the very same reason, deny the world to have been formed by Him," which, however, the reader, at this stage of the argument, is supposed to have conceded.]

(2) Although it would be proper for us to leave off here, since, to the intelligent, not a word more requires to be said ; yet, since *all* persons are not thoroughly intelligent, we

। २ । यद्यस्माभिरिहैव विरमितुमुचितं विदुषामधिकवचनापेचाविरहात् तथापि सर्वेषां जनानां सम्यक् पाण्डित्यस्याभावेनोक्ताचार्यदय

must endeavour to make intelligible, even to those of
lower capacity, the foregoing
words of those two great
teachers.   With reference,
then, to the question how it
is that its analogy to the constitution and course of nature
proves the Scriptural scheme
to be the work of God, we
propound an aphorism, to intimate, that, analogy, in the
shape of likeness, produces
only a probability of what it
is desired to prove, and that
probability, arising from the
contemplation of likeness,
though it is of the nature of
an inference, is yet an assurance lower in degree than that
of inference proper.

चांसि मन्दाधिकारिबोधा-
नि विधातुं यतितव्यमेव । तच
धर्मशास्त्रीयव्यवस्थायाः सां-
सारिककार्यकारणभावानुरू-
पलं परमेश्वरप्रणीतलख कथं
साधकमित्याकाङ्कायां सा-
दृश्यरूपखानुरूपलख तादृ-
प्रसाध्यसम्भावनामाचजनकलं
सादृश्यदर्शनोत्या सम्भावना
तु अनुमितिजातीया ऽप्यनु-
मितितो निकृष्टा प्रमितिरिति
सूचयितुं सूचयति ।

APHORISM II.

Analogy de-
scribed.   Analogy, though
akin to induction, is evidence
falling short of an induction.

(1) And, from the contem-
plating of likeness, assurance
of the following kind arises
[—in other words, the form of

सादृश्यमनुमानजातीयम-
प्यनुमानाद्पकृष्टं मानम्॥२॥

। २ । सादृश्यदर्शनाच्चैवंप्र-
कारा प्रमितिरत्यद्यते तथाहि
यौ द्वौ पदार्थावन्योन्यमेकेन

analogical reasoning is as fol-
lows] : " two things resemble
each other in one or more
respects ; a certain proposition is true of the one, therefore it is [probably] true of
the other."

(2) But [as Mr. Mill, in
his *Logic*, vol. ii., pp. 97-8,
goes on to say, " we have
here nothing to discriminate
analogy from induction, since
this type will serve for all
reasoning from experience,"
so] if it be asked, when the
unperceived is established
through perception of likeness, as is required in all
cases, in what respect is there
any falling short of induction ?
—we reply, that in induction
are employed the ascertained
invariable conjunction or non-
conjunction of certain properties ; but it is not so in the
case of a conclusion from analogy [or of assurance arising
from perception of likeness].

(3) But, it may be said,
the cause of a genuine inference is a genuine induction ;

वानेकैर्वा धर्मैः सदृशौ तयो-
रेकस्मिन् यो धर्मो निश्चितः
सो ऽपरस्मिन् सम्भाव्यत इति।

। २ । ननु सादृश्यस्य प्रत्य-
चाद्प्रत्यचसिद्धौ सर्वचोपयु-
क्त्यानुमानात् केनांशेनापक-
र्षं इति चेदुच्यते अनुमाने
तावद्न्वयव्यतिरेकौ निश्चि-
तावुपयुच्येते नलेवं सादृश्य-
दर्शनोत्यप्रमितिस्थले ।

। ३ । अथ सदनुमितौ स-
दनुमानं हेतुः सादृश्यस्य ल-

and what use is there then
for analogy, which you acknowledge to fall short of induction?   To remove this
doubt, we propound an aphorism.

नुमानादपक्षष्टलेन खीक्कतस्
क उपयोग दृत्याग्रङ्कां निर-
षितुं सूचयति ।

APHORISM III.

Practical value
of analogy.   Analogy, though
falling short of induction, is
universally the guide in practice.

(1) The import is this. It
is only in the case of beings
who are not omniscient that
knowledge, in the shape of
probability, and not consisting of certainty, arises from
the contemplation of likeness
[or from analogy]. For, in
the case of one omniscient,
nothing whatever — present,
past, or future—is matter of
probability, since He knows
with absolute certainty the
truth of what things are true
and the falsity of what things
are false.   But in the case of
the like of us, who are not
omniscient, it is probability

साटृश्रमनुमानादपक्षष्टम-
पि व्यवहारे सार्वचिकं प्रवर्त्त-
कम्॥ ३ ॥

।१। अयं भाव: । साटृश्र-
दर्शनात् केवलमसर्वज्ञानामेव
सम्भावनारूपमनिश्चयात्मकं
ज्ञानं जायते । सर्वज्ञस्य हि न
किमपि वस्तु वर्तमानमतीत-
मनागतं वा सम्भावनाविषय:
सत्यवस्तूनां सत्यताया मिथ्या-
पदार्थानां मिथ्यालस्त्यच तेन
सुनिश्चितलात् । असर्वज्ञानां
लस्मदादीनां सम्भावनैव प्रा-
येण व्यवहारप्रवर्त्तिकेति।

that pre-eminently furnishes
the motives of conduct.

[In the words of Bishop Butler, "Probable evidence,
in its very nature, affords but an imperfect kind of
information; and it is to be considered as relative only
to beings of limited capacities. For nothing which is
the possible object of knowledge, whether past, present,
or future, can be probable to an infinite intelligence,
since it cannot but be discerned absolutely as it is in
itself, certainly true or certainly false. But to *us*, probability is the very guide of life."]

(2) Now some one who, as
if he were omniscient, does
not acknowledge any authority in the probability which
results from the contemplation of likeness, and who is
accustomed [in the books of
Hindū philosophy] to cer-
tainty in respect of a thing's
being, or else not being, so
and so [—and whose language,
therefore, abundantly wealthy
as it is, almost grudges us
terms for the discussion of
probabilities], may doubt
whether error must not be
inevitable, if we follow evidence which falls short of per-
fection. To this doubt we reply as follows.

।२। अथ कश्चित् सर्वज्ञ इव सा-
दृश्यदर्शनजन्यसम्भावनाया:
प्रामाण्यमनादृत्य भावाभा-
वान्यतरविषयकनिश्चयशीलो
ऽपकृष्टप्रमाणानुसरणे ऽवश्यं
भ्रान्ति: स्यादिति शङ्केत त-
च्चोत्तरं सूचयति ।

APHORISM IV.

In the absence of superior evidence, evidence comparatively inferior is not to be despised, as a lamp in the absence of the daylight.

(1) "Not to be despised," etc. For if the inferior ought to be rejected because the superior is unattainable, then, since they are unable to fly through the air as birds do, people ought not either to walk with their feet.

(2) Again, the attendants of a certain child whose mother has died, seeing that he cannot survive without milk, desiring to procure milk, there being at hand no cow, or she-buffalo, or the like, become hopeless as they look around on stones, logs, pieces of cloth, etc., all very unlike in character to the cow or any other source of milk. Suddenly observing a female of the Bos Gavaeus, an animal of a

उत्कृष्टप्रमाणालाभे ततो निकृष्टं प्रमाणं नानादरणीयं सूर्यज्योतिषो ऽसन्निधाने दी-पवत् ॥ ४ ॥

। १ । नानादरणीयमिति । यदि त्कुत्कृष्टं न लभ्यत इति निकृष्टं परित्यज्येत तर्हि पचि-वदन्तरिचे सवेगोत्यनासाम-र्थ्यात् पादाभ्यामपि लोका न चलेयुः ।

। २ । किञ्च कस्यचिन्मृतमा-चिकस्य चिशोः परिजना वि-ना दुग्धं तस्य जीवनानुपपत्ति-दर्शिनो दुग्धसम्पादनेच्छवो गोमहिष्याद्यसन्निधाने पाषा-एकाष्ठपटखण्डादीन् दुग्ध-योनिगवादितो ऽत्यन्तविधर्म-कान् पश्यन्तो निराशाः सह-सा गवयामदृष्टपूर्वजातीया-मुपलभ्य साक्षाविरहितायेषा बङ्गभिर्धर्मैर्गोसदृशीति कदा-

kind they had never seen before, on the probability that
she, resembling a cow in many
respects, even though destitute of a dewlap, may perhaps give milk, putting her
to the proof, they obtain milk
from her. In this instance,
we see how analogy, though
falling short of a perfect induction, instigated [and rightly
too] the conduct of those persons.

(3) But then we see that,
in mundane affairs, the cause
of action is will, preceded by
knowledge; whereas, in the
Christian institute, action is
enjoined with a view to knowledge. To explain. We are
informed in Scripture [John
vii., 17], "If any man will
do His will, he shall know of
the doctrine, whether it be of
God;" so here there is no
analogy between the world
and the Scripture. To meet
this objection, we propound
an aphorism.

चिद्देषा दुग्धं ददादिति स-
म्भावनया तां परीचमाणास्त-
तो दुग्धमासादयन्ति । तथा-
चाच सादृश्यमनुमानादपक्र-
ष्टमपि तेषां पुरुषाणां व्यव-
हारं प्रवर्त्तयामास ।

। ३ । अथ लोके क्रियां प्रति
ज्ञानपूर्विकेच्छा कारणमिति
दृष्टं खष्टशास्त्रेच ज्ञानार्थं
कर्म विधीयते । तथाचि । श्रू-
यते यस्तस्येष्टं करिष्यति स
एव भगवतो धर्मो ऽयमस्ति
नवेति निश्चयं लप्स्यत इति ।
तथाचाच लोकानुरूपलं ना-
स्ति शास्त्रस्येत्याचेपं समाधातुं
सूचयति ।

APHORISM V.

Belief may be the reward of obedience. Belief in the doctrines of Christianity is indispensable; but this may grow from doing the will of God, and experiencing the benefit of so doing.

(1) "May grow," etc. A sick man, though doubting the skill of the physician who attends him, yet, by obeying his directions and by experiencing the benefit of such obedience, may come to place confidence in the physician. So is it in the case before us: such is the import.

(2) Moreover, whatever proofs, establishing the truth of the Christian Scriptures, have been set forth in Book II., so long as a man does not also *act* upon these in accordance with the Christian Scriptures, so long will they fail to confirm belief in him.

ख्रष्टधर्मंग्रन्थेषु श्रद्धा ताव-द्वर्जनीया किन्तु भगवदिष्टा-चरणेन ताटृशाचरणफला-नुभवेनच सा वर्धते ॥ ५ ॥

। १। वर्धत इति । कश्चिद्रो-गी निजोपचारकारिणो वैद्य-स्य ग्रिल्ये सन्दिहानो ऽपि त-दुक्ताचरणेन ताटृशाचरण-फलानुभवेनच तस्मिन् वैद्ये श्रद्धते तद्वत् प्रकृते ऽपीति भावः ।

। २। अपिच यानि ख्रष्टध-र्मंग्रन्थप्रामाण्यसाधकानि प्र-माणानि द्वितीये ऽध्याये नि-रूपितानि तेषामपि यावदयं पुरुष: ख्रष्टधर्मंग्रन्थानुसारि न व्यवहरति तावदस्य श्रद्धां दृढीकर्त्तं न समर्थानि ।

[As Mr. Fitzgerald remarks, at p. 6 of his edition of Butler's Analogy, "I am not sure that any one could be a fair judge of the sufficiency of the evidence to determine belief, until he had allowed it to determine behaviour."]

(3) But, it may be objected, we are told that belief results from doing the will of God; but doing the will of God just *consists* in believing,—for we are told in Scripture [John vi., 29], "This is the work of God, that ye believe on him whom he hath sent,"—and the sense of the proposition that "belief in Christ results from belief in Christ" is nugatory. With a view to removing this difficulty we propound an aphorism.

। ३ । अथेश्वरेष्टाचरणाच्छ्रद्धा जायत इत्युक्तं । ईश्वरेष्टाचरणञ्च श्रद्धरूपमेव । ईश्वरप्रेरिते अद्वैवेश्वरेष्टाचरणमिति धर्मग्रन्थोक्तेस्तथाच अद्धया श्रद्धा जायत इति वाक्यार्थो निराकाङ्क्ष इति श्रद्धां निरसितुं सूचयति ।

APHORISM VI.

Belief may have degrees of assurance. Belief may be of two kinds, attended by doubts, or entirely cleared from doubts.

श्रद्धा द्वेधा ससन्देहा निः-सन्देहाचेति ॥ ६ ॥

(1) To explain,—The expression employed, in addressing Christ [Mark ix. 24], "Lord, I believe, help thou mine unbelief," met with no rebuke from Christ. The import of the expression was

। १ । तथाहि खष्टं सम्बोध्य प्रयुक्तं हे प्रभो अद्दधे किन्नु ममाश्रद्धां दूरीकुर्विति वचनं खृष्टेन न तिरस्कृतं मदीया श्रद्धा स्थिरा न भवति तमेनं दुर्बलभक्तिमनं निः-

this,—"My faith is not steady:
—help thou this weak be-
liever by the bestowal of un-
doubting faith."

(2) And so the matter as-
certained is this : 1st, It is
fitting that, by reason of the
external evidences, we should
acknowledge the truth of the
Scriptures, as it is said in
Scripture [John xiv., 11], " or
else believe me for the very
work's   sake;"   and   again
[John v., 36], "the works
which the father hath given
me to finish, the same works
that I do, bear witness of me,
that the Father hath sent me."
2nd, It is fitting that the
faith thus originated, though
still encumbered by doubts,
should be ingenuously carried
out into action, as a child in
many cases acts according to
his father's directions, trust-
ingly, though not knowing
the motives which his father
has in view. And further, 3rd,
It is fitting that thoroughly
defecated faith, amounting to
knowledge, should be the re-

सन्देहभक्तिदानेनानुगृह्ळ्वेति
तदाक्यार्थः ।

।२। तथाचार्यं निष्कृष्टार्थः ।
बाह्यप्रमाणै: दृष्टधर्मग्रन्था-
नां प्रामाण्यं मन्तुमुचितमेभि-
रेवाद्भुतचरितैर्मयि   विश्वासं
कुरुतेति यानि चरितानि क-
र्त्तुं पित्राचं प्रेरितखान्येव मम
पित्रप्रेरितं   साधयन्तीतिच
धर्मग्रन्थवचनात् । अपिचेयमे-
वमुत्पन्ना श्रद्धा ससन्देहापि
निष्चपातमाचरणपर्यवसा-
यिनी कर्त्तव्या यथा बङ्बधा
पित्रर्भिप्रेतं प्रयोजनमजान-
न्नपि बालो विश्वासमानेण त-
दुक्ताचरणे प्रवर्त्तते तद्वदिति।
अपिच सत्खपि सन्देहकारणे-
ख्विवितर्कमुत्पन्नाया: श्रद्धा-
या: सम्यङ्निर्मलीक्तता ज्ञा-
नपर्यवसायिनी श्रद्धैव फल-
मिति ।

ward of that faith which sprang up uncavillingly even while there existed causes of doubt.

(3) Well, grant that all this is as you have said,—now it is alleged in Scripture that God governs both this world and the other world according to a fixed scheme. What, then, are the facts in that scheme? [or, in the words of Butler, " What things are implied in the divine government of both worlds, according to the Christian doctrine?"] To meet this inquiry, we propound an aphorism.

। २। अथ भवतु सर्वमिदं यथोक्तं परन्तु ख्रष्टमतग्रन्थे एतल्लोकपरलोकयोर्व्यवस्थां नियतदर्शनानुसारेणभगवान् करोतीत्युक्तं तच्च तादृशदर्शने कीदृश्याः सिद्धान्ताः सन्तीत्याकाङ्क्षां निरसितुं सूचयति ।

APHORISM VII.

What the divine government of both worlds implies, according to the Christian doctrine. The divine government of both worlds implies, according to the Christian doctrine, these propositions, viz., 1st, All souls are appointed to exist endlessly; 2nd, It is appointed that every one, after death, shall be either rewarded or punished; 3rd, The abiding of souls in this world is for

ख्रष्टधर्मग्रन्थानुसारिण्या लोकद्वयव्यवस्थाया गर्भे द्वे सिद्धान्ताः सन्ति । तथाहि जीवानामनन्तजीवनं नियत-मित्येकः । सर्वस्य मरणोत्तरं निग्रहानुग्रहान्यतरनियतमिति द्वितीयः । एतल्लोके स्थितिर्जीवानां परीचार्थं परलो-कानुगुणश्चिचार्यञ्चास्तीति ष-

the purpose of trial, and of discipline for the next world; 4th, Since this world, through wickedness, tends to ruin, and since men's knowledge both of their own condition and of duty has become corrupted, occasion was thus given for God's contriving a new remedy; 5th, The truth of this remedial dispensation, which consists of a special scheme carried on by a divine person, the Messiah, for the benefit of the world, is proved by miracles; 6th, And that means of salvation is not revealed to all, nor proved with the strongest possible evidence [with evidence not less strong than the strongest good evidence] to all those to whom it is revealed; but it is revealed only to such a part of mankind as God has chosen, and with such particular evidence as God has chosen.

(1) "To exist endlessly after death," etc. The import is this. It is unnecessary here to set forth proofs that

तीय: । अस्य लोकस्य पापव-
ग्रेन चयोन्मुखतया जनानां
खीयावस्थाधर्माचरणविषय-
कज्ञानापचयेनचापूर्वलोकमु-
त्क्षुपायरचनमीश्वरस्य प्रसक्त-
मिति चतुर्थं: । लोकहिताथं
दिव्यपुरुषेण ख्रष्टेन प्रवर्त्तनी-
यधर्मविग्रेषरूपस्य तादृग्रो-
पायस्य प्रामाणिकलमद्भुतच-
रितै: सिद्यतीति पञ्चम: । सच
मोचोपायो न सर्वान् प्रति
ज्ञापितो न वा यांश्च प्रत्येष
ज्ञापितस्तान् सर्वान् प्रत्यपि
बलवत्तमसाधुप्रमाणान्यूनब-
लेन प्रमाणेनैव ज्ञापित: कि-
न्त्वीश्वरेच्छाविषयीभूतं कञ्च-
न लौकिकदेशं प्रति भगवदि-
च्छाविषयीभूतप्रमाणविग्रेषै-
रेवचज्ञापित इति षष्ठ: ॥ ७॥

। १ । मरणोत्तरानन्तस्थि-
तिरित्यादि । अयं भाव: ।
एतादृश्स्थितिसत्त्वे तस्यास्त-

such [endless existence] is really the condition [of soul], and that this state will be in accordance with each soul's deserts, since our dispute is not at present with him who denies the soul to be other than the body; but we have entered on an argument with those only who accept as authoritative the Hindū Spiritual Institutes. But we do not, on the strength of the Hindū Institutes, accept the theory of transmigration, because we do not allow that the Hindū Institutes have any authority as proof. And it must not be said, moreover, that, since the existence of evil cannot be without some cause, transmigration is established as its cause, because we have already shown that even by the supposition thereof, the existence of evil cannot be accounted for. In the Christian Scripture, the truth of which has been established by the arguments set forth [in Book II.], it is declared that the endless condi-

त्तञ्जीवानां तत्तत्कर्मफलप्रा-
प्त्यनुकूलत्वेच प्रमाणोपन्यास-
स्तु नावश्यक: देहात्मवादिना
समं विवादस्याप्रस्तुतत्वात् ।
भारतवर्षीयाध्यात्मशास्त्रप्रा-
माण्याभ्युपगन्तृभि: सच्चैव वि-
वादस्योपक्रान्तत्वात्। भारत-
वर्षीयशास्त्रबलात् पुन: पुन-
र्जन्मवादस्तु न स्वीक्रियते भो-
रतवर्षीयशास्त्राणां प्रामाण्य-
स्यास्माभिरस्वीकारात्। दु:-
खसत्त्वस्याकस्मिकत्वासम्भवात्
तद्धेतुतया पुन: पुनर्जन्म सि-
द्ध्यतीत्यपि न वक्तव्यम्। तत्क-
ल्पने ऽपि दु:खसत्त्वोपपादना-
सम्भवस्य पूर्वं प्रदर्शितत्वात्।
प्रदर्शितयुक्तिसिद्धप्रामाण्के
स्रष्टधर्मग्रन्थे मरणोत्तरान-
न्तस्थिति: केषाश्चिदनन्तान-
न्दवती केषाश्चिच्चानन्तदु:ख-
वती भवतीत्युक्तम्।

tion after death is, in the case
of some, a condition of endless
happiness, and, in the case of
some, a condition of endless
misery.

(2) " State of trial and discipline," etc.　The special
means of salvation which have
been enjoined by God, constitute one trial for the proud
and rebellious heart of man.
The particulars of this have
been set forth in the section
on the Atonement [Book III.,.
Aph. V.]　For man, by rea-
son of pride, would fain obtain salvation, not through
what is done by another, but
by works of his own, such as
perseverance in austerities,
however wearisome, — by
something other than the
imputation to himself of the
merits of Christ's death.

(3) " The ruin of this world
through wickedness," etc. The
doctrine of the Hindū Institutes is, that ignorance is the
cause of the unhappy state of
the present life.　But this
doctrine is unproved, for we

।२। परीचाग्निचर्य्योरवस्त्रेति।
तच्च गर्वेद्रोद्वपरचेतसोमनु-
ष्यस्य मुक्त्यसाधारणकारणानि
यानीश्वरेणोपदिष्टानि तानि
परीचारूपाणि तद्विशेषाश्च पू-
र्व्वमेव प्रायश्चित्तप्रकरणे प्रति-
पादिताः। मनुष्यो हि गर्व्ववा-
त्सात् खृष्टमरणपुण्यस्यात्म-
न्यारोपादन्येन तपस्वर्य्यादि-
नात्यन्तश्रमदेनापि खकृतेन
कर्म्मणा मुक्तिमिच्छति नतु प-
रकृतेनेति।

।३। अस्य लोकस्य पापव-
शात् चयोन्मुखलमित्यादि।
इदानीन्तनदुरवस्थायाः का-
रणमविद्येति भारतवर्षीयशा-
स्त्रसिद्धान्तः सतु तच्चास्मा-
कां प्रामाण्यास्माभिरनङ्गी-

do not admit that those institutes are any proof. Nay, the further a man advances in vice, the less conscious of his sinfulness does he become; and so, from forgetfulness of his danger, he dreads not the pain of retribution [—thus owing to ignorance his *freedom* from mental distress]. On the other hand, the more truly a man discerns his own condition, the more is he distressed by the view of his own sinfulness, and he remains in dread so long as he has not found any means of deliverance from his sins.

(4) [If it be asked, "Whence is sin?" we reply that] we have already acknowledged, in the chapter on the Mysteries, that the source of the existence of sin, like the cause of the existence of evil, we cannot tell.

(5) "Not revealed to all men," etc. But it may be said,—Since all men are under apprehension of terrible and eternal misery, the means of escape from such misery ought

कारादसिद्ध एव किञ्च यथा यथायं दुष्कर्मणि प्रवर्त्तते त-था तथासौ खीयां पातकितां न्यूनमनुभवति तथाच खान-र्थविस्मरणाद् दण्डदुःखान्न बिभेति । प्रत्युतायं यथा य-थायं खीयामवस्थां वस्तुतः पश्यति तथा तथा खीयदुष्क-र्मदर्शनेन सन्तप्यते यावच्च क-श्चित् पापमोचणोपायं न प्रा-प्नोति तावद् व्याकुलितो भ-वति ।

। ४ । पापस्य सत्त्वे बीजं तु दुःखसत्त्वहेतुवद् दुर्वचमेवेति रहस्यप्रकरणे पूर्वमेव चिन्ति-तम् ।

। ५ । सर्वमनुष्यान् प्रति न ज्ञापितमिति । ननु भयावहे-नानन्तेन दुःखेन सर्वमनुष्या-णां व्याकुलितत्वात् तादृग्व-दुःखमोचनोपायः सर्वान्

to be told to all;—and so, why has it not been told to all? We reply, that we have not here undertaken to remove all the objections that have been raised or that may be raised either against the course of nature or against the will of God as revealed in the Christian Scripture; but [what we have undertaken is] to explain that the world, though established by the evidence of the senses, might be disbelieved on the ground of the very same objections, on the strength of which you say that the mysteries announced in the Christian Scriptures ought not to be believed.   And so it is fruitless to raise these same objections against the Scriptures, the truth of which is established by other unobjectionable proofs.

(6) But, it may be asked, since it was declared in Scripture [Revelations, xv. 3], "Just and true are all thy ways," how is it acknowledged by you who accept the Christian religion that you are unable to

प्रति वक्तव्यः तथाचेश्वरेण स-
र्वमनुष्यान् प्रति स कुतो नो-
क्तः इति चेदुच्यते प्रकृते जग-
द्ववस्थायां वा खृष्टधर्मग्रन्थ-
प्रकाशितेश्वरेच्छायां वोद्धा-
वितानामुद्भावयिष्यमाणानां
वा दोषाणां वारणे वयं न प्र-
वृत्ताः स्मो ऽपि तु चैर्दोर्षैर्ध-
र्मग्रन्थोक्तानि रहस्यानि न श्र-
द्धेयानीति लयोच्यते तैरेव
दोषैः प्रत्यक्षसिद्धमपि जगन्न
न श्रद्धेयं स्यादिति वक्तुं तथा-
च निर्दोषप्रमाणान्तरदृढी-
कृतप्रामाण्येषु धर्मग्रन्थेषु ते-
षां दोषाणामुद्भावनमफल-
मेव ।

। ६ । ननु परमेश्वरस्य तव
सर्वे व्यवहारा उचिताः सत्या-
श्च सन्तीति धर्मग्रन्थेषूक्तलात्
खृष्टमतखीकर्त्तभिर्युष्माभिर-
मेषत्त्वनिर्वचनासामर्थ्यं कथं

justify those ways in every respect? We reply [with Dr. Chalmers], To utter such an expression is fitting for those only to whom the day of the revelation of hidden things has come, whose condition of having the secrets of God hidden from them has ceased, or by whom the fulfilment of God's designs has been witnessed. But previously to such great and final manifestation of the hidden things of God, we have only to expect with humility; and the mysteries which in our present state we cannot comprehend we must silently acquiesce in.

प्रतिपाद्यत इति चेत्। अ-
चोच्यते तादृशं हि वचनं तै-
रेव वक्तुमुचितं यान् प्रति रह-
स्यवस्तुप्रकाशनदिनं प्राप्तं ये-
षां देवगुह्यगोपनावस्था विर-
ता भगवदिच्छासिद्धिर्वा यैः
प्रत्यचीक्षता । तादृश्या मह-
त्या अन्यायाश्च देवगुह्यप्र-
काशावस्थायाः पूर्वं तु केवल-
मस्माभिः सविनयं प्रतीचित-
व्यम् । इदानीन्तनावस्थायां
ज्ञातुमश्क्यानि रहस्यानिच
द्रष्णीमेव स्वीकर्त्तव्यानि ।

[The words of Dr. Chalmers, in his *Evidences*, vol. i., p. 310, are these:—"This [Rev. xv. 3] might well be said by those to whom the day of the revelation of hidden things has come, and to whom the mystery of God is finished—or who have witnessed its fulfilment. Previous to that great and final manifestation, it is our part to wait in humble expectancy, and to acquiesce in the mysteriousness of many things which at present we do not comprehend."]

(7) Further, whoever says that he can now everywhere discern God's wisdom and

। ७ । अपिच यः को ऽपि
साम्प्रतं भगवतो ज्ञानं साधु-

goodness, he, like one "lying for God," injures with great effort [or unintentionally does his best to injure], though loving it, the very cause which he seeks [thus disingenuously] to advance.

(7) Let us now recapitulate the matters that have been laid down in the several sections of this treatise. In Bk. I. is an account of the leading points in the Christian religion. In Bk. II. is an account of the arguments for the truthfulness of the Christian Scriptures. In Bk. III. it is shown that this world was made by an Intelligent Worker, possessed of power transcending that of mortals. In Bk. IV. it is shown that as there are learned, from the books which reveal God's will, things different from the visible, and which we cannot explain,— so, too, are there in God's created world things seen and yet mysterious, and by us at present inexplicable. In Bk. V. it is shown that as the mys-

ताञ्च सार्वचिकीं ज्ञातुं शक्नो-
मीति वदेत् स भगवत्स्वात्-
कार इव यं पचं स्थापचितु-
मिच्छति तमेव पचमिच्छन्नपि
मच्छता यत्नेन दूषयति ।

। ७ । तथा चास्मिन् ग्रन्थे त-
त्तदध्याये प्रस्तुतानां विषया-
णामेवमुपसंहारः । यथा । प्र-
थमेऽध्याये खृष्टमतसारांश-
निरूपणं । द्वितीये खृष्टधर्मग्र-
न्थानां प्रामाण्ये हेतूनां निरू-
पणं । तृतीयेऽस्य जगतो लो-
कातीतशक्तिमता बुद्धिपूर्वका-
रिणा कृतत्वनिरूपणं । चतुर्थे
यथा भगवदिच्छाप्रकाशकग्र-
न्थेभ्यो दृष्टविलक्षणानि दुर्वे-
चानि वस्तून्यवगम्यन्ते तथा-
स्मिन् भगवत्सृष्टे जगति दृश्य-
मानानि वस्तूनि रहस्यानी-
दानीमस्माभिर्दुर्वेचानि सन्ती-
ति निरूपणं । पञ्चमे परमेश्व-
रेच्छाप्रकाशकग्रन्थानां चैर-
स्वैरत्वद्वेयलं कल्पनोयं तानि
दृष्टे जगति वर्त्तमानानामपि

teries, because of which it is imagined that the Christian Scriptures ought not to be believed, are analogous to the mysteries which exist in the visible world, and which yet do not cause men to disbelieve in the world; therefore, they ought not to be brought as objections against the Scriptures, the truthfulness of which is established by the evidence already adduced [in Bk. II].

जगत्यश्रद्धामनुत्पादयतां र-

च्छानां तुल्यानि सन्यतश्च

प्रदर्शितप्रमाणदृढीकृतप्रामा-

णकधर्मंयन्त्येषूद्भावनं नार्ह-

न्तीति निरूपणमिति ।

(8) Thus strong reasons have been stated for the probability that the Christian Scriptures are true; and if they *are* true, it is quite clear that tremendous consequences must attend the rejection of them. We wind up, then, the present discussion of the leading points in Christianity, by indicating to those who desire to know the whole truth of these Scriptures, the method of satisfying that desire of knowledge.

। ८ । ऐवं तावत् खृष्टीयध-

र्मागमानां प्रामाण्यसम्भाव-

नाया: प्रबलानि कारणान्यु-

क्तानि तेषां प्रामाण्यपच्चेच त-

दनङ्गीकारे ऽतिभयावहानि

फलानि स्फुटान्येव। अथ ता-

दृग्मागमानामर्थेषार्थजिज्ञा-

सून्प्रति तज्जिज्ञासानिवर्त्तं-

नोपायं प्रदर्शयन्प्रस्तुतं खृ-

ष्टधर्मसारांश्विचारमुपसंह-

रति ।

APHORISM VIII.

Concluding advice to the inquirer. Search the Scriptures ;—search the Scriptures.

खृष्टीयधर्मागमा विचार-
णीया: खृष्टीयधर्मांगमा वि-
चारणीया दृति ॥ ८ ॥

(1) The repetition is to indicate [as it will do to the reader of the Sānkhya Aphorisms], that this is the conclusion of the section.

। १ । वीप्सा प्रकरणसमाप्त्य-
र्था ।

(2) "Search," etc. That is to say, they are to be studied diligently and candidly, not with the intention of finding objections, but with the desire of finding the truth. Further, at the time of thus studying, let him with sincerity and humility pray to the Lord of the universe, saying, "Show me the truth who am seeking to know it, and the way in which I ought to walk." Amen.

। २ । विचारणीया दृति ।
सपरिश्रमं निष्कपटं दोषदृ-
ष्टिवर्जनपूर्वकं तत्त्वजिज्ञासापू-
र्वकञ्चाभ्यासनीया द्त्यर्थः ।
किञ्च तथाविधाभ्यासकाले त-
त्त्वं जिज्ञासमानं मां नयमार्गे-
ञ्च दर्शयेति निष्कपटं शविन-
यञ्च जगदीश्वर: प्रार्थनीय
दृति ग्राम् ।

Here ends the Fifth Book of the Elucidation of the Christian Religion.

दृति खृष्टधर्मकौमुद्यां पञ्च-
मो ऽध्याय: ॥

APPENDIX

OF

NOTES AND DISSERTATIONS.

SEVERAL points involved in the preceding treatise appear to call for a fuller exposition than could have been given, where each point first presented itself, without the risk of injuriously interrupting the thread of the argument. Such points may be, perhaps, profitably treated in separate Notes, in which a somewhat familiar style of treatment, and an admixture of dialogue, —employed not less for the sake of perspicuity than of vivacity,—may be not displeasing to the reader. Our first dissertation is on the subject of "Matter," a most important topic where the missionary has to reason with idolaters,—much more with idolaters imbued, from the cradle, through the very language, with a system of metaphysics of such a nature that, if the missionary neglect or fail to master it and its strictly defined terminology, he will strive in vain to make his arguments against idolatry intelligible, even to the most candid among those whom he addresses. One missionary, for example (the case is not feigned), thinks that he has stated, with sufficient precision, the proposition that "God is not material," when he has stated to a Hindū

that God is not *dravya*, *i.e.* not a "substance," which an
idol certainly is;—but he omits to keep in mind that
there is (as Milton says), "spiritual substance" as well
as "material," both of them included under the head of
dravya = "substance;" so that his proposition conveys
to the Hindū the assertion that "God is neither Matter
nor Spirit." These things, though metaphysical, are not
trifling. The man who thinks them such, mistakes his
vocation when he ventures to become a missionary to the
Hindūs. Again, the missionary may perhaps feel equally
convinced that his meaning *ought* to be understood when
he has propounded that God is no *padārtha*,—this term
certainly being denotative of a "material thing,"—but
it denotes also *whatever is meant by any term*,—so that
the proposition here conveys to the Hindū the assertion
that the term "God" has *no meaning*, denotes nothing,—
not even the *non-existence* of anything. Another reasoner
suggests—for "Matter"—the term *Vastu*, which, where
it is a recognised and defined metaphysical term, denotes
the "Supreme Spirit," to the exclusion of whatever is *not*
spirit. But the reader who cares to see this question
discussed more fully need not be longer detained from
the note following.

NOTE A.

A DIALOGUE ON THE TERM "MATTER" AND ITS POS-
SIBLE CORRESPONDENTS IN THE HINDŪ DIALECTS.

You have frequently expressed a wish, my Theophilus,
that I should explain to you clearly and concisely those
opinions of my Hindū friends which, in the current expositions of them, appear to be so strange as to render it

scarcely credible that a thinking person should seriously
entertain them. It occurs to me that I may in some
measure perform what you require of me by giving
you—to the best of my recollection—an account of a
conversation, on the subject of " Matter," which took
place the other evening. You know Eusebius, our in-
defatigable missionary. He had just returned, rather
wearied, from preaching all day amidst the noise and
distraction of a *melā*, or religious fair ; but he brightened
up as he saw the inquiring young Brāhman, Tārādatt,
approaching. Eusebius and I had been sitting on the
high bank that overhangs the Ganges, where the sacred
stream glides past the garden of the excellent Philoxenus.
By the strangest of coincidences, Lawrence happened
to be with us. You know Lawrence, with his huge
quantity of reading, and his frequent, or, rather, habitual,
absence of mind. Tārādatt smiled as he sat down and
addressed Eusebius. " You have been labouring to en-
lighten the holiday makers at the *melā* to-day, my dear
Sir, if one may judge from your jaded look." " You
have guessed rightly," replied Eusebius; but why do
you smile?" " At the amusing inexhaustibleness of
your patience," replied the other. " Surely," exclaimed
Eusebius, " you do not expect that I shall ever give up
labouring in my vocation from despair at the apparent
ineffectualness of my efforts? It is my part to labour ;
it belongs to God to give the increase in his own good
time."

Tārādatt.—My being a Hindū does not prevent me
from appreciating and honouring your perseverance in
the face of difficulties. But I could not help smiling at

the thought of the discouragements to which you must
have been exposed to-day. Did your audience consist
entirely of the illiterate ?

Eusebius.—No. There was a forward young man who
interrupted me from time to time, declaring that all that
was true in my account of the Deity was to be found in
the books of the Hindūs, from which the Europeans had
borrowed, or stolen, without understanding the real import of what they were appropriating. He produced a
marked effect upon the people, by declaring that my
views of the omniscience and the omnipresence of God
were lamentably imperfect,—the true view of that subject
being conveyed, he contended, in a text of the *Veda*,
which he quoted in Sanskrit, and which, of course, not
one of them understood a word of."

Tārādatt.—" Can you repeat the text ?"

Eusebius declared he feared he could not, not having
fully understood it himself. Only he was sure it contained a pointed reference to the word " all," and sounded
somewhat like so and so,—reciting here certain sounds,
with which, O Theophilus, I cannot at this moment tax
my memory. The words which had appeared of so grave
import to the listeners at the *melā*, had quite a different
effect upon the Brāhman, who burst out laughing, assur-
ing us, as gravely as he could, that the words were
quoted from the Grammar of *Pāṇini*, and that they bore
reference to nothing beyond the fact that in *all* cases the
word "cow" was optionally amenable to a certain euphonic
rule. Eusebius himself could not help smiling at the
barefaced impudence of the trick which had been played
him ; and Tārādatt took advantage of the incident to

press a suggestion which it appears he had made more than once before.

Tārādatt.—You see, my dear Sir, that you would be the better of knowing our sacred language. I do not, indeed, promise you that, even with a knowledge of the Sanskrit, you would be able to convince the illiterate. Our low-caste Hindūs are too modest to think for themselves. They commit the keeping of their consciences to the hands of us Brāhmans just as, I have heard, the people on the continent of Europe make over the same trust to their own Brāhmans. The Europeans are unfortunate in this, that they are necessarily misled, their guides being blind leaders, or, at all events, guides groping in the dark; but in this more favoured land the people have reposed their implicit confidence in guides who have eyes and who have light. The people here are content with guidance; they do not seek for light, which might possibly dazzle them. Can it be, that you, Eusebius, shrink from meeting the learned of India on their own ground, preferring, as less arduous, to defy them from a safe distance, and to come to close quarters only with the avowedly uninstructed, who afford you an easy triumph in argument, though, you will admit, they afford you little else?

Eusebius.—You wish to provoke me, I perceive, to an argument with your learned self, friend Tārādatt; and you know very well that neither I nor my brother missionaries are wont to shrink from a contest with you, arduous as you may choose to think it. But you are not ignorant that a characteristic difference between the Gospel and the lights which the Brāhmans declare that

they possess is this, that to the poor the Gospel is
preached. By the poor we understand those whom you
look upon as of *low caste*, and hence unworthy, or incap-
able, of enlightenment. The Gospel acknowledges no distinctions among men, except to point out the lowly as the
especial objects of its care.

Tārādatt.—But are these to be the sole objects of its
care?

Eusebius.—By no means. How can you insinuate
that we have made them so? You have long had the
New Testament in your loved Sanskrit, and you have
more recently received the Pentateuch in the same. I
wish that, to us, as large a proportion of your *Veda* were
available, if it were only as a literary curiosity.*

Tārādatt.—Your mention of the *Veda* reminds me that
the portion of it which has been printed in Europe is
accompanied by an ample commentary, without which
even *we* could not understand the text. Now, much of
the text of your Scriptures is, to us, at least not less
obscure. Have you no explanatory commentary?

Eusebius.—We have, and more commentaries than
one. To select from these the portions most likely to be
needed by a Hindū reader, and to digest them into a
separate volume in the vernacular, or to print them along
with the text, would be a commendable work in one who
could do no better.

Tārādatt.—I should welcome such a work, though I
should like it in the Sanskrit rather than in the vernacular.

* The substance of this Note appeared in the *Benares Magazine* some years ago,
when only the first volume of the *Rig Veda* had been published by Max Müller.

Eusebius.—That is to say, you would prefer keeping it to yourself and your brother Brāhmans.

Tārādatt.—If I did, yet its being in Sanskrit would scarcely secure that end. But let that pass. I am not so anxious to keep all knowledge to my own class, but that I should be very well pleased if I could make you yourself understand and appreciate the sublime philosophy of the Hindū religion.

Eusebius.—Why, Mr. Colebrooke has enabled me to do that already. But that need not prevent you from indulging in some declamation on your favourite topic. I am all attention. Lawrence, who is watching the first glimmer of the rising moon on the ripple of the stream, will not interrupt you without good reason; and as for our other friend, he, for reasons of his own, is not likely to interrupt you at all.

This last observation, my Theophilus, was designed to convey a gentle sarcasm on myself; Eusebius holding, in spite of all my protestations to the contrary, that I am half a Hindū, because I am fonder than he is of their sacred language. You, my friend, know that the imputation is undeserved; but it would have been useless to remonstrate with Eusebius, so I contented myself with shrugging my shoulders in the way of protest, whilst Lawrence, removing his eyes from the moon, looked benevolently, yet mournfully, on Tārādatt. The latter, instead of becoming eloquent on the theme proposed, simply stated his belief that one thing alone existed.

Eusebius.—Well, what thing?

Tārādatt.—Do not accuse me of trifling with you if I answer " *that* thing." As one of your poets makes a lady ask, so I may ask here, "What's in a name?" If there be but one thing, then this one thing is all, and it may be (what nothing else supposable can be) *definitely* named by that which you Europeans call a pronoun, and which we, the followers of Pānini, call a *sarva-nāma*, or "name of all or any thing." We call the one thing, in Sanskrit, *tat*, *i.e.* "that."

Eusebius.—Good;—but if you, like your lady in the play, have no predilection for any name in particular, you will perhaps have no objection to give me some other name in exchange for this "that," which does not please me.

Tārādatt.—Let the name be *Brahm.*

Eusebius.—Has that name a meaning?

Tārādatt.—The word being derived from the root *vṛih*, "to increase," may signify "that from which all emanates."

Eusebius.—From which all *what* emanates?

Tārādatt.—All that which is no *thing*,—Brahm being the one only thing—the sole reality—according to the sense of that term as derived from the Latin *res*, a "thing," as I suppose it is.

Eusebius.—Well, laying aside for the present all that is *no* thing, pray tell us all that you can about the one thing.

Tārādatt.—All that can be told about it,—in fact, all that it *is*,—may be enounced very briefly. It is existence, knowledge, and joy. There you have the whole. It is not a something, of which these are the properties or qualities,—but these are *it*, and it these.

Eusebius.—And this material world?

Tārādatt.—That to which you give the name of a material world is an illusion.

At this moment, O Theophilus, Lawrence, who had seemed previously to be wrapped in his own thoughts, broke silence and spoke as follows :—

Lawrence.—" We are placed in a system in which mankind will deal with us, and we, in spite of all theories to the contrary, must deal with mankind, as if the objects of sense were real. Hence it does, I own, seem to me an unpractical philosophy which leads men to treat these things as if they were unreal."

On hearing these words, O Theophilus, the Brāhman seemed not a little perplexed. After pondering them for some time, with his eyes fixed upon the ground, he looked up, designing apparently to reply to the speaker; but, perceiving that the eyes of Lawrence were again bent intently on the moon, he turned to Eusebius, and remarked as follows :—

Tārādatt.—Men *do* deal with one another as if the objects of sense were real; and, for aught that I can say to the contrary, they possibly *must* so deal with one another, so long as the illusion of a world continues. I, for one, am not concerned with the inquiry whether this or that philosophy is "practical" or "unpractical." I ask simply, what is *true?* What you Europeans call "practical," is, I imagine, what we Hindūs call *vyāvahārika;* and we admit the importance of attending to such a consideration, so far as concerns this illusive world; but we do not see how the consideration bears upon the one reality, which is the sole object of sound philosophy. If I mistake not, your own Berkeley was

idly charged with inculcating an "unpractical" philosophy, when he questioned the existence of material
substance; but the best of your writers now-a-days
acknowledge, that, while he questioned the existence of
anything *under* the phenomena,—to be called material substance from its being *sub* or *under* these,—he did not deny
that there *were* such phenomena as required such and such
actions to be *practised*. For example, he did not neglect
to practise the action of getting out of the way of a loaded
wagon, although he held that the driver of the wagon no
more believed in the existence of a *material substance* of
the wagon, over and above all its powers and properties,
than he himself did,—the conception that there is any
such inscrutable substratum, being, he contended, the conception of his metaphysical opponents, and not that either
of himself—accused of over-refinement in speculation—
or of the wagoner not so accused. We do *not*, then,
treat phenomena as if they were unreal,—that is to say,
as if they were *not;* but we deny that they are *real*—
that they are *things*. Our *treatment* of them *is* " practical," our conception of them, at the same time, is
correct.

Eusebius.—We must look a little closer into that
word *real*;—but hark, Lawrence, who has seemingly been
in a brown study since he last spoke, appears to be again
about to speak.

Lawrence.—" And as *experience* is our guide, and not
theory, in practical matters; as, further, men often entail
upon themselves, and even upon others, very great
misery, even in this life, by obstinately following their
own theories of things, in opposition to the teaching of

men of experience, it becomes a very serious question
for you, whether you ought not to be able to prove the
Vedānta system far more demonstratively, before you let
it have the least influence upon your practice. And the
choice between Christianity and Brahminism is a *practical* question, and one which you will find, the more you
know of Christianity, to be materially affected by the
view you take of our relations to matter."

The Brāhman, O Theophilus, on hearing this, became
apparently more puzzled than before. He paused so long
that at length Eusebius interrupted his meditations by
asking what was the Sanskrit word for matter.

Tārādatt.—There is no Sanskrit word for " matter."

Eusebius.—You surprise me. Colonel Vans Kennedy,
I know, denied that there was a Sanskrit word answer-
ing to our philosophical term " matter ;" but Sir G.
Haughton immediately supplied him with a dozen.

Tārādatt.—What were they ?

Eusebius replying that he could not undertake to
recollect them, I, O Theophilus, being not unwilling to
aid, in some subordinate manner, a discussion which
interested me not a little, got up and fetched the book,
which happened to be among the borrowed volumes that
enrich my library, and occasionally reproach my punc-
tuality. Eusebius, turning to the place [the 221st page
of the (London) *Asiatic Journal*, vol. xviii., new series,
1835], read out the words of Sir Graves Haughton as
follows :—" I must, however, go beyond this refutation,
and inform your readers of what they might reasonably
have expected, namely, that the Sanskrit language contains many words for *matter*. Take the following examples:

11

*vastu, vasu, dravya, śarīra, mūrtti, tattwa, padārtha, prad-
hāna, mūla-prakriti ;* and, with the Jainas, *pudgala.*"

On hearing this list read, to each item in which it
struck me that Lawrence nodded a mild approval, the
Brāhman, O Theophilus, gradually opened his eyes wider
and wider. At the close, he rubbed them as if in doubt
whether he were awake ; and then he requested a sight
of the volume. Having certified himself that the words
were printed as they had seemed to strike his ear, and
that he was therefore probably awake, he asked Eusebius
whether he was content to receive each or any one of
these words as the synonyme of the term " matter,"—
the ὕλη of the Greeks.

Eusebius.—I am content to hear what you have got
to say against receiving them as such.

Tārādatt.—Let us look at them in succession. The
word *vastu* (as the *Vedānta Sāra* will tell you) means the
Divine Spirit, the one thing recognised as a reality in the
Vedānta. The whole of what we talk of as the world is,
according to the *Vedānta, a-vastu, i.e.* " not a thing."
What you speak of as the *material* world is what we call
not vastu. And the same applies to the term *vasu*, the
second in the list. Then the term *dravya*, as stated in
the *Tarka Sangraha* and a score of other works, is the
generic name of earth, water, light, air, ether, time, space,
soul, and mind.

Eusebius.—Soul, do you say ?

Tārādatt.—Certainly. Soul is one of the things belonging to the list headed *dravya.* Do you hold it to be
matter ?

Eusebius.—Heaven forbid.

Tārādatt.—Then I fear that this term will not suit; the more so as I imagine you will object to classing time and space as varieties of *matter.*

Eusebius.—Pray, on what principle do you class these with earth and water?

Tārādatt.—On the principle that *qualities*, etc., belong to them, as you may see by referring to the 23rd verse of the *Bhāshā-parichchheda*, the text-book of the *Nyāya*, that is in the hands of every schoolboy.

Eusebius.—Then you hold *time* to be a *substance?*

Tārādatt.—What do you mean by " substance?"

Eusebius.—Its meaning accords with its etymology. It is that which "stands under," and serves as it were for a support to the qualities which could not exist apart from it.

Tārādatt.—I like your definition, for it is my own; and so if time has any qualities, then time is the substance in which these its own qualities inhere. But tell me :—We mortals have wishes and we have fears ; we have doubts, difficulties, and, occasionally, joys. Do these exist apart and of themselves?

Eusebius.—No. A wish does not exist without a wisher, nor a doubt apart from one that doubts. Why do you ask a question the answer to which is so self-evidently obvious?

Tārādatt.—I ask it because I am curious to know whether you hold that these wishes and doubts can exist apart from *matter.* Is your wisher or your doubter necessarily material?

Eusebius.—By no means. I happen to remember that your own revered Gautama declares that " desire, aversion," etc. belong to the *soul.* The soul is a *spiritual* substance, not a material substance.

Tārādatt.—You remember rightly; you refer to the tenth aphorism of Gautama's first lecture. But you speak of *spiritual* substance as differing from *material* substance;—do you really then, in Europe, hold that there is such a twofold distinction in "substance?"

Eusebius.—Unquestionably. There are, indeed, men, calling themselves "materialists," who hold that there is only one substance; but those who recite the creed in which the persons of the Trinity are acknowledged to be "the same in *substance,*" speak, as Milton does, of *spiritual* substance, not of matter. If you will glance down the page that is before you, you will see an apposite remark of Cudworth's, which, as Sir G. Haughton observes, Lord Brougham, in his *Discourse on Natural Theology,* page 93, quotes with applause. Pray read it aloud.

Tārādatt.—Ah, here is what you refer to:—" Whatever is, or hath any kind of entity, doth either subsist by itself, or else is an attribute, affection, or mode of something that doth subsist by itself." Well, I agree with Sir G. Haughton that this is obviously true. But tell me, in your opinion, does the *Deity* "subsist by itself," or is it " an attribute, etc. ?"

Eusebius.—Of course you know my opinion. God exists of himself. His is a spiritual substance.

Tāradatt.—This I expected you to say; and I thoroughly agree with you. But I must now beg you to explain the passage which had just caught my eye on the opposite page.

Eusebius.—Read out the passage.

Tārādatt.—I find Sir G. Haughton, in page 220, declares as follows :—" Every one conversant with these subjects must know that, in philosophical language, *substance, body,* and *matter* mean all one and the same thing, and, as such, are opposed to *spirit.*" Permit me to ask you, when your creed speaks of the persons of the Trinity as being " the same in *substance,*" does it mean that they consist of the same *matter* ?

Eusebius.—Again, I say, God forbid. But allow me to look at the book ; for the passage that you have just read makes me suspect, as you did of yourself a little while ago, that I must be dreaming.

Taking the book, O Theophilus, Eusebius appeared the more perplexed the more he pondered and reperused the passage asserting the identity of " substance, body, and matter." At length he exclaimed :—" Indeed it seems to me that Col. Vans Kennedy, when he assailed Mr. Golebrook's account of the *Vedānta,* and Sir G. C. Haughton, when he defended it, must have been engaged in a game of cross-purposes, which the enlightened Mr. Colebrooke himself,—had he not been then, alas, upon his death-bed,—would have been able to bring to a satisfactory conclusion.

Tārādatt.—Pray explain what you refer to.

Eusebius.—I shall perhaps be the better prepared to do this, if you will first complete your detail of objections to the string of terms which Sir G. C. Haughton offered to Col. Kennedy as equivalents for the philosophical term *matter* ;—but see, here comes the cheerful Chrysostomus and his meek-eyed helpmate. Let us welcome them.

The cheerful Chrysostomus, you must know, O Theo-

philus, is a valiant polemic,—formidable in argument,
for his good-humoured imperturbability, as he is attractive at all times through his imperturbable good humour.
With a sigh that seemed to come from a heart as light as
heart could wish, he shook his head gently at Tārādatt,
who, receiving this not unexpected greeting with an
expression of countenance blending the comic and the
kindly, without further exordium addressed him.

Tārādatt.—We are enquiring, O Chrysostomus, whether there be any Indian term answering to the word
"matter."

"And where is the difficulty?" exclaimed Chrysostomus. "Down in the city, *padārtha* is one very good
word for it, and *dravya* is another."

Tārādatt recapitulated the objections to the term
dravya, which I have already recorded; and Chrysostomus shook his head, as if he thought that there were
here a splitting of straws; but just then Philoxenus,
hearing that a lady had arrived, hastened out to say
that tea was preparing; and the lady was led off,
followed by her worthy spouse.

The Brāhman then resumed his criticism of the list,
remarking that to place among the synonymes the term
śarīra, which (as rendered rightly in Wilson's Dictionary,
and also in Sir G. C. Haughton's own) means only *the*
body, looked almost like a punning design to burlesque
the proposition that "substance, *body*, and matter, mean
all one and the same thing." "The next term," he con-
tinued, "viz., *mūrtti*, which, in common language, means
a form or image (μορφη), means, in philosophical language,
whatever has definite limits. Earth, water, light, air,

and *mind*, we are told,[1] are of this description, while the ether is a substance *not* of this description. If the substance air extended as far as the substance ether, it would cease to bear the name in question, yet this would be very different from its ceasing to be *material*."

Eusebius.—But what do you hold to be the definite magnitude of the *mind?*

Tārādatt.—In the system to which the term under discussion belongs, the mind is held to be of the size of an atom.[2]

Eusebius.—Well, let that pass;—but pray continue your censures. The next term that you have to deal with is *tattwa.*

Tārādatt.—The term *tattwa* belongs more peculiarly to the Sānkhya school. Being, according to the ordinary etymology, an abstract derivative from the pronoun *tat*, "that," it answers to the *hæcceitas* of Duns Scotus; but in the Sānkhya it is employed as a concrete term to denote the eight "producers," the sixteen "productions," and "soul."

Eusebius.—In such an acceptation the term certainly does not correspond with matter; but, though the term bears a sense so extensive in the Sānkhya system, may it not answer to the term matter in some of the others?

Tārādatt.—In the Nyāya it bears a sense founded on its supposed etymology,—it means the nature of anything as it really is,—in short, *truth.*

Eusebius.—Its *supposed* etymology? Is the etymology called in question that you have just mentioned?

---

[1] See the *Bhāshā-parichehheda*, v. 24, and its commentary, p. 12.
[2] See *ante*, p. xxiv.

Tarādatt.—Certainly ; by those who know what truth is. There is but one truth that can be declared to any one ; and that one solitary truth,—obscured only by the unavoidable imperfections of language,—is conveyed in the formula *tat twam,* " That art thou." The hearer of this truth—(from the terms of which, you perceive, truth itself takes its designation of *tattwa)*—when he has rightly understood and accepted it, changing the " thou" to the first person, reflects thus—" *I* am Brahma." This is so far well;—but he must finally get rid of the habit of making even *himself* an *object* of thought. There must be no object. The *subject* alone must remain—a thought, a joy, an existence,—and the only one.[1]

Eusebius.—Take breath, I beseech you, and then let us finish the list, the next term in which is the word *padārtha,* which our friend Chrysostomus thinks a good one.

Tārādatt.—The term *padārtha*[2] means " substance" (including soul), " quality," " action," " com——."

" In short," interrupted Eusebius, " it seems to mean everything ;—is it so ?"

Tāradatt.—It means everything that is,—with the varieties of non-existence into the bargain.

Eusebius.—Very possibly it may do so in the philosophical systems ; but when the word recalls to the mind of the generality of hearers the idea of sticks and stones, and rivers and fruits, and so on, why is it not as good a word to use for matter, when speaking to those who are not philosophers, as any other ?

---

[1] See *ante,* p. xxxvii.   [2] *Tarka-sangraha,* p. 1.

At this question, O Theophilus, the Brāhman looked as if taken aback. After some reflection he replied.

Tārādatt.—Let me understand you, my dear Sir. The question in hand, if I am not mistaken, was this,— viz., Do such and such terms represent the European term "matter" so precisely, that the difference in opinion between Colonel Vans Kennedy and Sir G. C. Haughton could, so long as we employ one of those terms as the substitute for the term matter, be brought under the cognizance of learned Hindūs in such a manner that the difference of opinion could be intelligently entertained, and rightly adjudicated upon, by these competent judges? I deny that the terms are such as to allow of this. Few more competent judges could have been found than Rammohun Roy ; and yet he, when the dispute was laid before him,[1] was so absolutely ignorant of the meaning of the term matter, that he thought that he had settled the question submitted to him, by pointing to a passage in his own works, fully supporting Mr. Colebrooke's interpretation, "that," according to the Vedānta philosophy, "God was not only the *efficient* but the *material* cause of the universe." I have been all along talking on the supposition that the enquiry is, how you are to let Indian philosophers understand what you mean by matter,—not—what words may serve when speaking to the illiterate about material products, without any reference to the philosophical conception of matter at all.

Eusebius.—Well,—let it be so. I shall expect you to explain what bearing the remark of Rammohun

---

[1] *London Asiatic Journal*, vol. xxxv., new series, 1835, p. 214.

Roy has upon your *spiritual* Vedāntism, which it seems
to me to reduce to something very like simple materialism; but, in the first instance, pray finish your list of
terms.   What objection have you to *pradhāna?*

Tārādatt. — The term *pradhāna* belongs to the
Sānkhya philosophy, where it is interchangeable with
the next term in the list, viz., *mūla-prakriti*, as Professor
H. H. Wilson's translation shows.[1]   Either term is
usually translated by the term nature.   Such a term—
(for of the Jaina misuse of the word *pudgala*, I, like
other Brāhmans, know nothing)—comes, perhaps, nearer
to the term matter than any other in the list; but
yet it will not serve as a substitute for the ὕλη.   You
cannot speak of the *pradhāna* of a jar, or the *pradhāna*
of a web, as you speak of the ὕλη or matter of a goblet
or a statue, because *pradhāna* is the name of a single
power, like the "Nature" of European sceptics.   Further,
instead of this *pradhāna* being a substance, you may
learn from Professor Wilson,[2] that it is the aggregate
of the three *qualities*, " goodness," " foulness," and
" darkness."

Eusebius.—Aha, my friend,—but I happen to have
jotted down in my note-book an extract from the page
preceding that to which I presume you mean to refer
me.   There[3] Professor Wilson says that, "in speaking
of qualities, however, the term *guṇa* is not to be
regarded as an insubstantial or accidental attribute,
but as a substance discernible by soul through the

---

[1] " *Mūla*, 'the root,' *prakriti* 'nature,' is *pradhāna*, 'chief,'" &c.   See Wilson's
Sānkhya Kārikū, p. 16.
[2] *Sānkhya Kārikā*, p. 53.   [3] *Ibid*, p. 52.

medium of the faculties." What, then, is the use of
founding upon its being *called* a quality?

Here, O Theophilus, I ventured to express my own
opinion on this point. " Professor Wilson," I said,
" rightly reports the opinion of the *Sānkhya* when he
says that what are usually spoken of as the three
' qualities,' (*guṇa*) might with propriety be termed ' Ingredients or constituents of nature.' But while it
would follow logically that, if nature be substantial,
these its ingredients or constituents cannot be *insubstantial*, it also follows logically that, if these ingredients
or constituents are *not* substances but qualities, then
nature, the aggregate of them, cannot be substantial,
but is an aggregate of qualities." Here Eusebius showing symptoms of impatience, I paused deferentially, and
he exclaimed, as I had partly expected—" What room
is there for any such *opinion*, forsooth, when Professor
Wilson cites the very words of Kapila's commentator,
who tells us that *Satwa* and the rest are ' things,'
not ' specific properties.' "[1] " Forgive me," I here exclaimed in turn, " if I object to the rendering, in this
present connexion, of *Vaiseshikā guṇāh* by ' specific
properties,' instead of by ' the *Vaiseshika guṇas*.' According to the *Vaiseshikas*, the *guṇas*—the things to which
exclusively these philosophers allow the name of ' quality'
—are twenty-four in number, and to these they deny
the possession of, or the right of standing as substratum
to, any of the said four-and-twenty qualities. The
twenty-four ' qualities' of the *Vaiseshika* philosophy,[2] are

---

[1] सत्वादीनि द्रव्याणि न वैशेषिका गुणाः ॥
[2] See the *Tarka-sangraha.*

called *guṇa;*—and the *Sānkhya* commentator, dreading that his own *three* 'qualities' might be mistaken for these, took care to warn us that they are *not* the *Vaiśeshika guṇas;*—and, to make assurance doubly sure, he stated that they were spoken of by Kapila in terms which a *Vaiśeshika* or a *Naiyāyika* was bound to apply only to a substance,—viz., as 'themselves having qualities.'" "Well, well," interrupted Eusebius, "waiving that question, let me recall friend Tārādatt to the dictum of Rammohun Roy, 'that, according to the Vedānta philosophy, God was not only the *efficient* but the *material* cause of the universe.' If God be the material cause of a material universe, then what is God but matter? Really I begin to doubt how I am to avoid agreeing with Colonel Kennedy that it is impossible to suppose that Mr. Colebrooke, who employs the same terms—saying of God, that 'He is both efficient and material cause of the world'[1]—could be of opinion that such a system could be otherwise than material. I see, indeed, that Mr. Colebrooke, by what Sir G. C. Haughton calls 'a fortunate departure from his usual reserve,'[2] has left an explicit record of his opinion of the Vedānta philosophy that removes all doubt as to his conception of its nature. The Vedānta, he says, 'deduces from the text of the Indian scriptures a refined psychology, which goes to a denial of a material world.'[3] But is not this contradictory to the other assertion? Deny a material world, and what do you mean by its material cause? Sir G. C. Haughton

---

[1] Colebrooke's *Essays*, vol. i., p. 371. [2] *Asiatic Journal,*, vol. xviii., p. 215.
[3] Colebrooke's *Essays*, vol. i, p. 227.

appears to have been conscious that there was some
inconsistency here, for he seeks to shift the blame from
Mr. Colebrooke to the Vedāntists themselves. Mr.
Colebrooke held the Vedānta to be a refined psychology, and 'consequently,' argues Sir G. C. Haughton,
'should it appear to be, as Colonel Kennedy asserts,
a system of gross and material pantheism in the writings
of Mr. Colebrooke, such an inference must be deduced
from the expressions of its Indian interpreters, who are
faithfully rendered by him.'¹ I must say, I think
Sir G. C. Haughton had better have confined his defence
of Mr. Colebrooke to this single assertion that the
inconsistency belongs to the system itself which Mr.
Colebrooke faithfully expounded. No more then needed
to be said. The most marvellous thing of all is the
fact that Colonel Kennedy, with the inconsistency star-
ing him in the face, could speak of the *Vedānta* as
'the most spiritual system that ever was imagined by
man.'² Solve this riddle, friend Tārādatt, if you have
the power,—which I greatly doubt."

Tārādatt.—The riddle can be solved without difficulty. There is *no* such inconsistency as you imagine
in the system, and neither is there in Mr. Colebrooke's
exposition. Colonel Kennedy misunderstood Mr. Colebrooke, and Sir G. C. Haughton, with his well-intended
interference and his pet dogma of the co-extensive
signification of the terms "substance" and "matter,"
bewildered the Colonel still further. The Rajah, Rammohun Roy, was right in declaring that Mr. Colebrooke
was right. Had the Rajah been as thoroughly well

versed in the technical terminology of European philosophy as in that of the Vedānta and the Nyāya, he could at once have placed his finger on the misconceived term which lay at the bottom of the strange logomachy recorded in these papers of the *Asiatic Journal*. Mr. Colebrooke, had he been in health, could have done this; and I can fancy the readiness with which that most candid of scholars would have given up the use of a term which was liable to such misconception. When Mr. Colebrooke, or Rammohun Roy, speaks of the Vedāntic tenet that God is the *material cause* of the universe, do you suppose he means a cause consisting of the *matter* which we have been hitherto in vain seeking to find a name for in the list offered by Sir G. C. Haughton?

Eusebius.—If not, then what is it that he does mean?

Tārādatt.—Why, surely,—if we have had such difficulty in finding—what we have not yet found—a term in the philosophic vocabulary of India answering to *matter*, does it not strike you as an odd circumstance that the same vocabulary should so readily supply a term for a "*material* cause?"

Eusebius.—Now that you mention it, the circumstance does seem indeed somewhat odd. But may we not turn it to good account? We want a word for "matter;"—tell me then your word for "material," and I imagine that we shall only have to lop off the adjectival termination in order to find what we were in search of.

Tārādatt.—It grieves me to disappoint you, but in the present instance your disappointment is unavoidable.

The Sanskrit term rendered "material cause" is *samavāyi-kāraṇa*. In the Vedānta books the term *upādāna-kāraṇa* is more commonly used, but the same thing is meant. The portion of the term (viz., *samavāyi*) so frequently rendered, by Mr. Colebrooke and his successors, "material," is the adjectival derivative of the word *samavāya*—which Mr. Colebrooke rightly renders "intimate and constant relation."[1]

Eusebius.—"Intimate and constant relation?"—this will never serve as an equivalent for matter.

Tārādatt.—No. But it will serve very well to denote the relation between a substance and its qualities, as it is employed, in our philosophical vocabulary, to do. Hence the logomachy of Colonel Kennedy and Sir G. C. Haughton might have been prevented if Mr. Colebrooke had rendered *samavāyi-kāraṇa* by " *substantial* cause" instead of " *material* cause." That Mr. Colebrooke did not confound substance with matter, like his well-intentioned defender, is evident from his speaking of *soul* as a substance. "Being a substance," he says, "though immaterial, as a substratum of qualities, it is placed in Caṇāde's arrangement as one of the nine substances which are there recognized."[2] Now, pray observe,—Soul, though immaterial, is a substratum of qualities:—qualities, according to Plato and the Vedāntists alike, have not an *esse* such as their substratum has:—hence, soul, the immaterial, is the only *real* essence;—Mr. Colebrooke was right in saying that the Vedānta is a "refined psychology;" Colonel Kennedy, rightly entertaining the same view of the Vedānta, was

---

[1] Colebrooke's *Essays*, vol. i., p. 267.   [2] *Ibid*, vol. i., p. 268.

to blame for boggling at Mr. Colebrooke's employment
of the technical term "material cause" for what might
better have been called "substratum;"—and Sir G. C.
Haughton was to be condoled with for a confusion of
ideas in regard to the co-extensiveness of matter and
substance, which are no more co-extensive in meaning
than cow is co-extensive with quadruped.

Having heard this, Eusebius, as it appeared to me,
became thoughtful. He shook his head several times,
as if doubtful. At length he looked up briskly and
exclaimed:—"Why do you talk of soul, as if there were
but one? I have a soul; you have a soul; even our
friend here——" "Stop, my dear sir," exclaimed the
Brāhman, "we have separate *minds*, but soul is one
only—pure and unchangeable." But here, O Theophilus, as you will observe, the conversation diverged from
the question of matter;—so I will not at present report
the discussion that ensued. Ultimately left alone, I
joined the circle at the tea-table of Philoxenus, where
the conversation, cheerful and miscellaneous, bore little
reference to the notions of the Hindūs.

NOTE B.

ON THE HINDŪ EMPLOYMENT OF THE TERMS "SOUL" AND "MIND."

You ask me, O Theophilus, what the Brāhman was
going to say, when my last communication was abruptly
brought to a close by the diverging of Eusebius from
the question of the term "matter." Eusebius, then, in
reply to the Brāhman's assertion of the unity of soul

and the plurality of minds, exclaimed—" You talk most strangely, explain yourself if possible."

Tārādatt.—You observe the moon, which Lawrence has kept gazing at,—indifferent to our conversation, on the subject of which his mind is apparently made up. Now look into any of these large earthen vessels which Philoxenus keeps filled with water for the benefit of his beloved shrubs and trees. If it should seem to you that the moon is visible in every one of these, as well as in the sacred stream that ripples before us, would you conclude that there are many moons, some of them at rest, as in the water-tub, and some in agitation, as in the rippling stream ?

Eusebius.—No; because there is but one real moon, and the others are reflections.

Tārādatt.—Good:—and if the water, to which these reflections are due, were removed, what would remain ?

Eusebius.—Why, as regards the present question, the moon itself.

Tārādatt.—True. Now, in like manner remove the ignorance or delusion, out of which men's minds are made, and then there will be no dim or disturbed *reflections* of soul, but soul itself will remain alone.

Eusebius.—You ought to be very sure indeed that you have good evidence for the authenticity of a revelation which asserts things so repugnant to reason and common sense.

Tārādatt.—On the contrary, I think, we may dispense with the trouble of enquiring into the credentials of a revelation conveying a doctrine which so irresistibly approves itself to the reason.

At this declaration, O Theophilus, Eusebius shrugged his shoulders, Lawrence sighed, and I myself felt moved to speak, which I proceeded to do as follows:—" That the doctrine of the Vedānta so entirely approves itself to the reason ought to lead you to doubt, O Tārādatt, whether the doctrine required a revelation, and was therefore likely to be the subject of one. I do not refer to those queer observances, such as inhaling the breath by one nostril and expelling it by the other, which are inculcated in the system, and which, in my opinion, are so far from approving themselves to the reason, that an unquestionably authenticated revelation alone could justify their being gravely considered. I refer solely to the great tenet that only One exists, and that nothing but One ever really existed, or will exist, or could exist."

Here Eusebius, starting up, put on his hat, and, turning on his heel, walked off. Tārādatt, who seemed to waver between the inclination to follow his friend and some curiosity to hear me out, laughingly welcomed me as a convert to Vedāntism ; while, disregarding the interruption, I proceeded,—until ultimately left alone, as I mentioned before.[1]

NOTE C.

ON "LOGIC" AND "RHETORIC," AS REGARDED BY THE HINDŪS.

He who undertakes to argue with a learned Hindū will be the better of knowing how a Hindū reasoner

---

[1] See *ante*, p. 34.

arranges his arguments, and why. This has been generally and often mischievously misconceived. A misconception of this matter suggested [*Benares Magazine*, 1852, vol. viii., p. 251] the following

REMONSTRANCE TO SIR WILLIAM HAMILTON ON HIS INJUSTICE TO THE HINDŪS.

The reader may probably recollect the notable paradox of Dr. Campbell's, that "there is always some radical defect in a syllogism, which is not chargeable with that species of sophism known among logicians by the name of *petitio principii*, or a begging of the question" (*Phil. of Rhet.*, vol. i., p. 174). This "epigrammatic, yet unanswerable remark," as Mr. Dugald Stewart styles it, was well answered by Archbishop Whately, when he observed (*Logic*, bk. i. § 4) that Dr. Campbell little dreamt, "of course, that his objections, however specious, lie against the *process of reasoning itself*, universally; and will therefore, of course, apply to those very arguments which he is himself adducing. He should have been reminded of the story of the woodman who had mounted a tree, and was so earnestly employed in lopping the boughs, that he unconsciously cut off the bough on which he was standing."

Sir William Hamilton (in his *Discussions*, p. 615) has answered this "unanswerable" epigram of Dr. Campbell's, less epigrammatically, but more searchingly, in a passage which we transcribe the more readily, as it will afford us an opportunity of vindicating what Sir William calls "the Hindū syllogism," against his undeserved disparagement of it. He says:—"Mentally

one, the categorical syllogism, according to its order
of announcement, is either *analytic* (A), or *synthetic* (B).
Analytic, if (what is inappropriately styled) the conclusion be expressed first, and (what are inappropriately
styled) the premises be then stated as its reasons.
Synthetic, if the premises precede, and, as it were
effectuate the conclusion." He then goes on, in a note,
to say, " This, in the *first* place, relieves the syllogism
of *two one-sided views.* The Aristotelian syllogism is
exclusively synthetic; the Epicurean (or Neoclesian)
syllogism was—for it has been long forgotten—exclusively analytic; whilst the Hindū syllogism is merely
a clumsy agglutination of these counter forms, being
nothing but an operose repetition of the same reasoning
enounced, 1st, analytically, 2nd, synthetically. In
thought the syllogism is organically one; and it is
only stated in an analytic or synthetic form, from the
necessity of adopting the one order or the other, in
accommodation to the vehicle of its expression —
language. For the conditions of language require that
a reasoning be distinguished into parts, and these detailed before and after other. The analytic and synthetic orders of enouncement are thus only accidents of
the syllogistic process. This is, indeed, shown in
practice, for our best reasonings proceed indifferently in
either order.

" In the *second* place, this central view vindicates the
syllogism from the *objection of petitio principii*, which,
professing logically to annul logic, or at least to reduce
it to an idle tautology, defines syllogistic—the art of
avowing in the conclusion what has been already con-

fessed in the premises. This objection (which has at least the antiquity of three centuries and a-half) is only applicable to the synthetic or Aristotelic order of enouncement, which the objectors contemplate as alone possible. It does not hold against the syllogism, considered aloof from the accident of its expression; and being proved irrelevant to this, it is easily shown in reference to the synthetic syllogism itself, that it applies only to an accident of its external form." He goes on to say, that the synthetic form of the syllogism is the "less natural. For if it be asked, 'Is C in A?' surely it is more natural to reply, 'Yes' (or C is in A); for C is in B and B in A (or, for B is in A and C in B), than to reply, B is in A, and C in B (or C is in B and B in A), therefore, C is in A.

"In point of fact, the analytic syllogism is not only the more natural, it is even *pre-supposed* by the synthetic. To express in words, we must first analyse in thought the organic whole—the mental simultaneity of simple reasoning, and then we may reverse in thought the process by a synthetic return. Further, we may now enounce the reasoning in either order; but certainly, to express it in the essential, primary, or analytic order, is not only more natural, but more direct and simple, than to express it in the accidental, secondary, or synthetic. This also avoids the objection of P. P." [*i.e.*, the objection that the syllogism involves a *petitio principii*.]

Well, let us first consider how this debars Dr. Campbell's objection, and then we may proceed to the vindication of the Hindū Philosophers.

The synthetic syllogism is of this form :—

> " All things smoking are fiery,
> The mountain is smoking,
> Therefore the mountain is fiery."

This is the form of syllogism contemplated by Dr. Campbell, and he says that here *the question is begged.* The question is, whether the mountain be fiery or not; and he alleges that you *beg,* or *take for granted,* the very question in dispute, when you lay down the premise, " *All* things smoking [and among these the smoking mountain] are fiery." This seems plausible; but let us now look at the analytic form of the same syllogism, which is as follows :—

> " The mountain is fiery,
> Because it is smoking,
> And all things smoking are fiery."

In this form of expression we do not begin by laying down anything which can be charged with taking for granted the point in dispute; we propound affirmatively, for discussion, the point in dispute itself, and then assign a reason, and then propound a condition in the absence of which the reason would avail nothing. The objection of "avowing in the conclusion what has been already confessed in the premises," does not apply to the argument in this analytic form ; and as the argument in this form is none other than the same argument in the synthetic form, neither does the objection really apply to the latter.

But now, however far the Scotch Philosophers may have gone astray, we should like to be told what there is in all this that the Hindū Philosophers have failed to

discern. Let us follow Sir William through his analysis
of the syllogistic process just quoted, and see whether
there be any one single step in it for which our Sanskrit
books do not supply the counterpart, and no "clumsy"
counterpart, but something as perfectly elaborated (at
least) as ancient Greece or modern Germany (or "modern
Athens" either) can offer us.

To begin with the beginning. Sir William Hamilton,
as we have seen, observes, that, "In thought, the
syllogism is organically one; and it is only stated in
an analytic and synthetic form, from the necessity of
adopting the one order or the other, in accommodation
to the vehicle of its expression—language." Good :—
and have the Hindūs failed to discern *this?* So far from
it, that they have endeavoured, and, as far as we are
aware, at least as successfully as any that ever attempted
it, to embody *this organic unity of the syllogism in thought*
in a linguistic unity of expression. When they discuss
the laws of the mind syllogizing "*for itself*,"—*i.e.*, to use
Sir William's language, "*in thought*," — they notify
the organic unity of the process by wrapping the two
premises in one sentence so constructed (viz., in the
shape of a period), that, until the last word of the sentence is uttered, no demand is made—or rather no pretence exists — for either affirmation or negation. In
reference to the stock example above quoted, the premises "*in thought*," are propounded, in their unity,
by writers on the Nyāya, thus:—"By smoke, invariably attended by fire, is attended this mountain." We
subjoin the Sanskrit[1] (from the *Tarka-sangraha*, ed. 2,

[1] वह्निव्याप्यधूमवानयमर्वतः ॥

p. 39). Can Sir William Hamilton point out, anteriorly to his own statement regarding the organic unity of the syllogism "in thought," any expression, in a European work, evincing a more thorough conviction of the truth in question than this *periodic* form of expression adopted by the Hindūs for conveying the premises in their simultaneity? To our mind it was a noble, and far from unsuccessful, effort to emancipate their exposition of the mental process, in its unity, from those hampering "conditions of language," which, as Sir William remarks, "require that a reasoning be distinguished into parts, and these detailed before and after other." In a *period*, strictly, nothing is detailed "before and after other." The "yes" or the "no" can no more legitimately leave the lips of the auditors till the last word of the period has been heard, than the bullet can leave the gun before the process of loading is finished and the trigger pulled.[1]

Let us now follow Sir William in his next step. "The analytic and synthetic orders of enouncement are, thus, only accidents of the syllogistic process. This is, indeed, shewn in practice, for our best reasonings proceed indifferently in either order." Good again;—but have the Hindūs failed to discern *this?* Not a bit of it, as we shall show. The Aristotelic syllogism may be, as Sir William observes, "exclusively synthetic," and the "long

---

[1] Some one may perhaps say—Nay; but when you have uttered thus much of your period, viz., "by smoke invariably attended by fire," then we may legitimately interrupt you, and deny the invariable attendedness. To this we reply, that you have no legitimate right to do any such thing. For anything that *you* know, before you have heard me out, my period might have been intended to run thus—"By *smoke invariably attended by fire* this mountain is *not* attended, because [I choose to hold that] there is *no* such kind of smoke." You have no pretence to understand me till I finish my period.

forgotten" Epicurean or Neoclesian syllogism "exclusively analytic;" and Dr. Campbell and Mr. Stewart, conversant only with the former, may have written (as indeed they have) most dismal nonsense on the whole subject; but have the Hindūs done so? Again we reply,—not a bit of it. We have seen how the *Tarkasangraha* (following hundreds of consentient writers), recognized, and sought to symbolize, in language guardedly periodic, the unity of the syllogism " in thought,"—the " reasoning for one's-self."[1] Let us now see how the Hindūs regard " the analytic and synthetic orders of enouncement,—the mere ' accidents,' " as Sir William justly observes, "of the syllogistic process;" and let us see whether *they* failed to discern the fact that " our best reasonings proceed indifferently in either order." Let us turn to the *Vedānta-paribhāshā*, section second. There we read as follows :—" Reasoning is divided into that which is for one's-self, and that which is for another. Of these, that which is for one's-self has been already described ; but that which is for another is effected by a process. This process is an aggregate of parts ; and the parts are three only, in the shape of—1st, the proposition, the reason, and the example [—making up Sir William's analytical, or more natural, form of exposition] ;—or, 2nd, the example [—equivalent to the major premiss—], the application, and the conclusion"[2] [Sir William's synthetical, or less natural form].

---

[1] स्वार्थानुमानमिति ॥

[2] तच्चानुमानं स्वार्थपरार्थभेदेन द्विविधम् । तत्र स्वार्थनूत्तमेव परार्थनु न्यायसाधनम् । न्यायो नामावयवसमुदायः । अवयवाश्च चय एव प्रतिज्ञा-हेतूदाहरणरूपाः उदाहरणोपनयनिगमनरूपा वा ॥

And here, before we go further, let us remark in
passing, that Sir William's parenthetical protests against
things being "inappropriately styled" the premises, or
"inappropriately styled" the conclusion, do not apply
at all to the language of Hindū philosophers.   When
the matter in question is stated first, as in the analytical
form, they style it the proposition (*pratijñā*); when it is
stated last, they style it the conclusion, or issue (*nigamana*).   The "clumsy" instances of want of terminological foresight in Western speculators, thus noticed by
Sir William, do not occur in the Indian scientific language,
where things are not named from their *separable accidents*.

But why did the author of the *Vedānta-paribhāshā*
think it necessary to impress upon his readers long ago
the essential equivalence of the analytic and synthetic
forms of the syllogism, to which Sir William Hamilton
has found it necessary to call the attention of Western
sages in the year 1852 ?   He tells us, when, in continu-
ation of the passage last quoted, he says that the *five*
members of what Sir William Hamilton calls the "clumsy
agglutination," are not, as some Hindū learners by rote
might have imagined them to be, indispensable; "for,"
to quote the work itself, "since no more than three members are required to set forth the general principle and
its relevancy to the subject, the other two members [of
the five-membered exposition] are superfluous."[1]   Here,
then, we see that the Hindūs were just as well aware as
Aristotle, that three members suffice to contain all the
essentials of a process of reasoning, and just as well

---

[1] न तु पञ्च अवयवचयेनैव व्याप्तिपचधर्मंतयोरुपदर्शंनसम्भवेनाधिकाव-
यवद्वयस्य व्यर्थंत्वात् ॥

aware as Sir William Hamilton, that these three members may be arranged indifferently in either the analytic or the synthetic order. What, then, becomes of Sir William's scornful remark that "the Hindū syllogism is merely a clumsy agglutination of these counter forms?" It is irrelevant altogether,—the five-membered exposition, which it alludes to, not being the Hindū *syllogism* at all, but the Hindū *rhetorical exposition.*. Sir William Hamilton might, with the same (absolutely the same) propriety, accuse Euclid of a " clumsy agglutination" of the analytic and synthetic syllogisms, because he begins by stating his proposition *as a proposition*, and ends by re-stating it *as a conclusion.* Sir William very well knows that logic and rhetoric are not the same thing. At page 641 of his *Discussions,* he says, "Here we must not confound the logical with the rhetorical, the necessary in thought with the agreeable in expression." Good: may we, then, cherishing, as we do, the profoundest admiration for Sir William Hamilton, entreat that he will not[1] (in imitation of those who have on this point erred before him) continue to confound the logical with the rhetorical when again writing or speaking of Hindū speculation? We have shown him that the Hindūs have the analytic syllogism of Epicurus, the synthetic syllogism of Aristotle, and an expression (not excelled in precision by any similar attempt that we are aware of) for his own syllogism "in thought," in its organic unity. Is all this to be ignored, and the error of the earlier investigators of Sanskrit literature, misrepresent-

---

[1] [This was written in 1852, after a letter, the last received by me, from Sir William Hamilton.]

ing the *oration* as the syllogism,[1] to be for ever perpetuated? Sir William Hamilton is not unknown to living successors of the old Indian sages on the banks of the Ganges. But had the unfortunate passage on which we have animadverted been the first on which the eye of one of these readers alighted, the chance is that it would have gone some way to confirm the impression, here yet too prevalent, that the Europeans, though capital workers in brass and iron, had better leave the discussion of things intellectual to those whose land was the birth-place of philosophy.

[In justification of the foregoing remarks, we quote from the familiar text book, the *Tarka-sangraha* (Benares, 1852), as follows:—]

THE CHAPTER ON INFERENCE.

अनुमितिकरणमनुमानम्। परामर्शजन्यं ज्ञानमनुमिति: ।
व्याप्तिविशिष्टपक्षधर्मताज्ञानं परामर्श:। यथा वह्निव्याप्यधूमवानयं
पर्वत इति ज्ञानं परामर्श: । तज्जन्यं पर्वतो वह्निमानिति ज्ञान-
मनुमिति: । यत्र यत्र धूमस्तत्राग्निरिति साहचर्यनियमो व्याप्ति: ।
व्याप्यस्य पर्वतादिवृत्तित्वं पक्षधर्मता ।

TRANSLATION.

"An induction (*anumāna*) is the instrument of an inference (*anumiti*). An inference is knowledge that results from syllogizing (*parāmarśa*). Syllogizing is the taking cognizance that the subject (*paksha*) possesses

---

[1] See this point explained more fully at p. 45 (2nd Edition) of the English version of the *Tarka-sangraha*.

what is constantly accompanied [by something which is thus seen to belong to the subject]. For example,—the taking cognizance that ' This hill has smoke—which is constantly accompanied [at the point where it originates] by fire'—is [an instance of] syllogizing [*i.e.*, of apprehending, in connection, an induction and an observation]. The knowledge resulting therefrom, viz., that ' The hill has fire [somewhere about it],' is an inference. ' The being constantly accompanied ' (*vyāpti*) is such an invariableness of association as this—that wherever there is smoke there is fire. By the ' subject's *possession*' [of something that is constantly accompanied], we mean the fact that there *exists*—in a mountain, for instance,—that which is constantly accompanied [by something else]."

REMARKS.

In order that we may be enabled to trace the analogy which, disguised by differences arising from diversity in the point of view or in the form of expression adopted, must yet necessarily exist between any two expositions of the reasoning process, neither of which is unsound, let us examine the terms in the foregoing passage, which we have rendered, as nearly as we could, by equivalents borrowed from the logic of Europe.

The first formal difference that requires to be noticed, is the fact that, whilst the European logic employs a phraseology founded on classification, the *Nyāya* goes to work with the terms on which the classification is based. The former infers that kings are mortal because they belong to the class of men. The latter arrives at the same inference by means of the consideration that mor-

tality is present wherever there is the human nature,
and the human nature wherever there is that of a king.

In the argumentative expression, "This hill has
invariably-fire-attended smoke," there are wrapt up,
in one, the major premiss, "wherever there is smoke
there is fire," and the minor premiss, "this hill is
smoking." The reason for preferring to regard these
as two constituent parts of a single statement appears
to be this, that it is only when simultaneously present
to the mind that the premises compel the inference.
When they are stated separately, they are no other than
the premises of an Aristotelian syllogism.

The term which we have rendered "the being constantly accompanied," viz., *vyāpti*, means, literally, "pervadedness." In regard to the import of a proposition
which the logic of Europe calls a universal affirmative,
such as "all men are mortal," the *Naiyāyika* would say
that there is pervadedness (*vyāpti*) of humanity by
mortality;—and he would state the proposition thus:
"Where there is humanity there is mortality." In a
universal affirmative, the predicate or major term connotes the "pervader" (*vyāpaka*), or constant accompanier
of that, connoted by the subject or minor term, which is
"pervaded" (*vyāpya*), or constantly accompanied by it.

অনুমানং দ্বিবিধং স্বার্থং পরার্থং চ ৷ স্বার্থং স্বানুমিতিহেতুঃ ৷
তথাহি স্বয়মেব ভূয়ো দর্শনেন যন্ন যন্ন ধূমস্তত্রাগ্নিরিতি মহান-
সাদৌ ব্যাপ্তিং গৃহীত্বা পর্বতসমীপং গতস্তঙ্গতে চাগ্নৌ সন্দিহানঃ
পর্বতে ধূমং পশ্যন্ ব্যাপ্তিং স্মরতি যন্ন ধূমস্তত্রাগ্নিরিতি ৷ তদনন্তরং
বহ্নিব্যাপ্যধূমবানয়ং পর্বত ইতি জ্ঞানমুত্পদ্যতে ৷ অয়মেব লিঙ্গপ-

रामग्रं इत्युच्यते । तस्मात् पर्वतो वह्निमानिति ज्ञानमनुमिति-
रुत्पद्यते । तदेतत् स्वार्थानुमानम् ।

" An induction is of two kinds [inasmuch as it may
be employed], for one's-self and for another. That which
is for one's-self is the cause of a private conclusion [in
one's own mind]. For example, having repeatedly and
personally observed, in the case of culinary hearths and
the like, that where there is smoke there is fire, having
gathered the invariable attendedness [of smoke by fire],
having gone near a mountain, and being doubtful as to
whether there is fire in it, having seen smoke on the
mountain, a man recollects the invariable attendedness,
viz., ' where there is smoke there is fire.' Thereupon
the knowledge arises that ' this mountain has smoke,
which is constantly accompanied by fire.' This is called
[by some] the ' pondering of a sign' (linga-parāmarśa).
Thence results the knowledge that ' the mountain is
fiery,' which is the conclusion (anumiti). This is the
process of inference for one's-self."

यत् तु स्वयं धूमादग्निमनुमाय परप्रतिपत्त्यर्थं पञ्चावयव-
वाक्यं प्रयुङ्क्ते तत् परार्थानुमानम् । यथा पर्वतो वह्निमान् । धूम-
वत्त्वात् । यो यो धूमवान् स वह्निमान् यथा महानसः । तथा
चायम् । तस्मात् तथेति । अनेन प्रतिपादिताल्लिङ्गात् परो
ऽप्यग्निं प्रतिपद्यते ।

" But after having, for one's-self, inferred fire from
smoke, when one makes use of the five-membered form

of exposition, with a view to the information of another, then is the process one of 'inference for the sake of another.' For example : (1) The mountain has fire in it; (2) because it has smoke; (3) whatever has smoke has fire, as a culinary hearth; (4) and so this has; (5) therefore it is as aforesaid. By this [exposition], in consequence of the sign [or token] here brought to his notice, the other also arrives at the knowledge that there is fire."

प्रतिज्ञाहेतूदाहरणोपनयनिगमनानि पञ्चावयवा । पर्वतो वह्निमानिति प्रतिज्ञा । धूमवत्त्वादिति हेतु: । यो यो धूमवान् स वह्निमानित्युदाहरणम् । तथा चायमित्युपनय: । तस्मात्तथेति निगमनम् ॥

TRANSLATION.

" The five members [of this exposition are severally named]: (1) the proposition (*pratijñā*), (2) the reason (*hetu*), (3) the example (*udāharaṇa*), (4) the application (*upanaya*), and (5) the conclusion (*nigamana*).   'The mountain is fiery,' is the proposition; ' because of its being smoky,' is the reason; 'whatever is smoky is fiery,' is [the general proposition or principle founded on] the example [of culinary hearths and the like]; ' and so this [mountain] is' is the [syllogistic] application; ' therefore it [the mountain] is fiery,' is the conclusion."

REMARKS.

The five-membered argumentative exposition has been the object, sometimes of undeserved censure, and sometimes of commendation equally undeserved.   When it is commended, at the expense of the Aristotelian syllogism, on the allegation (see a quotation in Sir G. C. Haughton's *Prodromus*, p. 215), "that it exhibits a more natural mode of reasoning than is compatible with the compressed limits of the syllogism, and that its conclusion is as convincing as that of the syllogism," the commendation is based simply on a misconception of the syllogism thus disparaged. On the other hand, when it is censured as "a rude form of the syllogism," the censure is misapplied, because what corresponds to the syllogism is the two-membered expression, which, we have already seen, comprises neither more nor less than the syllogism does; whereas the form now under consideration is proposed as the most convenient for communicating our convictions to others. Being a matter of exposition, it is therefore a question of rhetoric whether the form be, or be not, the most convenient in which to arrange our proposition, our proofs, and our illustrations. The five-membered expression, so far as its arrangement is concerned, is a summary of *Kanāda's* views in regard to rhetoric, "an offshoot from logic," (see Whately's *Elements of Rhetoric*, p. 6), and to which, after "the *ascertainment* of the truth by investigation," belongs "the *establishment* of it to the satisfaction of *another*." Disregarding what is called rhetorical artifice, which, in his system, would have been out of place, as it would have been out of place in Euclid's *Elements of Geometry*, Kanāda directs his rhetorician to commence, as Euclid does, by stating the proposition to be proved. The reason is next to be alleged, and then instances are to be cited in order to show that the reason is sufficient to establish the fact in regard to all cases of a certain given character. The auditor is then to be

13

reminded that there is no dispute that the case in question is of the given character, and the oration winds up with the re-introduction of the original proposition, in the new character of an established conclusion, just as Euclid's argument winds up by re-introducing the triumphant proposition with a flourish of trumpets in the shape of a " Quod erat demonstrandum."

Thus, rhetorically considered, the five-membered expression is a very suitable framework for a straight-forward argumentative speech, making no appeal to the passions, and not hesitating to table, without exordium, the proposition which it proceeds to establish.

Logically considered, the five-membered expression is a combination of the inductive with the deductive syllogism.[1] The instances which led the speaker to an inductive generalization, are cited [in the shape of some one or other example, followed or not by a suggestive " etc."] for the satisfaction of the auditor, in the third division of the rhetorical address; from which circumstance it has happened that those who suppose the intended function of the model oration and of the Aristotelic syllogism to be identical, have come, either to regard the oration as an illogical monstrosity, or else to fancy that it is a great improvement upon the syllogism. The former misconception is that of those who, like Ritter (*History of Ancient Philosophy*, vol. iv., p. 365), were familiarly conversant with the logic of the schools. The other misconception was to be looked for in the case of those whose notions of the logic of the schools were derived from Locke's Essay and Campbell's Rhetoric.

---

[1] [As well as of the Epicurean and the Aristotelian syllogism. See *ante*, p. 147.]

Thus it is quite unfair to say, with Ritter (*History of Philosophy*, vol. iv., p. 365), that two of the five members of Kanada's argument "are manifestly superfluous, while, by the introduction of an example in the third, the universality of the conclusion is vitiated:"—for, as we have shown, the citation of the example serves, as a matter of rhetorical convenience, to bring to the recollection of the hearer instances, in regard to which all parties are unanimous, and which are such as should constrain him to admit the universality of the principle from which the conclusion follows.

स्वार्थानुमितिपरार्थानुमित्योर्लिङ्गपरामर्श एव करणं तस्मा-
ल्लिङ्गपरामर्शो ऽनुमानम् ।

TRANSLATION.

"The instrument [in the making] of an inference (*anumiti*), whether for one's-self or for another, is simply the consideration of a 'sign' (*linga*); therefore an induction (*anumāna*) [which was previously stated to be the instrument of an inference], is (just) this consideration of a sign."

लिङ्गं त्रिविधमन्वयव्यतिरेकि केवलान्वयि केवलव्यतिरेकि
चेति । अन्वयेन व्यतिरेकेण च व्याप्तिमदन्वयव्यतिरेकि यथा वह्नौ
साध्ये धूमवत्त्वम् । यत्र धूमस्तत्राग्निर्यथा महानस इत्यन्वयव्या-
प्तिः । यत्र वह्निर्नास्ति तत्र धूमो ऽपि नास्ति यथा महाह्रद इति
व्यतिरेकव्याप्तिः । अन्वयमात्रव्याप्तिकं केवलान्वयि यथा घटो
ऽभिधेयः प्रमेयत्वात् पटवत् । अत्र प्रमेयत्वाभिधेयत्वयोर्व्यतिरे-
कव्याप्तिर्नास्ति सर्वस्य प्रमेयत्वादभिधेयत्वाच्च । व्यतिरेकमात्रव्या-

त्रिकं केवलव्यतिरेकि यथा पृथिवीतरेभ्यो भिद्यते । गन्धवत्त्वात्।
यदितरेभ्यो न भिद्यते न तद्गन्धवद्यथा जलम् । न चेयं तथा ।
तस्मान्न तथेति । अच यद्गन्धवत् तदितरभिन्नमित्यन्वयदृष्टान्तो
नास्ति पृथिवीमाचष्ट पचलात्।

TRANSLATION.

" A sign [or characteristic token] (*linga*) is of three
sorts : 1, that which is [a token in virtue of its being
constantly] accompanied [by what it betokens], and absent [when what it would betoken is absent] (*anwayavyatireki*); 2, that which is [a token in virtue of its
being constantly] accompanied only [and never absent
through the absence of what it should betoken, the
thing betokened being in this case one everywhere pre-
sent] (*kevalānwayi*); and, 3, that which is [a token in
virtue of its being invariably] absent only [in the case
of everything that could be cited in addition to the
subject of the proposition itself] (*kevalavyatireki*). [To
illustrate these three in order],—that which is accompanied and absent (*anwayavyatireki*) is that which is
pervaded by [or, in other words, of which there is invariably predicable] accompaniment (*anwaya*) [on the
part of what it betokens], and absence (*vyatireka*) [on
its own part, when what it might betoken is absent], as
the possession of smoke, when fire is what is to be established. [For example], 'Where there is smoke there
is fire, as on the culinary hearth [where the fire is
assumed never to be extinguished] :' — here there is
'pervadedness by attendance' (*anwayavyāpti*) [*i.e.*, it
is predicable of the token, smoke, that it is attended

by fire which it betokens]. 'Where fire is not, there
smoke is not, as in a great lake [where it is taken for
granted that fire cannot be] : '—here there is 'pervadedness by absence' (*vyatirekavyāpti*) [*i.e.*, it is predicable of
smoke, as a token, that it will be absent where what it
would have betokened is absent]. [In the second place],
that [sign] which is accompanied only (*kevalānwayi*) is
that which is 'pervaded by [or, in other words, of which
there is invariably predicable] accompaniment only' [on
the part of what it betokens]. For example : 'A jar is
nameable because it is cognizable, as a web is :'—here
there is no [case of] 'pervadedness by absence,' in
cognizability and nameableness, because *everything* [that
we can be conversant about] is both cognizable and
nameable. [Thirdly, and lastly], that [sign] which is
absent only (*kevalavyatireki*) is that which is 'pervaded
by [or, in other words, of which there is invariably pre-
dicable] absence only,' [on its part, in the case of whatever could be cited, as an example, in addition to the
subject of the proposition itself]. For example :—

    (1) 'Earth is different from these others [of the
        elements] :

    (2) Because it is odorous :—

    (3) What is *not* different from these others is not
        odorous,—as water, [for example, is in-
        odorous] :

    (4) But this [earth] is not so [*i. e.*, is not in-
        odorous] :

    (5) Therefore it is not such [as the other elements,
        but different from these others].'

Here [we are obliged to employ, in the third member, a universal negative, because] there is no analogous example [to cite in confirmation], in the case of [the universal affirmative] 'What possesses odor is different from the others,' seeing that earth alone [according to the *Nyāya*] can be the subject [of a proposition in which *odor* is affirmatively predicated]."

सन्दिग्धसाध्यवान् पचो यथा धूमवत्ते हेतौ पर्वतः । निश्चि-
तसाध्यवान् सपचो यथा तचैव महानसः । निश्चितसाध्याभाववान्
विपचो यथा तचैव महाह्रदः ।

TRANSLATION.

" That, whose possession of what is to be established is doubted, is called the subject (*paksha*); as the mountain, when the fact of its smoking is [adduced as] the reason [for inferring the presence of fire]. That which certainly possesses the property in question is called an instance on the same side (*sapaksha*); as the culinary hearth, in the same example. That which is certainly devoid of the property in question, is called an instance on the opposite side (*vipaksha*); as the great lake, in the same example."

REMARKS.

The *sapaksha* corresponds to Bacon's *instantiæ convenientes* " quæ in eadem natura conveniunt, per materias licet dissimillmas." The *vipaksha* corresponds to the instantiæ " quæ natura data privantur."—*Novum Organum*, Lib. 2, Aph. XI. and XII.

NOTE D.

ON THE "VEDAS."

[IF the Indian missionary be staggered by the contemplation of the bulky published volumes (Sanskrit and English) of the *Veda*, the following remarks, penned in 1851, on receipt of the first volume in Benares, may possibly either satisfy or excite his curiosity.]

(From the *Benares Magazine*, for June, 1851).

Professor Wilson's version of the *Rig-Veda* is a book to be received with thanks. The *Friend of India*—no friend to the Sanskrit—with grumbling acknowledgment admits this. The *Friend's* opinion, further, that the book is dryish reading as it stands, appears to be the opinion of the periodical press generally. Reflecting upon these facts, it occurs to us that there may be readers who would thank us for something like a bit of the kernel of the volume,—being content to read it as the Lord of Session read the Waverley Novels, which he used to buy for his wife, as they came out, with the understanding that she was to tell him the story.

In his " Introduction," filled with matter interesting to the philosophical inquirer, Professor Wilson comes to the conclusion that the Vedas are *very* old, though it is difficult, if not impossible, to say how old they are. For our own part we believe the determination of their age to

be a point so little likely to be settled between this and
the end of the world, that we should almost be tempted,
if hard pressed, to profess doggedly the Hindū belief in
their existence from all eternity, rather than pledge ourselves to the discussion of the question until we should
have found out how much younger than eternity the
books really are.   The materials for forming an opinion
as to the *positive* date of the books, are, if possible, more
scanty than those which served the antiquary and the
knight for common battle-ground, when they disputed
as to the Teutonic or the classical origin of the Pictish
language, the only extant word of which was, if we remember rightly, *pen-vall*—which the one declared to be
" caput valli," and consequently Latin, while the other
—admitting the interpretation—insisted that it was
"head of the wall," and consequently Saxon.   To
" breathe the thin air of the mountain-top "—where
there is such a lung-trying lack of respirable matter, is
what we ourselves—un-condor-like — have no sort of
relish for.   Presuming that the reader to whom we
address ourselves has as little, if not less, we leave this
question,—satisfied that the Vedas are very old, and
that, like an old maid who happens to be, like Junius,
the " sole depositary of her own secret," they are not
very likely to give up the secret of their age without being put to a degree of torture which we nowise
feel called upon to apply in the face of the admission on
all hands that they are " certainly aged."

The hymns of the *Rig-Veda* are in verse.   Professor
Wilson, pledging himself to a literal version of them,
writes of course in prose.   Almost all verse is heavy

when turned into prose. We shall take the liberty of turning some of the hymns into metre, not copying the measure of the original but employing what form of English verse seems to us to suit the subject. The first hymn of the *Rig-Veda* is addressed to Agni, the god of fire, the favourite character of the book. According to Professor Wilson, with whom we are disposed to agree, the "author" of this hymn is Madhuchhandas, the son of Viswamitra. At all events, if Madhuchhandas is not the author—(and his name, signifying, as it does, "the man whose verse is sweet," has somewhat of an impersonal air about it)—we are not prepared to mention a likelier claimant of the authorship. When we spoke of this the other day to a learned Hindū friend, he exhibited very marked dissatisfaction and distress, begging us to write and tell Professor Wilson that the hymn had *no* author—that it had existed from everlasting—and that Madhuchhandas was only the fortunate seer to whom, on the last occasion of its revelation, it had been revealed. In the meantime, till Professor Wilson's retractation of the obnoxious epithet could be obtained, he begged us to draw our pencil through the word "author," or to allow him to do it himself. We assured him that it was useless, and that we knew enough of Professor Wilson to make us certain that he would not alter the word for anything that we could, with a good conscience, urge against the use of it. The Brāhman mournfully acquiesced in our proposal, that the matter should be left as it stood—only with the pencilled protest in the margin ;—and here follows the hymn versified, without rhyme, licentiously, but with a tolerably close adherence to the letter.

Hymn to the God of Fire.

I.

" Glory to Agni the high priest,
The ministrant divine, who bears aloft,
And offers to the gods the sacrifice,—
Wealth-saturated Fire!

II.

May He, the radiant, by the seers of eld
And later sages sung,
Invite for us the presence of the gods.

III.

'Tis all to fire we owe our wealth,
Kindred and fame;
Through Him descends each blessing from the skies.

IV.

Borne up to heaven,
Safe in thy flaming arms, the sacrifice
How sure to reach the gods!

V.

And when the gods attend well pleased,
May He, renowned, the true, divinely bright,
Be with us to present the offering.

VI.

Bless thou the giver of the sacrifice
With all thy blessings, for the well-placed gifts
Shall sure revert to thee.

VII.

At morn and even,
With reverential homage in our hearts,
To thee, bright deity, we turn;—

VIII.

To thee the guardian of the sacrifice,
Illustrious,
Expanding in thy glory, as thou tak'st
The offering to thy keeping.

IX.

Be ever present with us for our good ;—
And as the father to the son he loves
  Is easy of access,
    So be to us, O Fire ! " [1]

The second hymn is addressed to the god of the winds, Vāyu by name. Our version of this hymn has a sprinkling of rhyme, which militates somewhat against fidelity ; but we have been as faithful as we could contrive to be under the circumstances.

Hymn to the God of the Winds.

I.

" Vāyu, pleasant to behold,
  Approach :—for thee this offering,
Juice of the moon-plant, is prepared ;—
  Drink whilst we thy praises sing.

II.

Holy praises sing we now
  To the Air-god ;—'tis the hour
We have chosen for our hymn,
  When Vāyu cometh in his power.

---

[1] We annex the prose version of this hymn, as given by Professor Wilson :—

" 1. I glorify Agni, the high-priest of the sacrifice, the divine, the ministrant, who presents the oblation (to the gods), and is the possessor of great wealth.

2. May that Agni who is to be celebrated by both ancient and modern sages conduct the gods hither.

3. Through Agni the worshipper obtains that affluence which increases day by day, which is the source of fame and the multiplier of mankind.

4. Agni, the unobstructed sacrifice of which thou art on every side the protector, assuredly reaches the gods.

5. May Agni, the presenter of oblations, the attainer of knowledge, he who is true, renowned, and divine, come hither with the gods.

6. Whatever good thou mayest, Agni, bestow upon the giver (of the oblation), that verily, Angiras, shall revert to thee.

7. We approach thee, Agni, with reverential homage in our thoughts, daily, both morning and evening.

8. Thee, the radiant, the protector of sacrifices, the constant illuminator of truth, increasing in thine own dwelling.

9. Agni, be unto us easy of access, as is a father to his son ; be ever present with us for our good."

III.

Ha! thy soft approving speech
  Greets mine ear,—I know thy voice;
Thou com'st to drink the soma-juice—
  We see it vanish,—we rejoice.

IV.

Another rich libation pour,
  Now the Thunderer summon we;
Indra come!—with Vāyu come!
  Partake the juice prepared for thee.

V.

Conversant with every rite
  Of sacrifice—full well ye know
These libations are prepared
  For you,—on us then favour show.

VI.

Lord of skies and Lord of air,
  Indra come and Vāyu too,
Manful gods both,—we shall soon
  Gain all we wish, if helped by you.

VII.

Now call the regent of the sun,
  Mitra, lustrous in his powers,
And ocean's ruler, Varuna,
  The joint bestowers of the showers.

VIII.

Ye that treasure up the floods,—
  Lords of the sun and of the seas!—
To be dispensed in grateful showers,
  Requite our present services.

IX.

Sun and Ocean, for the sake
  Of many were ye born,—most wise,
Most kind to multitudes, are ye,—
  Prosper this our sacrifice."

There are some noticeable points in this hymn. In the first place, the author—(begging our friend the Brāhman's pardon for the phraseology)—speaks of the wind as "pleasant to behold." Pigs, as we all know, are proverbially said to see the wind; but here the poet would seem to claim participation in the privilege. Professor Wilson here remarks—" *Vāyu* is invoked in a visible form as the deity presiding over the wind; it is doubtful if the expressions, which in this and similar instances intimate personality, are to be understood as indicating actual figures or idols: the personification is probably only poetical." We incline to the opinion that the personification is only poetical, for two reasons— first, because we never saw any Hindū idol that could be conscionably spoken of as "pleasant to behold"— (except those of Hanumān, the monkey-chief, which our friend the archæologist assures us are long posterior to the date of the Vedas),—and, secondly, because we find a remark of Professor Wilson's in another page which seems to throw a different light upon the matter. The remark to which we allude occurs in the 24th page of the Introduction, where Professor Wilson observes that, in these hymns, " the power, the vastness, the generosity, the goodness, and even the *personal beauty* of the deity addressed, are described in highly laudatory strains." Now what could be more highly—more *implicitly*— laudatory than for the poet to laud the visible loveliness of the wind which he had never set eyes on in the whole course of his life?

The next point noticeable is the sacrificer's assurance that the wind has drunk up the exhilarating

juice of the moon-plant, when the juice has evaporated.
Here we have chemistry itself adumbrated in poetical
mythology.

Then we have the poet, at a loss for anything beyond
it as a climax of commendation, patting the wind and
the firmament on the back, with the protestation that they
are *men*—stout fellows both of them. There is something
hearty in this ;—he is evidently in earnest.

Lastly, the description of the sun and of the ocean as
the joint bestowers of the showers that refresh the earth,
is, to our mind, as beautiful as it is philosophical.
"Aurum latet in hoc," as Leibnitz said of the writings
of the Schoolmen. We may turn the Vedas to account,
if we but eschew the lazy blunder of a lazy scorn. It is
a glorious point gained when you can find any truth
enwrapped in language which the man that you have to
deal with has sucked in as with his mother's milk.

We may further remark—(in conclusion, after the
"lastly")—that their thankfulness for showers of rain
goes far to prove that the Hindūs (as Professor Wilson
observes at page 41 of his Introduction), were an agri-
cultural people at the time when this hymn was composed, and not a nomadic, as has been by some contended.
Nomads, though not independent of rain, are usually less
anxious about it than agriculturists.

The third hymn introduces us to the Hindū Castor
and Pollux—the Aswins—"the two sons of the Sun,
begotten during his metamorphosis as a horse (*aśwa*),
endowed with perpetual youth and beauty, and phy-
sicians of the gods." The invocation of the hymn is not
confined to these,—Indra, the thunderer, with his "tawny

coursers," certain miscellaneous deities, and the goddess of eloquence, being also invoked.

HYMN TO THE TWIN-BORN OF THE SUN, AND OTHERS.

I.

Twin-sons of heaven's bright orb,
Friends of the pious,—whose far-reaching arms
Avail to guard your worshippers, accept
The sacrificial viands. Ye whose acts,
Mighty and manifold, declare your power,
Ye that direct the hearts of the devout,
With favouring ear attend our hymn of praise.
Faithful and true, destroyers of the foe,
First in the van of heroes, As'wins, come!
Come to the mixed libations that we pour
On the lopped sacred grass.

II.

Now on Indra we call, on the wondrously bright;
See—we press from the moon-plant the juice of delight,
The juice, ever pure as enchanting, that longs [1]
To be quaffed by thy lips;—come and list to our songs.
The wise understand Thee—'tis only the wise
That the knowledge of Indra full rightly can prize;
Approach and accept then the prayers of thy priest,
Let thy fleet tawny steeds bear thee swift to the feast.

III.

Next the throng divine invite
Of deities that guard the right,
Ever watching o'er us all,—
Call them to our festival.
Come, ye swift-moving spirits, ye spirits that run
Through the universe—swift as the rays of the sun—
That preside o'er the rain-showers, accept of our cheer,
Nor despise the libation we pour for you here.

---

[1] In the prose version—"these libations, ever pure, expressed by the fingers (of the priests) are desirous of thee," p. 9.

Omniscient immortals, whose might is for aye,
In the youth of its vigour exempt from decay,
In whose souls void of malice all kindly thoughts spring,
Deign to look on the gifts that your worshippers bring.

IV.

Now to Saraswatī address the song,
Saraswatī to whom all gifts belong,
The recompenser of the worshipper
With food and wealth,—our hymn be now to her.
　　Joy !—for Saraswatī, whose inspiration
　　　　Is theirs alone that in the truth delight,
　　Accept our sacrifice ;—pour the libation
　　　　To her, the guide of all whose hearts are right.
　　Behold the present deity !—the stream,[1]
　　　　The mighty stream named hers,—behold it roll,
　　Bearing on its fair bosom such a gleam
　　Of light as she alone can stream upon the soul.''

Some of the most graceful of the hymns are addressed
to the goddess of the morning—Ushas—the Aurora of
Hindū mythology. Here is a portion of one,—for the
entire hymn would be rather long.

HYMN TO AURORA.
I.

Daughter of heaven,—Aurora, dawn on us ;
　Diffusing light, and bringing wealth with thee,
　　Bountiful goddess, dawn.

II.

Rousing the flocks and waking up the birds,
Nourishing all, yet onward to decay
Conducting all her transitory charge,
Even as a matron to her household cares,
　Daily the dawn comes forth.

---

[1] As Professor Wilson observes, *Saraswatī*, the divinity of speech, "is here identified with the river so named," p. 10. The river, we believe, is now nowhere to be
met with,—ominous, one might think, that the genius of India had run itself out,
for the time at least.

III.

Shedder of dews, delay she knows not. See
How her approach inspires the diligent ;
The client early seeks his patron's gate,
The soaring birds suspend their flight no more,
Up-springing with the dawn.

IV.

All living things invoke her, and adore ;
Bringer of good, she lighteth up the world,
While the malevolent that love the dark
Flee at her blest approach.

These may suffice as a sample of the hymns, in which
there is much sameness of character both as to style and
subject. From the remaining hymns we shall now glean
a few noticeable passages.

In the 3rd verse of the 9th hymn, Indra is addressed
as "thou, who art to be reverenced by all mankind."
In a note on this passage, Professor Wilson says that the
epithet *viswa-charshane* is literally "oh! thou who art
all men," or, as the commentator explains it, "who art
joined with all men,"—which is further qualified as
"to be worshipped by all institutors of sacrifices." Professor Wilson adds—"It may be doubted if this be all
that is intended." It strikes us that what is intended
may be that now familiar conception of the chief ener-
gising deity—*iswara*, "the lord"—as being not other
than the aggregate of all embodied souls, "as a forest
is not other than the trees that compose it,"—a conception which may be seen elaborated in any work on the
Vedānta, such as the *Vedānta-sāra*. Dr. Rosen's rendering of the epithet as "omnium hominum *domine*" is not
opposed to this view. It is curious to trace, in these the

14

most ancient portions of the *Veda*, anything like the
dawning of those conceptions which, gradually elaborated
through the subsequent portions entitled the *Upanishads*,
took at length the form which they now hold in the
Vedānta philosophy.   In the 3rd verse of the 6th hymn
there is another passage, which appears to have puzzled
the commentator, and which has to our eye a Vedāntic
aspect.   The verse runs thus—"Mortals, you owe your
(daily) birth (to such an Indra), who with the rays of the
morning gives sense to the senseless, and to the formless
form."   Indra, according to Professor Wilson, is here
"identified with the sun, whose morning rays may be
said to re-animate those who have been dead in sleep
through the night."   This is the obvious explanation,
and probably the correct one ; but there is something
strange in the construction,—the word for "mortals"
being plural, whilst the verb is in the singular.   The
commentator "is of opinion that the want of concord is
a *Vaidik* license." This it possibly is ; but the assumed
indifference between the singular and the plural reminds
us not only of the Vedāntic tenet of the indifference
between the collective and the distributive aggregate of
humanity,—"as between the forest and its constituent
trees,"—but also of another tenet, viz., that, during pro-
found sleep, the world *actually* as well as apparently
ceases to exist for the sleeper, whose disembodied spirit,
at that time merging in the Infinite Spirit, re-assumes,
in the processes of awakening, a body with its senses and
its outward form.

But whether there be or not in these ancient hymns
faint indications of the philosophy which was gradually

elaborated in the Vedānta, the indications are abundantly
plentiful of those myths which have supplied topics for
the poets. The combats of Indra, the thunderer, especially with the demons of drought, remind us of the
fights of the Scandinavian Thor with the Jötuns.
In the 7th verse of the 11th hymn we read :—"Thou
slewest, Indra, by stratagems, the wily Sushna : the wise
have known of this thy (greatness); bestow upon them
(abundant) food." On this Professor Wilson remarks,
that Sushna is described as a demon slain by Indra, but
that "this is evidently a metaphorical murder. *Sushna*
means dryer up, exsiccator .... heat or drought; which
Indra, as the rain, would put an end to." The greatest
of Indra's foes is *Vritra*, who ought by rights to be the
father of *Sushna*, or the drought, seeing that he repre-
sents the retentive power of the clouds whereby they
withhold from the earth the waters that they contain,
until Indra, "with his thunderbolt or electrical influence,
divides the aggregated mass, and vent is given to the
rain, which then descends upon the earth."

Dr. Müller's edition of the Sanskrit text of these
hymns is a monument both of his own diligence and
of the liberality of the Honourable Court, without whose
patronage the publication could not have been ventured
upon. The volume is a handsome quarto of nine hundred and ninety pages. The bulk of these is occupied
by the commentary, which is a very ample one. The
text of the hymns, in its translated form, does not
occupy much more than the half of some three hundred octavo pages, the other half being devoted to
the notes of the translator. Sāyanāchārya, the com-

mentator, makes something like an apology for the
amplitude of his exegesis.

This edition of the *Rig-veda*, Dr. Müller remarks,
"is not intended for the general scholar, but only for
those who make Sanskrit their special study," etc. To
such students this massive tome presents a supply of
pabulum, such as a helluo librorum may well be expected to lick his lips at. And then, to think of the
other volumes that are to come, this first instalment,
with its thousand pages, being but the one-eighth part
of one Veda out of the four! But the other volumes
are not likely to be so big; for, as the commentator
Sāyana remarks of his work, in some introductory
verses,—"The first section of this, deduced as it is
from traditional doctrine, is to be listened to. An
intelligent person, perfect in thus much, can understand the whole." He then proceeds to explain why
the Rig-veda, rather than any one of the others, is taken
for commentatorial illustration first in order. To justify
the selection, he brings forward various arguments,—
among others, the fact that when the separate Vedas
are enumerated in the Veda itself, the Rig-veda stands
first in the enumeration. The objector then, acquiescing
in the proposed order, falls back upon the more perilous
doubt whether there is any such thing as the Veda
at all! "The short and the long of it is," he insists,
"there is *no* Veda: how, then, can there be a *Rig*-veda,
—an integrant portion thereof? For there is no sign
whereby one can recognise anything as being the Veda,
nor is there any proof of it; and nothing can be established when there is neither the one nor the other

of these. For those that understand logic, hold that a thing is established by characteristic signs and by proofs." And so the hardy objector goes on, while Sāyana, calm in the consciousness of strength, abides his time. When the objector has finished, the other disposes of the objection; whereupon our objector, conceding—for the sake of argument—that there *may* be "a certain thing called the Veda," demurs to there being any occasion for making a commentary on it. The Veda, he argues, is no authority, some of its texts being downright nonsense. Such charges, it may be presumed, Sāyana did not deck out in all the pomp of regular disputation, without feeling tolerably sure of his own power to dispose of them satisfactorily. He allows to both sides of the question ample elbow-room, and it is not till after three-and-forty of Dr. Müller's broad quarto pages that we come to the first line of the first hymn of the Rig-veda. Four pages of comment on this hemistich bring us to the second line, and so the work goes on.

The exegetical part of Sāyana's commentary is quite exhaustive. For example:—on the first verse, beginning "I laud Fire, the priest," etc., he remarks—"I laud Fire, *i.e.*, the deity so named; laud, *i.e.*, praise, the verb here being *īd*, 'to praise,' the letter *d* in which is changed to *l* by Vaidik license," and so on.

We may mention to our Hindū friends that this edition is intended not only for Sanskrit scholars, but also Dr. Müller tells, "for those among the natives of India who are still able to read their own Sacred Books in the language of the original." The price of the volume is a trifle compared with that of a good manuscript; and no manuscript in the market can vie with it in point of accuracy. The copyists of the Veda admit their liability to error; and, in the verses which they are in the habit of appending to a completed transcript, they frequently complain of the hardships and difficulties of their task. One of the most touching of these penmen's plaints is the following, which Dr. Müller instances:—

"My back, my hips, and my neck are broken; my sight is stiff in looking down: keep this book with care, which has been written with pain."

NOTE E.

THE ETERNITY OF SOUND; A DOGMA OF THE MĪMĀNSĀ.

[This dogma being of vital importance to the *Veda*, he who argues against the *Veda* ought to understand what the dogma means. We reprint the following remarks of ours on it from the *Benares Magazine*, August, 1852.]

At page 305, vol. i. of Mr. Colebrooke's *Collected Essays*, where he is treating of Jaimini's system of philosophy, the *Mīmānsā*, we read as follows:—" In the first chapter of the lecture occurs the noted disquisition of the *Mīmānsā* on the original and perpetual association of articulate sound with sense." What this dogma means, and why the question forced itself upon

Jaiminī at the opening of his work, we here propose
to consider.

"The object of the *Mīmānsā*," to employ the words
of Mr. Colebrooke, "is the interpretation of the *Vedas*."
As he adds, "Its whole scope is the ascertainment of
duty." This is declared in the opening aphorism, which,
interspersing an explanatory comment, we may render
as follows:—"Well, then [O student, since thou hast
read the *Vedas* while residing in the family of thy
preceptor], therefore a desire to know *duty* [which knowledge, without further aid, thou wilt scarcely gather
from the texts with which thy memory is stored, ought
now to be entertained by thee]."[1] But what do you
mean by "duty?" inquires the student. To expound
the entire import of the term would be difficult, if not
impossible, at the outset; so Jaiminī, following the
recognised method of laying down a "characteristic"
(*lakshana*), by which the thing, though not fully described, may be securely *recognised*, declares as follows:
—"A duty is a matter which may be recognised [as
a duty] by the instigatory character [of the passage of
Scripture in which it is mentioned]."[2] As Mr. Colebrooke observes, "Here *duty* intends sacrifices and
other acts of religion ordained by the *Vedas*. The same
term (*dharma*) likewise signifies *virtue*, or moral merit;
and grammarians have distinguished its import according to the gender of the noun. In one (the masculine),
it implies virtue; in the other (neuter), it means an
act of devotion. It is in the last-mentioned sense that
the term is here employed." We may add, in expla-

---

[1] अथातो धर्मजिज्ञासा ॥ १ ॥   [2] चोदनालक्षणो धर्मः ॥ २ ॥

nation of this, that the discussion of the gender of the
word was provoked by Jaimini's choosing to employ
the masculine form (as may be observed in the original
aphorism given in the note), instead of the neuter. To
the query, why Jaimini was guilty of this grammatical
solecism, one of his commentators coolly replies, "take
[and be content with] as the reason thereof, the fact
that he [Jaimini] is a great sanctified sage [and therefore entitled to give the word what gender he pleases]."
Arguments of this lofty Pope Hildebrand order, which
were doubtless rolled out with unction, *et ore rotundo*,
in the palmy days of Hindūism, the Brāhmans now-
a-days are most amusingly ashamed of; those of
them, at least, who are not prepared to join cordially
in a broad grin over the "bumptiousness" of the pretension.

Whilst Jaimini contents himself with giving, in the
first instance, a "characteristic" by which *duty* may be
recognised, his commentator supplies an account of its
nature (swarúpa), *i.e.*, what constitutes that a duty to
which the characteristic in question belongs. According
to him, what constitutes anything a duty is "the fact of
its not producing more pain than pleasure [or, in other
words, its being calculated to produce more pleasure
than pain]." The agreement of this with the Ben-
thamite definition of the Useful is noticeable. Another
thing which we wish here to take an opportunity of
noticing, is a correspondence, in point of terminology,
between the systems of the East and of the West. That
which constitutes anything what it is, was called by
Plato its *Idea*. Aristotle disliked the term; and he

sought to convey the same meaning by a term which the Schoolmen rendered *Form*. Bacon adopted the word *Form* in this sense, and the exactly corresponding Sanskrit word, viz., *swarūpa*, is the one here employed, and generally employed, to convey the notion of what is the abiding cause of a thing's being what it is. When a Hindū writer, at the opening of a treatise on anything, says "I shall declare the *lakshana* and the *swarūpa* of the thing in question," he means to say, that he will tell first, how we are to recognise the thing as *the* thing that we are talking about, and that he will next tell, *all about it*. The *lakshana* is the mark on the sealed package, by which we recognise it among other packages ; the *swarūpa* is the contents of the package. The reason why we think it worth while to advert to the import of the phraseology in question is this, that we ourselves once took a good deal of pains unprofitably to reconcile these two terms with the "genus" and the "specific difference" which together make up the "definition," according to European logic. The one set of terms and the other, however, belong to different aspects of thought.

To return to Jaiminī:—Having intimated that the cause of our knowing anything to be a duty was simply an instigation, in the shape of a passage of Scripture holding out the promise of a reward for the performance of a given act, he next thinks proper to show how nothing else *could* be the evidence for it. "An examination," he says, "of the cause of [our recognising] it [viz., a duty, is to be made];"[1] and he ex-

---

[1] तस्य निमित्तपरीष्टिः ॥ ३ ॥

plains, as follows, how our organs of sense cannot supply
the evidence of it. " When a man's organs of sense
are rightly applied to something *extant*, that birth of
knowledge [which then takes place] is perception—[and
this perception is] *not* the cause [of our recognising a
duty], because the apprehension [by the senses] is of
what is [then and there] extant, [which an act of
duty is *not*]."[1] Since perception is not the evidence
of a thing's being a duty, it follows, according to the
commentator, that inference or analogy, or anything
else, " which has its *root* in perception," cannot be
the evidence ; and, consequently, precept—express or
implied—is the only evidence of a thing's being a
duty.

But here the doubt presents itself, whether the
evidence in favour of a thing's being a duty may not
be as fallacious as is the evidence of the senses. According to the objector,—" after words and meanings have
presented themselves, since the connection between the
two is one devised by *man*,—consisting, as it does, of
the conventions which man has devised ; therefore, as
sense-knowledge wanders away from truth when it mistakes mother-o'-pearl for silver, so language is liable
to part company with veracity in matters of assertion,
and consequently the instigatory nature of a passage
which, being couched in words, is liable to be misunderstood, cannot be the instrument of certain knowledge
in respect of duty." Jaiminī, in reply, denies that this
doubt affects the evidence of Scripture. " But the

_____

[1] सत्सम्प्रयोगे पुरुषस्येन्द्रियाणां बुद्धिजन्म तत्प्रत्यक्षमनिमित्तं विद्यमा-
नोपलब्धात् ॥ ४ ॥

natural [*i.e.*, the *eternal* and not conventional] connection of a word with its sense, *is* [the instrument of] the knowledge thereof, and the intimation [of Scripture which is] infallible, though given in respect of something imperceptible. This, [according to our opinion, as well as that] of Bādarāyana, [the author of the *Vedānta* aphorisms], is the evidence [by means of which we recognise a duty], for it has no respect [to any other evidence, such as that of sense]."[1] Assertions in regard to ordinary things, such as the assertion that there is fire in this or that place, meet with credit, because people have opportunities of verifying such assertions by ocular inspection. This is not the case with regard to the assertion that this or that act is a duty; and therefore Jaimini—in the absence of the possibility of verification—rests the evidence of testimony, in the case of Scripture, on its *infallibility*. The mention of the name of Bādarāyana (who is the same as Vyāsa), in this fifth aphorism, goes to prove that Jaimini's work, the *Pūrvva-mīmānsā*, was not antecedent in time to Vyāsa's *Uttara-mīmānsā*. Mr. Colebrooke's rendering of the terms *pūrvva* and *uttara* by "prior" and "later" (see *Essays*, vol. i., pp. 227 and 295), would seem to have led Dr. Ritter to suppose that Jaimini's system was the earlier in order of publication. Dr. Ritter says (at p. 376, vol. iv., of his *History of Philosophy*, Morrison's version) that, "according to Colebrooke, the adherents of this school may be divided into the earlier and the later;" and then he goes on

---

[1] श्रौत्यक्तिकस्तु शब्दखार्थेन सम्बन्धस्य ज्ञानमुपदेष्ट्री व्यतिरिकखार्थे ऽनुपलब्धे तत्प्रमाणं बादरायणख्यानपेचलात् ॥ ५ ॥

to speak of "the older and genuine *Vedānta*:" but in
fact the terms "prior" and "later" refer not to time,
but to the divisions of the *Veda* which Jaimini and
Vyāsa respectively expound, the latter directing his
attention to the *Upanishads*, or theological sections,
which stand last in *order*. The word *mīmānsā* means
"a seeking to understand," and the *pūrvva-mīmānsa* is
"a seeking to understand the prior (or ritual portion
of the *Vedas*)," while the *uttara-mīmānsā* is a "seeking
to understand the later (or theological portion of the
Vedas)." These two compounds, in short, to speak
grammatically, are not *Karmadhāraya*, but *Shashthī-tat-
purusha*.

Jaimini, we have just seen, denies that the connection
of a word with its sense is dependent on human conven-
tion. This he was obliged to do in order to remove the
Vedas beyond the imputation of that fallibility which
attaches to all that is devised by man. The *eternal* connection between a word and its sense, the commentator
here remarks, "is dependent on the eternity of *sound*,"
—seeing that if sound were not eternal, then words
which consist of sound could not be eternal, nor consequently could the relation of such to their significations
be eternal. Being compelled, therefore, to demonstrate
that sound *is* eternal, Jaimini, in pursuance of the established method of procedure, first grapples with the
arguments which, *primâ facie*, might seem to countenance an opposite view of the matter. The first objection
to the eternity of sound is its being made by effort.
Thus, according to Jaimini, "Some [viz., the followers
of the Nyāya] say that it is a product, for, in the case

of it, we *see* [the effort made for its production]."[1] Jaiminī is far too secure in the strength of his own position, to be under any temptation to stop the mouths of objectors before they have said their say. Half a dozen objections he allows to be tabled against the eternity of sound, the second of them being, "Because of its transitoriness,"[2]—because, "beyond a moment it is no longer perceived." Moreover, the Naiyāyikas contend, in the third place, that sound is not eternal, because it is stamped as factitious by the usage of language,—"Because of [our employing, when we speak of sound] the expression '*making*.'"[3] When you talk of *making* something, as a jar for instance, you talk of something that has a commencement, else where were the need of its being *made?* Fourthly, according to the Naiyāyikas, the alleged eternity of sound is incompatible with its undeniable *multeity*: and the fact that multeity *does* belong to it is inferred "From its being simultaneously in another person [occupying a different place from some first person whom it also affects]."[4] According to the explanation of the scholiast, "The scope of the present objection is this, that an argument which establishes the *eternity* of any sound will equally establish its *unity*; and thus we should have to admit that a numerically single and eternal entity is simultaneously present to the senses, both of those near and those far off—which is an inconsistency." And the Naiyāyikas infer that sound is not eternal, because,

---

[1] कर्मके तच दर्शनात् ॥ ६ ॥

[2] अस्थानात् ॥ ७ ॥

[3] करोतिशब्दात् ॥ म ॥

[4] सत्त्वान्तरे यौगपद्यात् ॥ ए ॥

" Also, of the original and altered forms"[1] of words—
a condition incompatible with the changelessness of
eternity—and, finally, because, "Also, by a multitude
of makers there is an augmentation of it."[2] A thousand
lamps, rendering a jar manifest, do not make the jar
seem larger than a single lamp does: yet a thousand
persons uttering any sound in concert, make a propor-
tionately greater sound than one person does; so this
must be a case not of manifesting a previously extant
sound, but of *making* one.

Before stating the arguments in support of his own
view, Jaimini addresses himself to the refutation of the
foregoing objections; and antecedently to this, also, he
judiciously seeks to narrow the ground of contention by
determining how far both parties *agree.* "But alike,"
he says, "is the *perception* thereof,"[3]—according to both
views,—both agreeing that the *perception* of sound is only
for a moment, whatever difference of opinion there may be
as to sound itself being momentary. But though acqui-
escent so far as *this* point is concerned, Jaimini cannot
allow that the sound which we perceive for the moment
was *produced* at the moment. He explains:—" Of this
[sound], while it really exists, the non-perception at
another time [than that when the sound is perceived] is
due to the non-application [of a manifester] to the object
[the then unheard sound]."[4] In like manner, a jar, seen
by a flash of lightning, is not then *produced*, nor does it
cease to exist on its ceasing to be perceived. The same

---

[1] प्रकृतिविकृत्योश्च ॥ १० ॥   [2] वृद्धिश्च कर्त्तृभूमास्य ॥ ११ ॥
[3] समनु तच दर्शनम् ॥ १२ ॥
[4] सतः परमदर्शनं विषयानागमात् ॥ १३ ॥

jar may be manifested for another moment by a subsequent flash. According to the commentator, " Sound is eternal [as we are constrained to admit], by force of the recognition that, ' This is that same letter K" [viz., the same[1] sound that I heard yesterday, or fifty years ago], and in virtue of the *law of parcimony*,"—one of the fundamental laws of philosophising acknowledged by philosophers both of the East and of the West, and implying that we must never assume more causes of a given effect than are sufficient to account for it. Europeans hold that sound is due to vibration. Jaimini's commentator admits that it is not perceived when there is *no* vibration : but, with perverse ingenuity, he argues that the *absence* of vibration, or the *stillness* of the air, is what prevents us from perceiving the sound, which never ceases to *exist*, whether perceived or not. " The conjunctions and disjunctions [or undulations] of the air issuing from the mouth, remove the *still* air which was the obstacle to the perception of sound, and thence it becomes perceptible."

Replying to the objection conveyed in Aph. 8, Jaimini says, " This [expression ' making'] means *employing ;*"[2]—we talk of *making* a sound when we only make *use* of it. Then, as for the objection that a sound cannot be *one*, because its perception is present to many at a time, he replies, " The simultaneousness is as in the case of the sun :"[3] which is explained to mean, that,

---

[1] In opposition to the Mīmānsakas, the Naiyāyikas contend that the form of expression, " This is that same letter K" is grounded merely on the fact that the things referred to are of the same *kind*,—just as is the case with the expression, " He has taken the same medicine that I did." See the *Siddhānta Muktāvalī*, p. 103 ; and compare the remarks of Whately (in the Appendix to his *Logic*) on the ambiguity of the word " Same."

[2] प्रयोगस्य परम् ॥ १४ ॥ [3] आदित्यवद्यौगपद्यम् ॥ १५ ॥

"As the sun, which is but one, is seen simultaneously by those stationed in different places, so, like the sun, a sound is a great object, not a minute one"—such as cannot come at once under the cognizance of persons at any distance from one another. Then, as for the objection that a sound cannot be eternal, since it undergoes changes in the hands of the grammarian, he says, "This [*e.g.*, the letter *y* coming in the room of *i*] is another letter, not a modification"[1]—of that whose place it takes. As the commentator adds, "The *y* is not a modification of the *i*, as a mat is a modification of the straw. If it were so, then, as the maker of a mat is under the necessity of providing himself with straw to make it of, the man that employs the letter *y* would be under the necessity of taking the letter *i* to make it of." Finally, to the objection that a sound must be a product, because there is the more of it the more numerous are those employed in making it, he replies, "It is the increase of the *noise* that becomes great,"[2]—and not of the *sound*.

Here we begin to perceive that this notable dispute is somewhat of a verbal one, and that Jaiminī does not mean by sound what his opponents mean by it. Sound, according to Jaiminī, like the music spoken of in Othello, is of a kind "that may not be heard,"[3]—a "silent thunder" in its way. But let us hear Jaiminī, who, having disposed of the offered objections, proceeds

---

[1] वर्णान्तरमविकारः ॥ १६ ॥   [2] नाद्वृद्धिः परा ॥ १७ ॥

[3] *Clown.*—If you have any music that may not be heard, then to 't again : but, as they say, to hear music, the general doth not greatly care.
Musician.—We have none such, sir.
Clown.—Then put up your pipes——

                                        Othello, Act iii, sc. 1.

to defend his own theory. "But it must be eternal [this or that articulate sound], because its exhibition is for the sake of another;"[1] and the commentator adds, in explanation—"If it were not eternal, then, as it would not continue till the hearer had understood our meaning [the *perception* of the sound ceasing on the instant that it reaches the ear], the understanding [of what was uttered] would not take place because of the absence of the cause;—for, to explain further, the understanding of what is uttered must *follow* —at however short an interval—the perception of the sound uttered; and if the sound perish on the hearing, as the *noise* does, then being no longer in existence, it cannot be the *cause* of anything." If, on the other hand, it continue to exist, for any period however short, after ceasing to be perceived, it is impossible to assign any other instant at which there is any evidence of the discontinuance of its existence,—whence its eternity may be inferred. Moreover, as it is prospectively eternal, so was it antecedently, which he considers to be proved, " By there being everywhere simultaneousness"[2] in the recognition of it by ever so many hearers, who could not *recognise* it if it were a new production. For example, when the word *cow* is uttered, a hundred persons recognise the word alike; and, the commentator adds, a "hundred persons do not simultaneously fall into an error,"—this being as unlikely as it is that a hundred arrows discharged simultaneously by a hundred archers should all by *mistake* hit the same object. Then, again, a sound is proved

[1] नित्यस्तु स्याद्दर्शनस्य परार्थत्वात् ॥ १९ ॥
[2] सर्वत्र यौगपद्यात् ॥ २० ॥

to be eternal "By the absence of number;"[1] for, *e.g.*,
"When the word *cow* has been uttered ten times, we
say 'The word *cow* has been uttered ten times,' but not
' ten words of the form *cow* have been uttered." Further,
sound, as being indiscerptible, is proved to be eternal,
"By there being no ground for anticipation"[2] of its
destruction. "As, on the mere inspection of a web, one
feels certain that 'this web was produced by the conjunction of threads, and it will be destroyed by the destruction of the conjunction of the threads,' so,—from the absence of the knowledge of any cause that should lead to
the destruction of a *sound*, we conclude that *it* is eternal."

But some one may contend that a sound is a mere
modification of the air, and he may cite the *Siksha*—
that appendage of the Vedas which treats of pronunciation, which tells us that "air arrives at the state of
being sound" after undergoing such and such treatment;—so Jaiminī anticipates and repels this, "Because
[if it were so], there would not be perception [by the
organ of hearing] of an object appropriate to it."[3] He
means to say that "modifications of the *air* are not what
the organ of hearing takes cognizance of, sound not being
something *tangible*," as the air is held by the Naiyāyikas
to be, while sound, they hold, has an altogether different substratum, viz., the ether. Here Jaiminī, though
he does not himself hold sound to be a quality of ether,
does not however disdain to avail himself of the *argu-
mentum ad hominem*.

Finally, to put the seal upon the evidence of sound's

[1] संख्याभावात् ॥ २१ ॥
[2] अनपेक्षत्वात् ॥ २२ ॥   [3] प्रख्याभावाच्च योग्यस्य ॥ २३ ॥

eternity, he refers to the Hindū scriptures:—"And [each articulate sound is proved to be eternal] by our seeing a proof"[1] of this, in the text which the commentator supplies, viz., "By language, that alters not, eternal," etc. Here ends the topic of sound; and assuredly Jaiminī does not make it very clear what he means by the term. Let us therefore turn to a fuller exposition of the dogma in question, and this may be found in the *Mahābhāshya* and its commentaries.

Patanjali commences the *Mahābhāshya,* or "Great[2] Commentary," on the Grammatical Aphorisms of Pānini, by saying "Now, the teaching of sounds:"—"Of *what* sounds?" he asks;—and he replies, "Of those secular and those sacred." Kaiyaṭa remarks on this as follows: "Since the word 'sound' signifies sound in general, having reflected that—since, but for the question in hand, etc., there would have been nothing to determine the species,—the teaching also of the sounds of fiddle-strings, and of the cries of crows, etc., might have suggested itself, he asks, ' *Of what,*' etc." Then, "having further reflected, that since Grammar is an appendage of the Veda, from the sense of the terms the species [of sounds with which Grammar is concerned] may be inferred, he says [in order to give a useful reply to his own question], ' *Of secular,*' etc." After several pages of such disquisition, which provoke twice as many more

---

[1] लिङ्गदर्शनाच ॥ २४ ॥

[2] Its "greatness,"—though the commentator Kaiyata, with allusion to its bulk, styles it an "ocean of a commentary,"—is explained by *his* commentator, again, Nāgeśa Bhaṭṭa, to consist in its being, unlike ordinary commentaries, a supplementary authority, and not a mere exegesis.—See vol. i. of the Benares College edition of the *Mahābhāshya*, p. 1 of translation.

from Nāgeśa Bhaṭṭa, Patanjali is allowed to go on again.
"Of these, the secular, in the first place, are such as
cow, horse, man, elephant, bird, deer, brāhman. The scriptural are verily indeed such as *sauna devīrabhīshtaye*
('may the goddess be propitious to my prayers,')" etc.
He goes on to say—"Well—'cow'—here which is the
word? That which is in the shape of a thing with dewlap, tail, hump, hoofs, and horns,—pray, is *that* the
word? Nay, replies he, that is verily a *thing.* Then
the hints, gestures, and winking,—is *that* the word?
Nay, he replies, that verily is *action.* Then the white,
the blue, the tawny, the spotted,—is *that* the word?
Nay, he replies, that verily is *quality.* Then, that which
in [many] different is [one and] not different,—and which
is not destroyed in things which [by disintegration] are
destroyed,—that which is the common nature,—is *that*
the word? Nay, he replies, that verily is the *form*—
[implying the genus, or Platonic 'idea'—the ἐν ἐπὶ
πολλῶν]. What then *is* the word?[1] The word ['cow']
is that through which, when uttered, there is the cognition of things with dewlap, tail, hump, hoofs, and
horns." We must not at present indulge in a *réchauffe-
ment* of all the drolly sagacious things that Kaiyaṭa and
Nāgeśa take occasion to propound with reference to these
remarks of his Snakeship[2] Patanjali. We must confine
ourselves to the question of what is *eternal,* or held to be
eternal, in the matter of sound.

Everybody allows that the constituent *letters* of a word

[1] The inquirer is supposed to ask this after having run through all the categories,
which the grammarians reckon to be four,—the four above-mentioned.

[2] Whilst the author of the *Mahābhāshya* (and of the *Yoga* Aphorisms) honoured
the world with his presence, he is understood to have been a serpent.

are non-significant; because, says Kaiyaṭa, " if letters severally were significant, the pronunciation of the second, or of any subsequent [letter in any word] would be purposeless. But, assuming that they are severally non-significant, then, on the theory that they *arise*, since they cannot arise *simultaneously*; and [then again] on the theory that they are *manifested*, since, from their being manifested *successively*, there is no [stable] aggregate,— if those that are impressed on a single [page of] memory were what express [the meaning connected with these letters so recorded], then we should find no difference between the sense gathered in the case of *sara*, 'an arrow,' and *rasa*, 'a taste,' [the letters of which are the same]. In the *Vākyapadīya* [of Bhartrihari] it is diffusely established, that what denotes [the thing denoted] is [so to speak] a ' disclosure' (*sphoṭa*), other than these [letters, and, at the same time], revealed by utterance." What is here called *sphoṭa*—a ' disclosure'—is what Jaiminī meant by the term sound (*sabda*), though he chose, for prudential reasons of his own, not to point out to his opponents—what they ought to have had perspicacity enough to discern for themselves—that he was " paltering with them in a double sense." Possibly, again, the case may have been an exemplification of the Hudibrastic principle, that

> Sure the pleasure is as great
> Of being cheated, as to cheat.

The Naiyāyikas had no interest in really clearing up a confusion of ideas which allowed Jaiminī to settle the eternity of the *Veda*, on which all the six schools repose, while at the same time it left a world of cloudland available for endless and luxurious logomachy. The Naiyāyikas were *humbugs* when they did not come down upon Jaiminī with the sledge-hammer of Gautama's 52nd aphorism. They *knew* that he was "paltering in a double sense,"—but then their philosophical virtue was not of the termagant order, but rather of the kind that coyly resists with sheathed claws. Paying no further attention to the Naiyāyikas, let us attend to the conception which the grammarians, in accordance with the Mīmānsakas, denominate *sphota*.

At page 305 of the first volume of his *Essays*, Mr. Colebrooke says, " Grammarians assume a special category, denominated *sp'ho'ta*, for the object of mental perception, which ensues upon the hearing of an articulate sound, and which they consider to be distinct from the elements or component letters of the word. Logicians disallow that as a needless assumption." Of this *sphota*, which the grammarians—as being Vedāntins—assume to be the only real entity in the universe, Nāgeśa Bhaṭṭa speaks as follows: "The cognition, ' This is one word,' ' This is one sentence,' is proof of there being such a thing as *sphota*, and of its unity [it being held to be one with knowledge, or one with God]; because, too, there is no solid evidence of the fact that memory is exactly according to the order of apprehension [so that *sara* and *rasa* might come to suggest each the same idea] since we *see* things that were apprehended in one order, recollected even in the inverse order. But, in my opinion, as there becomes gradually, in a web, a tincture of various hues deposited by various dye-stuffs, so in that [*sphota*] which is perfectly single, by the course of utterance does there take place a quite gradual tincture in the shape of each letter; and this is permanent, and it is this that the mind apprehends." He adds, that this *sphota*—this substratum of unqualified, but diversely qualifiable, knowledge—is *one* thing, though "common to the [particular] denominations of jars, webs, etc.;" and he mentions, that, in another work of his, the *Manjūshā*, he has shown how "the apprehension of the difference is reflectional,"—as when the pellucid crystal[1] assumes successively the hue of the red, blue, or yellow flower beside it.

This illustration of the web, to which a succession of tints may be communicated, reminds us of the contrivance of an editor in the backwoods of America, where printing materials were scarce. Each of his subscribers was provided with a towel, on which the current number of the journal was stamped, not with ink, but with the black mud from the neighbouring swamp. When this had been duly perused by the family, the towel was washed and sent back to receive the next day's impression. The towel of the subscriber, like the *sphota* of the grammarian, remained one and the same towel throughout, whether serving as the substratum of a democratic harangue, a defence of repudiation, or an advertisement of wooden nutmegs.

We observed that, by the Vedāntin grammarians, the *sphota* is regarded as the sole entity:—with them th " word" (*śabda*) is " God" (*Brahma*). This remark-

---

[1] Cf. *Sānkhya Aphorism*, Bk. I., § 19, *c*. The word *sphota* is derived from *sphut*, " to open as a bud or flower," being that by means of which each particular meaning is opened out and revealed. It means *meaning in general*, the foundation of all particular meaning.

able expression would require to be carefully considered, when the question has reference whether to the adoption or the avoidance of such and such terms in conveying the doctrines of Christianity.[1] The pandits furnish a striking exemplification of Bacon's remark, that, by men in general, "those things which are new in themselves will still be understood according to the analogy of the old." Employ a term that holds a definite place in any of the current systems, and the whole of the pandit's thoughts will immediately run in the mould of that system, to which he will strive to accommodate what he hears, rejecting whatever refuses to be so accommodated. A pandit remarked to us one day,[2] for example, that the opening verses of the Bible contained a palpable contradiction. "It is stated here," said he, pointing to the first verse of the Sanskrit version of Genesis by the Baptist Missionaries, "that God, in the beginning, created Earth (*prithivī*) and Ether (*ākāśa*); and then it is added that the Spirit of God moved upon the face of the *Water*,—an element, the creation of which is nowhere mentioned in the chapter, the next verse going on to speak of the creation of Light. If Water and Air did not require to be created, why did the other three?" Here the unfortunate employment of the terms *prithivī* and *ākāśa* had marshalled his thoughts at once under the categories of the *Nyāya*. Our explanation, that the one term was intended to denote all the matter of this globe, and the other term all that is material, external to this globe, satisfied him that the contradiction did not exist which he

---

[1] [See Preface, p. iv.]   [2] [As already observed in the Preface, p. v.]

had supposed; but he felt sure that the words would raise precisely the same notions in the mind of every Naiyāyika that they had raised in his own. The terms *bhūmi* and *diva*, not being technically appropriated, would be free from the objection.

NOTE F.

ON "TRANSLATION INTO THE LANGUAGES OF INDIA."

[THE dispatch of the Honourable Court of Directors, of the 19th of July, 1854, ordaining a great extension of the means for the education of India, gave a fresh interest to the question how the books to be employed in carrying out the work of enlightenment and civilization ought to be constructed. From a *Discourse* addressed to the Government of the North-west Provinces, and printed by the Government at the time, extracts are subjoined].

As regards our educational proceedings, the importance of native learning in India is not to be measured by the value—real or supposed—of the amount of information contained in the Arabic and in the Sanskrit. The disparagers of the one or the other literature will scarcely be found among those who really possess any knowledge of either. The best judges have long ere this decided that the Arabic and the Sanskrit languages are noble disciplinal studies, and that they are fountain-languages, from which the vernaculars can be indefinitely supplied with fresh forces. But, in order that the fresh additions may become

What the value of native learning in India consists in.

naturalised, it is indispensable, first, that the additions should be made by persons thoroughly qualified to make them rightly; and, secondly, that the learners should have access to complete information respecting the reasons why each particular addition was made exactly as it was. In other words, a permanently vital system of education in modern science, through the medium of un-barbarized Urdū, implies the possibility of reference at all times to learned and well-informed Maulavīs; and, analogously, in the case of Hindī dialects, to learned and well-informed Pandits; just as a scientific English education implies the possibility of reference to reliable sources of information relative to the classical languages from which the terms of science are taken in Europe. Where this access to the fountains is not open, or not made use of, the terms will be found to degenerate rapidly into a gibberish—such as we find in the *digarī* of our law-courts, for a "decree," the *tārpīn-kā-tel* of our laboratories, for "turpentine," or the *māmlet* of our kitchens, for an "omelette."

Through what practical agency. India is to be educated. If these views are just, then the first question which requires to be distinctly settled, and not thereafter to be perpetually opened up again, or to be kept hovering vaguely as a mirage before the eyes of the speculator, is the question—whether we are going to undertake the education of the Indian millions through an English agency or through a native agency? The idea of its being possible to employ a direct English agency in the tuition of all India, is perhaps explicitly entertained by no one; but the legitimate consequences of the impossibilty are constantly and most mischievously overlooked. The labour and difficulty of reproducing —really, and not merely in fallacious appearance,— European terms of science in the languages of the East, originate that "indolent impatience" which seeks to cut the Gordian knot by de- ciding that the English language ought to be the lan- guage of science for all the world,—a decision which it is further sought to recommend by the plausible plea that a cosmopolitan language of science offers ob- vious advantages. My reply rests on the fact, which I have asserted and illustrated, that scientific terms, cut off from the possibility of reference to their sources, tend headlong towards degeneracy. Under an English agency employed in the tuition of all India, this natural and experienced result might be partially staved off; but with the agency which, as already agreed, we must go to work with—if the work is to be done extensively at all—the English names will rapidly alter to such a degree, that no one who has not watched the pro- gress of their degeneracy will be able to recognise them; and thus the fancied advantages of a cosmo- politan terminology vanish into smoke. The degenerated English terms of our law courts, our laboratories, and our kitchens, are just as unintel- ligible to the English new comer as if they were native terms which he had never before met with. A shout of laughter usually accompanies the discovery of what the transmogrified vocable was intended for; but the word is no help towards mutual understanding. The same would be eventually the fate of an English scien- tific terminology in the hands of the only agency which,

How the indolently im- patient cut the Gordian knot.

Chimerical hope of a cos- mopolitan ter- minology.

by the hypothesis, is at our disposal for the education
of the millions.

Having set forth reasons for holding that an extended vernacular terminology, to have any chance of
becoming profitably naturalized, must be fed from the
sources of the Arabic or of the Sanskrit; and having
declared my conviction that neither of these can be
made—except in most delusive semblance—to supply
the place of both, I should now proceed to exemplify
the application of an Eastern fountain-language, the
Sanskrit, to the production of new terms of science;
but, before entering upon the terminology of the sciences,
I must state my reasons for taking them in the order
in which I take them.

Neither the end nor the means, in the attempt to educate India, unanimously or clearly determined. In designing an educational course, if we
are to go to work methodically, systematically,
and profitably, then regard must be had to the
end and to the means. Where no distinct end,
or not the same end, is kept in view by those who take
part in a discussion, agreement as to the means is pretty
well out of the question. And how can we hope, as
Bacon says, to achieve the course if we have not first
distinctly fixed the goal ? It may be said, indeed, that
there are more goals than one, inasmuch as we do not
expect all our pupils to go as far as the one who goes the
furthest. Be it so; but let us first settle the goal for
that *one*, and then the various stages which the others
may content themselves with reaching, will all lie along
that more extended course.

Shall our absolutely ultimate end, then, be the production of a first-rate engineer, or of a valuable revenue

officer, or of an accomplished native magistrate? With this I am not prepared to be satisfied. My proposed end is the making of each educated Hindū a Christian, on principle and conviction. This *The end, according to my own view.* end, as I propose here to indicate, implies every thing that the amplest course of education can comprise. Let us trace this assertion backward,—as thus. That a Hindū should, on principle and conviction, embrace a religion which, like Christianity, bases its claims on historical evidence, presupposes not merely an acquaintance with historical assertions, but a cultivation of the critical faculty, so as that the force of the historical evidence may be intelligently felt. The immediate preparation for a critically intelligent study of history is the study of Physical Geography. A history, all of whose assertions are found quite consistent with the multifarious information supplied by Physical Geography, must be felt to present very different claims on our respect from those of a *Purāna*, with its nowhere discoverable oceans of treacle, cane-juice, and butter-milk. But, to apprehend with full intelligence what is presented of Physical Geography, a knowledge of Zoology, Botany, and Geology are required. The full appreciation of these, again, presupposes Chemistry, in all its extensive bearings on Meteorology, climate, etc. The study of Chemistry must be preceded by that of Physics. Physics demands an anterior acquaintance with the sciences of Number and Magnitude,—sciences which present the most elementary exemplification of applied Logic. Such is a rapid enumeration of the great steps in the intellectual course. How the moral course combines with

this, we shall see, when, returning on our steps synthetically, we enquire what apparatus of educational materials the course above indicated will require.

Science the   Now, it may be objected as follows :—
only solid foun-
dation of art. "You call this an intellectual course,—it is
all science,—mere knowledge ; but are we to have no
applied science?—are we not to teach the *arts?*" I
reply,—assuredly you have got to teach these ; and if
you wish to teach them effectually, you will take care
that your exposition of each of them shall emanate from
a previously well-digested exposition of the sciences from
which the arts draw their life-blood. Your instructions
in Surveying will bear reference to your scientific exposition of Geometry and Arithmetic, and will be given
in the accurately determined language of those scientific
expositions. Your Pharmacy will be founded on your
scientific exposition of Chemistry, and will avail itself of
chemical language and chemical principles. You will
not—it is to be hoped—when penning practical instructions for the miner, ignore the scientific views and terms
of your Geology. In short, all treatises on the arts
ought to bear reference to the parent sciences, and should
be constructed in such exact accordance with the exposition of the parent sciences, that the artist may have
nothing to unlearn, or to confuse him, when he turns to
the expositions of the parent sciences for fresh suggestions in the prosecution of his art. Hence, in a systematic preparation of a literature, we must, except in
cases of urgency, attend to science first ; and, even in
the exceptional cases, you must regard your first rude
manuals of art as merely provisional, and as awaiting the

rectification which a thorough exposition of the parent sciences will subsequently render possible.

A second probable objection is this, that the course indicated above presents the sciences in an order which is not adapted to practical education. That you should begin with Logic,—then proceed to Mathematics (including all its branches),—go next to Physics, and so proceed through the whole series of the sciences, before reading a page of history, or a chapter of Zoology, is not feasible. True,—nor do I intend that anything of the kind should be attempted. A boy may with great advantage store his mind with passages of history before he is at all qualified to decide on the historian's claims to respect; and he may, not unprofitably, become acquainted with the chemical characters of the gases, though he may not have studied Physics so as thoroughly to understand the physical principles on which the manipulation of the gases depends;—and he may profitably become familiar with the mechanical powers, even when his mathematical acquirements are but slender;—and he may advisably prosecute his mathematical studies pretty far, before he turns his attention to the general laws of reasoning,—to that abstract science, of which all other sciences are the concrete embodiments. But still, the books which he reads ought all to be constructed in prospective contemplation of his eventually coming to recognise the chain of evidence in all its strength and in the logical order of its links. This cannot be expected, if no attention, in the preparation of the course, be paid to the order of the links.

Independent translational labours a source of wasteful expenditure. A third objection may be this, that so systematic a course as that proposed could not be the result of the independent working of the numerous persons who would be required to work upon it. This I most readily allow; and therefore it is that I grieve over the comparative waste of a great quantity of independent working, which has hitherto produced loads upon loads of books, and yet, by general admission, no educational course. Look at the voluminous catalogue of the [Benares] Centralizing Book Society, and see what sort of a course could be culled out of it;—what course such as could train a man's mind, and lead his convictions, with any sort of certainty, in the direction which I have indicated as desirable.

How co-operation, with saving of much useless labour, and of great needless expense, might be effected. How co-operation, as contra-distinguished from a mass of simultaneous but irrespective labour, might be secured, I must not here allow myself the space which would be necessary for discussing. Suffice it to say that my views in regard to the desirableness of a college of translators, coincide with those set forth by Mr. B. H. Hodgson in his published letters on *The Pre-eminence of the Vernaculars.*

No wish to drag valuable English teachers into vernacular studies where they have no turn for these. Let me now enumerate the sciences, and show how I think each ought to be dealt with, in presenting it to India through those of the vernaculars which hang upon the Sanskrit. Let it be remembered that I am not proposing any substitute for English education, where English education is available; and that I am not proposing that English teachers who have neither taste nor turn for vernacular teaching, should trouble themselves for one moment by attempting it. My suggestions have reference to that purely native agency, which I contend we must employ, if the millions are to be really educated; and in the hands of which agency I would seek to place an educational literature containing nothing that is insoluble, in the absencè of the power of reference to that European erudition which, by the hypothesis, is not available. The native erudition, competent to the solution of all the terminology which I advocate, *is* available, and would remain available if the English, by any strange chance, should have been driven from India into the sea.[1] It is scarcely worth while to remark, parenthetically, that to those who, in such event, care not what might become of India, I am not now addressing myself.

All science, or knowledge, rests on its appropriate evidence, direct or indirect. Sense and consciousness are direct evidence. Inference and testimony are indirect or mediate. In a synopsis of the sciences, these topics come properly at the outset; though they are not, I repeat, the topics which first demand the attention of a learner. In our Sanskrit synopsis, designed to furnish the terminology for versions in the Hindī, Bengālī, Mahratta, Telugu, etc., we treat these topics in the order of (1) the senses and the mind, (2) inductive investigation, (3) deduction, (4) demonstrative exposition, *i.e.* rhetoric, and (5) formal logic. The philosophical writings of the

The order of the sciences.

---

[1] [This was first published in 1855. The contemplated possibility did not then appear at all so near as it did to us at Benares on the 4th of May, 1857].

Hindūs furnish a tolerably ample terminology for the
satisfactory treatment of the first four of these topics;
but, to be wielded with any effect at all, this terminology requires to be carefully and critically sought

<small>Translators,</small> out, and estimated, *in situ*, not to be taken
<small>by dictionary,
of little avail,</small> on trust from the pages of a dictionary. More-
<small>except to spoil
paper.</small> over, where an appropriated term exists, if
we fail to discover it, and if we invent a different term
of our own, the established and appropriated term will
be almost sure to prevent the new term from being
understood; because the hearer naturally supposes that
you must mean something else than what is meant by
the appropriated term, else why not have made use of
it? For example,—Archbishop Whately explains *induction* to mean the "bringing in" of instances sufficient to support a general conclusion. Dr. Whewell,
again, holds that the word properly means the "super-
inducing" of a general conception upon the observed
facts. Now any attempt to translate the word according to either of these views, would only mystify a
Pandit, who really has already the required idea in
his mind, but a very different term—and, in my opinion,
a much better one—to express it by. The term is
vyāpti-graha—literally, "the cognizance of pervadedness,"—*i.e.* the cognizing that some given nature or
property, *e.g.* "human nature," is invariably attended
by some given nature or property, *e.g.*, "mortality."
It may be objected that we have nothing to do with
this, when dealing with the *tabula rasa* of a student's
mind; to which objection I give the reply—requiring
with such sad frequency to be reiterated—that when

we have settled that a native agency must be employed
in the education of the millions, and this agency one
owing its value to the possession of a fountain-language,
and a classic literature, we do ill to obtrude terms which
tend to keep the learner from understanding the *right*
views embodied in the time-honoured phraseology of
his teacher. Why do we, in any case, obtrude our
uglier term, when the finer one might be found, if
dug for, like a diamond, in the proper mine? It is
because of that "indolent impatience," which has so
long cankered all translational efforts in India, and
made the hasty and ill-concocted results so comparatively valueless.

But, without dwelling further on the ad- Construction of necessarily new terms.
visableness of learning what the Hindūs *know*,
before we undertake to *teach* them, let us advert to the
construction of new terms, where ·established terms are
avowedly *not* available. Formal logic, a subject neglected or overlooked by the Hindūs, demands a construction of new terms. The nomenclature of the parts
of the syllogism, adopted in concert with Pandit Vitthal
Sāstrī, may here suffice for illustration. To explain
how we rendered "illative conversion," and why; or
"conversion by negation," or "reduction to the first
figure;" would take up too much space: and, besides,
the information can be found, if wanted, in the published synopsis. As regards the syllogism, taken as
a sample of our treatment of the science, equivalents
were required for *proposition, term, major premiss, minor
premiss, conclusion, subject, predicate, major term, minor
term,* and *middle term.*

Now, a proposition is " a sentence indicative ;" and
there is no one word in Sanskrit which distinguishes
a proposition from other sentences (questions or com-
mands), by implying its indicative character. The
matter required, therefore, to be looked at from a different point of view, as thus :—a syllogism, or argument in regular form, is called *nyāya ;* and each of
its three members (*avayava*) is called a *nyāyāvayava.*
As each of these is necessarily a proposition, it follows
that the term *nyāyāvayava*, though it does not etymo-
logically signify " a sentence indicative," is yet, for
the purposes of logic, its precise equipollent ; and as
such we employ it. Next, there is no Sanskrit word
for *term.* The terms of a proposition are the subject
(*uddeśya*) and predicate (*vidheya*); and Hindū speculators, having a separate name for each of these, did
not take the trouble of devising an expression which,
like our word *term*, might refer the two to one common genus. An equipollent expression being, however,
wanted in our exposition, instead of seeking to obtrude
the novel and infructuous conception of the two as being
alike the boundaries (termini) of a proposition, we accommodate ourselves to the language already in use ;
we dissolve the expression which will fit no Sanskrit
mould, and we recast it in a *shape which dispenses with
the necessity of any accompanying explanation*, as " that
which expresses a subject or a predicate" (*uddeśya-
vidheya-bodhaka*). It may be objected that an expression like this is cumbrous ; but even cumbrous instruments are not unmanageable in powerful hands,—and
the Pandits of Benares are no children.

Just as we dealt with the word *term*, making our expression denote explicitly the subject and predicate which we found already provided with separate names, so have we dealt with the word *premiss*. There is no Sanskrit word for premiss; but there is a word for what we denominate the *major premiss*, and another for what we denominate the *minor premiss* (*udāharaṇa* and *upa-naya*). The aggregative compound of the two—*udāharaṇo-panayanau*—is equipollent to "the premises." For the other words above-mentioned, there were available terms already in use.

We pass now to those sciences in which Mathematics. logic, the most abstract of the sciences, the science of the forms of thought, first becomes concrete, by applying itself to those object matters of the widest generality,—space, time, and number. For Arithmetic, Algebra, and Geometry, an exact and tolerably exten-sive terminology exists in the mathematical books of the Hindūs. In devising additional terms—as is neces-sary, for example, in the case of the differential and integral calculus—regard should be had to the analogy of the existing terms, none of which ought to be rashly set aside and replaced by new names. New names will almost certainly prove (it could easily be shown that they *have* proved) inferior to the established ones; and, further, they have a tendency to prevent the native mathematician from seeing, so clearly as he otherwise might do, that our higher Mathematics are the legiti-mate development of his own science. The only kind of man, therefore, to be trusted with the formation of new mathematical terms for the Hindī vernaculars, is

one who unites to the most familiar conversancy with
Hindū mathematics, an accurate and extensive knowledge of the modern European methods. Such a man
we possess in the accomplished Bāpū Deva Sāstrī, to
whose care and superintendence I could wish that the
preparation of the whole of our Hindī vernacular course
of Mathematics were confided; and to whom, in the
matter of mathematical terminology, I have not the
presumption to fancy that I could offer any needful
suggestion.

Formal Astro-
nomy.
The first subject—in the order of simplicity
—to which the Mathematics are applicable, is
motion; and a science of pure motion is found in formal
astronomy. Here again I have nothing to suggest, but
that this department also may be safely confided to the
superintendence of Bāpū Deva, whose published *Euclid*,
Arithmetic, *Algebra*, and *Trigonometry*, are models of what
educational works ought to be.

Physics.
Force, the cause of motion, is the next element, the conception of which introduces the matter of a
new science,—the so-called "Physics." The modern
application of this term ought, consistently, to relegate
chemistry and physiology to the region of metaphysics or
of ethics. But there is no use, at this moment, in
quarrelling with English terms. Let us endeavour that
our Indian term shall not be open to the same reproach.
To ensure this, we must guard against being led away by
the etymology of the name, and·we must take an unbiassed view of the nature of the thing. On examining
the sciences which are clubbed under the name of
" Physics," we find that, while in common they treat of

force, they differ from the subsequent sciences of Chemistry and Physiology, in this, that the forces considered
in the sciences called physical, produce motion or rest,
but no permanent and essential change of property. The
aggregate, therefore, constitutes the science of the causes
and conditions of motion and rest, *gati-sthiti-kāraṇa-vidyā*,
or, in the vernacular Hindī, *gati aur sthiti ke kāraṇoṅ kī
vidyā*. Under this aggregative heading we find the
mechanics of the solid, of the fluid, of the aeriform, and
of the imponderable. It might seem at first sight as if
our designation were inappropriate in the cases where, as
in acoustics and optics, we take cognizance of sounds and
colours, which are not modes of motion or rest. Strictly,
however, the sounds and the colours are phenomena of
physiology, and not of the physical science, to whose pro-
vince belong only the motions on which the physiological
phenomena depend. There seems no use, however, in
our attempting here to disjoin these physiological develop-
ments of the physical sciences from the physical sciences
to which they are related. Our general term, then, being
equivalent to "Statics and Dynamics," the four sub-divi-
sions readily accept the names of *ghana-padārtha-gati-
sthiti-vidyā*, the statics and dynamics of solids; *drava-pa-
dārtha-gati-sthiti-vidyā*, those of fluids; *vāyava-padārtha-
gati-sthiti-vidyā*, those of airs; and *gurutwa-rahita-padārtha-
gati-sthiti-vidyā*, those of the imponderables. To a mere
English eye, these names may appear terribly Names may
seem long,
long; but to a Hindū, familiar with the sense which in actual
effect are not so
of each several member in the compound, they are not
long at all. And as they carry their own meaning with
them, their employment puts an end to those prevalent

confusions of memory, under which a school-boy blurts
out confidently, in reply to his examiner, that the radia-
tion of heat belongs to the science of Stereostatics, or that
the pressure of fluids is a phenomenon of Optics.   Where
the memory loses its hold upon the sense of terms insoluble as are these Greek ones to the Hindū, it possesses
no resources in itself for regaining it.   This I have repeated very often.   I wish I could believe that I have
repeated it sufficiently often.

Terms in
mechanics.   Of the terms employed in the exposition of
the physical sciences, in our *Synopsis of Science*
—and which can be found there if wanted—I shall here
cite only two, in illustration of two principles.   The
The lever. *lever* we name *uttolana daṇḍa*, " the lifting-
rod."   Now, it may possibly seem to some that the word
"rod" implies a solidity which does not belong to the
" lever" of rational mechanics ;—but the word "lever"
originally meant a solid lifting-rod; and if the English
mathematician, after his training in mechanics, has come
to associate with the name the notion of an absolutely
rigid line devoid of weight, the notion is due to that
training, and not to any inherently suggestive power in
the word, which it could carry with any profit into a
Hindī treatise.   Whatever rationalization of the originally
solid " lever" can be effected by the explanations of the
science, can be effected precisely in like manner with
the *uttolana daṇḍa* of our *Synopsis*.   The other term on
Impenetra-   which I would offer a remark is " impenetrability.   bility."   This term must have proved a source
of much misery to successive generations of lecturers on
physics ; for no sooner has the lecturer announced that

matter is "impenetrable," than he must breathlessly follow up the announcement with the explanatory assurance
that he does not at all mean what he seems to mean ; for
he is perfectly willing to admit that a deal board is pene-
trable by a nail or by a pistol-bullet. To render the
term "impenetrability" by *abhedyatā*, "incapability of
being cleft,"—as I have seen it rendered,—is needlessly
to multiply the terminological inconvenience just referred
to. What is it, then, that physicists actually *do* mean
when they speak of matter as "impenetrable?" It is
not that it cannot be pierced,—not that it cannot be
divided,—not that it cannot be compressed into smaller
space,—the degree of smallness being limited apparently
only by the limit of the compressing force available ;—
but what they mean to deny is, that matter can be so
compressed as to occupy *no* space. It may be indefinitely but it is not *infinitely* compressible. This important philosophical conception,—much more obscured
than illustrated by the term "impenetrability,"—we
convey, in our *Synopsis*, by the self-explanatory term
parimānātyantatyāgāsambhava, "the incapability of entirely resigning bulk." It may be asked,—what Hindū
will gain the conception by the mere enunciation of this
term? I reply,—what human being, Hindū or European,
will gain the conception by the enunciation of the word
"impenetrability?" Both terms—like other technical
terms—require explanation at the outset ; and the Indian
term has the merit of being to the purpose, which the
English term has not. It may be worth while to notice
the fact that, when such a term as "impenetrability" has
been once explained by a writer, the conception is taken

for granted throughout the remainder of his treatise, and the term itself scarcely ever recurs, if it recur at all. Such being the case, the apparent cumbrousness of the term by which we communicate the conception intelligibly at the outset is of very little moment. But our term is not really cumbrous. "Civil-disabilities-removal-bill," is a term not at all cumbrous for an Englishman, though it would sorely tax the memory of the foreigner who should be required to remember it as one sound simply denotative of a document upon a particular shelf.

Chemistry. The next conception, the introduction of which marks out the object-matter of a new science, is that of essential change of character. That the yellow substance sulphur, and the silvery fluid mercury, should combine to form the brilliant red vermilion, compels us to think of some other force than that - which results merely in motion or rest. This special force is termed "chemical." Chemistry being nothing else than purified alchemy, we reclaim to our own use the *rasāyana* of the Hindūs; designing to show, under that familiar title, what the true science is. Ancillary to chemistry is the section of natural history called mineralogy, *khanija-padārtha-vidyā*, "the knowledge of things produced in mines," which we treat as an *anga*, or "appendage," of the science.

Mr. Mack, in the preface to his treatise on Chemistry, published in Bengālī and English at Serampore, in 1834, tells us that he was advised to discard all European terms in his Bengālī version, but that he could not persuade himself to adopt the advice. He retained therefore many of the European names, and adapted Sanskrit terminations to them. European names I entirely discard. As an educational instrument,—and it is in *this* capacity that we at present seek to employ it,—the science of chemistry loses more than half its value when its compound terms do not tell their own meaning; and it is impossible that they should rightly tell their own meaning to one who is not familiar with the language from which they are derived. To an Englishman, unacquainted with the classical languages, the study of a work on chemistry is very far from being such a mental exercise as it is to a classical scholar. The long compound names which exercise the reflection and excite the admiration, or provoke the criticism of the latter, more frequently torture the memory and bewilder the understanding of the former. How entirely is the scientific beauty of the nomenclature thrown away upon the man who must look out hydro-chlorate and sesquioxide in his glossary in order to make sure which is which! It is all very well to teach long chemical names by rote to a youth who is to be employed as an apprentice in wielding a pestle. Him you perhaps do not seek to educate; you merely make a convenience of him; and if he does not practically mistake corrosive sublimate for coloquintida in making up a prescription, why all is well. The case is otherwise where the aim is to educate and to instruct. Where chemistry is to be efficiently employed for such a purpose, the learner must be conversant with Latin and Greek, or else the language of the science must be rendered into the language of the learner, as has been in a great measure done by the Germans for themselves.

The teaching of a trade is not education.

Acting as if under the impression of this truth, that the educational value of terms lies in their connotation and not in their mere denotation, the Germans have indigenated for themselves the language of chemistry; so that the study is far more profitable, as a mental exercise, for the German villager who knows no language besides his own, than it is for the English villager who does not know Greek and Latin. I wish the Hindū to enjoy in this respect the same advantage as the German. Of course the German who inclines to go deeply into chemistry will not rest until he learns also the Græco-Latin terminology of Europe in general. He can then talk of *bi-tartrate of potassa,* which does not tell its own tale to a plain German ear as his *Doppeltweinstein-saures Kali* does, and of *sulphuretted hydrogen,* which, to the plain German ear, would be but a baldly denotative and sense-eviscerated substitute for his own instructively connotative *schwefelwasserstoffgas.* As with the German, so with the Hindū. Let the study of foreign languages be encouraged to the utmost; but do not spoil the education offered to the millions, by using sense-evacuated foreign terms with a view to the imaginary convenience of the possibly exceptional few. Let the exceptional genius be sent up to College, and be set to study the sciences in English. His acquisition of the foreign terminology (just like the German's acquisition of it at the University) will be very far indeed from being impeded by his previous acquaintance with a kindred, though as yet less fully elaborated, vernacular phraseology; and, further, he will, by that previous training, be the better able to teach to his countrymen those new matters which he might else have found himself destitute of indigenous terms for teaching at all. Ask Liebig or Berzelius whether his own previous knowledge of *wasserstoff* and *schwefelsaure* stood in the way either of his learning about *hydrogen* and *sulphuric acid*, or of his explaining anything about these to a plain German (a dyer, for example) who knew them only by the names which, to *his* ear, carried a meaning in their component parts. I might, with tolerable security, peril the issue on a reference to Liebig or Berzelius or Humboldt, and acquiesce in the adoption (so congenial to mental indolence) of "transliteration" in the room of translation, if any one of these philosophers should consent to discountenance the principle on which the indigenous German terminology of chemistry is based. At all events, I wish that the discountenancers of veritable translation would clear up their ideas by trying to convert the Germans, before dealing with the scientific education of the Hindū millions as if the Germans were unquestionably in the wrong.

Having given examples from the German, let me illustrate the matter further from the language in hand, —say the Hindī.

Suppose an Englishman unacquainted with any Oriental language, and a Hindū unacquainted with any European language. Exactly as is the difficulty to such Englishman of recollecting and distinguishing between *jīvāntakik* and *gāndhakik*, is, conversely, the difficulty to the Hindū of recollecting and distinguishing between *nitric* and *sulphuric*. The supposed Englishman, again, though constantly liable to confound *gāndhakik* with *jīvāntakik*, cannot, by any lapse of memory, fall into a doubt whether *sulphuric* be the one related to *sulphur ;* nor, conversely, can the Hindū fall into a doubt whether *gāndhakik* be the one related to *gandhak*. If, therefore, it would be unadvisable to make that Englishman who is never going to study Hindī, employ Hindī terms which would leave him unceasingly upon a sea of doubt, it is scarely advisable to make that Hindū who (typifying millions on millions of our contemplated village pupils) is never going to study English, employ English chemical terms which would leave *him* unceasingly upon a sea of doubt. Now to proceed.

Indian nomenclature for the simple bodies. The first question, in settling a chemical nomenclature, regards the naming of the simple bodies. The common metals, as well as sulphur and carbon, have names in most languages which there is no occasion for changing. All the other simple bodies require to have names devised for them. First, there are the four simple gases. The name of oxygen, "the generator of acids," might readily be rendered by a corresponding Sanskrit compound; but this (as Mr. Mack has remarked) would only tend to preserve the exploded theory that there is no generator of acids besides oxygen. Its old name of vital air connotes one of its most important characters, and therefore we name it *prāṇaprada,* or *prāṇaprada-vāyu,* "the air that emphatically gives us breath." Nitrogen (or azote) we call *jīvāntaka,* "that which would put an end to life." Hydrogen is *jalakara,* "the water-former;" and chlorine *harita,* "the greenish-coloured."

Of the nine simple non-metallic bodies that are not gaseous, two, viz., sulphur (*gandhaka*) and carbon (*angāra*), have Sanskrit names. Boron, as it is the basis of borax (*tanka*), we therefore call *tanka-janaka ;* Silicon is the generator of flint—*agniprasthara-janaka;* Selenium —so named after the moon—we have likewise named after the moon—*chāndra,*—it being a matter of moonshine what so rare and unimportant a substance be denominated. Phosphorus is *prakāśada,* "the giver of light;" bromine is *pūṭa,* "the fetid;" iodine is *aruṇa,* the name, like the Greek one, referring to the violet colour of its vapour; and fluorine is *kāchaghna-janaka,* "the generator of that (fluoric acid) which corrodes glass."

Of those metals which have no names in Sanskrit, platinum, the "heaviest" of metals, is, with allusion to its weightiness, named *gurutama ;* and potassium, the "lightest," *laghutama.* Sodium is "the basis of culinary salt"—*lavana-kara ;* and calcium, "the basis of nodular limestone"—*śarkarā-kara.* Zinc, the Urdū name of which is *dastā,* we have named *dasta,* in allusion to the way in which its oxide, the "philosophical wool," is "tossed about" in the air.

Taking such, then, as the names that we have to deal with in forming the names of Of binary compounds. compounds, we come first to binary compounds. Compounds must have names suggestive of the fact that they are *acid* or otherwise. The termination *ic* belongs to the Sanskrit as well as to the Latin, so that sulphur and sulphuric acid can be satisfactorily rendered *gandhaka* and *gāndhakikāmla.* To the acids in *ous,* another termination (*ya*) has been appropriated. To the non-acid binary compounds, without attempting at present to fix separate terminations for the several varieties, the general termination *ja*, meaning "produced from," has been assigned. Thus an oxide is *prānaprada-ja;* a chloride, *harita-ja;* and so on. The alkalis, potassa and soda, take feminine names, according to the analogy of the Latin, from those of their metallic bases; thus —*laghutamā* and *lavana-karā*. The oxide of calcium may be termed *chūrna*, analogously to the English "lime."

Compounds of compounds. Coming to the compounds of compounds, as the acid affix *ic* changes to *ate* in the name of the resulting salt, the Sanskrit *ika* is replaced by *āyita*. Thus, as the sulphuric acid gives a sulphate, the *gāndhakikāmla* gives a *gandhakāyita*. It should be unnecessary to remark, that the suitableness of these names is not to be estimated on the principle which led the British sailor to set down the Spaniards as a nation of fools, because they call a hat a *sombrero*. To the British sailor the word hat sounds much more natural than *sombrero;* and, for like reasons, sulphate of soda may seem to sound much more natural than *lavana-karāyā gandhakāyitam*. But as "hat" is not good Spanish, so "sulphate of soda" is not good Sanskrit; and this leads us to forestall another criticism of kindred calibre. Is the sombrero-like expression, *lavana-karāyā gandhakāyitam*, good Sanskrit? The question is not to be resolved by submitting the term to a Sanskrit grammarian ignorant of physical science, to whom, without an attentive, serious, ingenuous, and uncavilling study of the tract in which it appears, the term has a *right* to be as obscure as the term binoxalate of potassa to the grandfathers of Lindley Murray.

Having shown, by the publication of our Chemical section in the Sanskrit Synopsis of Science, that the nomenclature of chemistry *Objections to the translation of scientific terminology dissected.* can be reproduced in an Indian language; and, finding that my Pandits now take a lively interest in the science, which formerly they regarded with indifference, looking as they did upon our *āksijen* and *haidrajen* as things of no more concern to Indian life than tomahawks and wampum are to ours; I think it worth while to dissect the following remarks (those of a gentleman highly and deservedly esteemed[1]), which appear in a recent fasciculus of *Selections from the Records of Government, N. W. P.* The remarks are these. " I cannot imagine any one proposing to translate all the nomenclature and terminology of the *Futile objections stated.* arts and sciences: even were it easy of performance, it would in many cases be useless; in chemistry, for instance, it would establish the misnomer oxygen (I may add hydrogen) and the indefinite names, chlorine, bromine, ammonia, etc. Were hydriodate of potash translated into Arabic or Sanskrit, a Maulavee or Pundit would perceive that the name was composed of words meaning water, purple, a saucepan, and ashes; but he would never be able to select that substance from several placed before him, for it is a dry, white, cubical, crystallized solid."

Now it has been already seen that I expressly *reject*

[1] Mr. Vincent Tregear, massacred in the mutinies of 1857.

the sense suggested by the term "oxygen," and ground my denomination of the element on that characteristic feature, its being the "vital air," which no revolution in chemical theory is likely to deprive it of. So much for the reverence shown in the Benares College for the supposed obligation to perpetuate misnomers in translation.

Now look at the rest of the passage. The writer says we should also have to perpetuate " indefinite~ names," such as chlorine. And, pray, do we escape the indefiniteness by adopting the indefinite name itself, and writing it *klārin gess*? If the indefiniteness is productive of no evil in Europe, where the name reminds us at least of the characteristic " greenness" of the gas, why should a like indefiniteness in the Indian term be dreaded *here*? To reject a self-explanatory name (our *harita vāyu*,— green air), which is precisely as definite or as indefinite as the European one, in favour of a name which here suggests nothing at all, seems to me most strange. The besetting delusion in the passage under review is what may be found admirably described in Whately's *Logic*, under the denomination of the " Fallacy of Objections." Suppose two ferry boats. Our friend objects to one of them that it is cumbrous ; and having thus condemned it on the strength of the objection, he steps unhesitatingly (as the necessary alternative) into the other, which, rotten and leaky, will sink under him before he has got a third of the way across.

At a risk of being tedious, since the case of the

oxygen suffices to dispose of the principle in *Further, and perhaps supererogatory, exposure of the fallacy.* question, I cannot refrain from remarking on the treatment of *hydriodate of potash* in the passage under review. The writer alleges that the term hydriodate of potash, if translated into Arabic or Sanskrit, would be seen by a Maulavī or a Pandit, "to be composed of words meaning water, purple, a saucepan, and ashes; but he would never be able to select that substance from among several placed before him, for it is a dry, white, cubical, crystallized solid." The reasoning here is unsatisfactory. The sense of the Sanskrit translation would never enable the Pandit to recognise "a dry, white, cubical, crystallized solid;" but does the writer conceive that in the term hydriodate of potash, formed of Greek and English, the sense of the same linguistic elements is of itself qualified to suggest "a dry, white, cubical, crystallized solid?" He will reply, that the name will suggest the thing, when the thing has been shown and the applicability of the name has been explained: but precisely so will it be in the case of the properly constructed Sanskrit term; so where is the relevancy of the objection? To have the shadow of a leg to stand upon, it must borrow the principle of the British sailor already cited, who held that the word "hat" was *naturally* significant, and that the Spaniards were fools for calling it a *sombrero*. "Why can't they call it a *hat*, when they must know it *is* one?" And, analogously, "why can't they call it hydriodate of potash, when they must know it *is* hydriodate of potash?"

Let me show how little, in the Benares College,

we find ourselves encumbered with the fan-
ciedly inevitable "saucepan" and "ashes,"
when reproducing the term hydriodate of potash in a form suited to furnish matter for the *judgment*
and not merely for the *memory ;* in a form, that is to
say, educationally valuable and not educationally valueless. Well, then, knowing that the more strict designation is *iodide of potassium* (just as chloride of sodium
is scientifically preferable to muriate of soda), we look,
in our list of elements, for *potassium,* and we find it
designated not with reference to the "ashes" of the
" saucepan," but with reference to its being the "*lightest*" metal (*laghutama*). Iodine, again (*aruṇa*), is named ·
after the colour of its vapour, just as in the European
nomenclature. Our term, therefore, is *laghutamasyāru-
ṇajam,* or, vernacularised, *laghutam kā aruṇaj,*—"the
iodine-product of potassium." Now, to one who has
been instructed regarding the elements, and the principles of nomenclature in designating compounds, this
is *self-explanatory.* If any doubt or dispute arise regarding its sense, a reference to the account of the
elements determines the question ; and, again, the etymological sense of the names assigned to the elements
can, in case of doubt, be ascertained by consulting a
Pandit. There is no occasion for a reference to an
educated Englishman. By such and similar means, and
by such only, shall we ever succeed in *naturalizing* our
knowledge among the Hindūs. The lazy barbarous plan
of talking (to those who are not intended to learn English) about *klārin gess,* and *haidraiyadet āf patāss,* is,
frankly, a wretched accommodation to the mental in-

dolence of English teachers and of incompetent translators.

Many of the names which I have proposed must necessarily, as I have already said, appear very long ones to the mere English reader, to whom the elements of the names convey no sense; just as "tithes-commutation-amendment-bill" must appear a very long name to a person ignorant of English. But if it would be cruelly unprofitable to attempt to impose on the mere English reader the employment of a terminology, to him key-less and non-significant, so cumbrous as our Sanskrit terminology would necessarily prove to him, is it less cruelly unprofitable to attempt to impose on the teachers and pupils of the purely native schools, the employment of a terminology to *them* key-less and non-significant, and just as cumbrous? It is not for *English* teachers that the vernacular terminology is required, but for the hundreds of *native* teachers whom I hope to see trained; and for the trainers of those teachers, in the normal classes which I hope to see cre long rapidly filling up.

We have seen it urged that the Arabic has not disdained to borrow from the Greek. True; and its borrowings are blots upon the language. What, for example, is gained by styling an introduction to logic *īsā ghojī;* because, forsooth, the Greek term is *eisagogē?* Nothing but mystification and pedantry is advanced by the sanctioning of cabalistical gibberish like this. Had the Arabs kept up a knowledge of the Greek language, as has been done in Europe, *then* the case would have stood very differently.

Greek words in the Arabic the reverse of beneficial to the latter.

Worthlessness of Greek contributions to Arabic illustrated. To make this point sufficiently clear, I shall avail myself of some observations on language by the Rev. Chenevix Trench. Quoting "a great writer not very long departed from us," Mr. Trench (at p. 4 of his delightful little volume, *On the Study of Words*, says—"There are few modes of instruction more useful or more amusing than that of accustoming young people to seek for the etymology or primary meaning of the words they use. There are cases in which more knowledge of more value may be conveyed by the history of a word than by the history of a campaign." Let us test this principle by the case of a Greek word borrowed by the English and by the Arabic : let us take the word *philosophos*. The English teacher, learned in Greek, or having access to the learning of those who are, can explain to his pupil how the "philosopher" was he who modestly disclaimed the proud title of *sophos*, or "wise," and professed himself merely a "*lover*" of wisdom." How much of this teaching can the modern Maulavī extract from the exanimate sound *failsūf?* Ignorant of Greek, and without access to those who know it, the Arabs can boast of a very poor linguistic acquisition indeed, when they point to the defunct *failsūf* of their lexicon.

The worse than uselessness of Greek contributions to Arabic illustrated. Further, Mr. Trench (at p. 182 of his *English, Past and Present*), says—"One of the most frequent causes of alteration in the spelling of a word is a wrongly assumed derivation. It is then sought to bring the word into harmony with, and to make it by its spelling suggest, this derivation, which has been erroneously thrust upon it." He continues (at

p. 188), "It is foreign words, or words adopted from foreign languages, as might beforehand be expected, which are especially subjected to such transformations as these. The soul which the word once had in its own language having departed from it, for as many as do not know that language, or not being now any more to be recognised by those who employ the word, these are not satisfied till they have put another soul into it, and thus it becomes alive to them again. Thus—to take first one or two familiar instances, but which serve as well as any other to illustrate my position—the Bellerophon becomes for our sailors the 'Billy Ruffian,' for what can they know of the Greek mythology, or of the slayer of chimaera?" Now, may we not discern something of this process in the *īsā ghojī* above referred to? The word, when the Arabs left off studying Greek, became exanimate; and may we not trace a "Billy-Ruffian"-like attempt to reanimate it by splitting the *eisagogē* in two, and spelling the first half like a proper name? The word *īsā* means "Jesus." "Jesus ghojī" might perhaps (to the Arab analogues of the sailors of the "Billy Ruffian") adumbrate some supposed author or patron of the work.

If such, and such-like, are the gains which Arabic has made by borrowing from the Greek, does the example hold out encouragement to the lazy plan of deluging the Indian vernaculars with our Greek scientific terminology; *The argument founded on the superficial and fancied analogy, when looked at more deeply and seriously, proves the very reverse.* or does it not rather hold out a caution and a warning? We may smile at the successful resurrection of "Bellerophon" in the shape of "Billy Ruffian," and shrug our shoulders at the barely half re-animation of the Greek *eisagogĕ* as *īsā ghojī*, where the *ghojī* means nothing and so remains dead ; but what ingenuity of Hindū thought is to re-animate, and in what vampire-shape, the *hai-draiyadet āf patāss*, after it shall have been reposited as a mummy in the catacombs of the sham-vernacular ?

The hinge of the cosmopolitan analogy.
That a Graeco-Latin terminology of science is cosmopolitan throughout Europe, is the natural and appropriate consequence of the fact that every nation in Europe has *retained its hold* upon the Greek and upon the Latin. This is the one sole cardinal element in the analogy,—the hinge on which it hinges if it is to hinge at all. This, the one solely and cardinally important element in the analogy, is non-existent in the case of the Indian vernaculars, just as I have shown it to be absent in the case of the Arabic. To the logical reader what need I say more ? To others, what is the use of anything that could be said ?

Rootless branches do not flourish.
The difference between a scientific terminology backed up by the means of access to its radicals, and the same dissevered from such means of access, suggests the illustration of the electro-magnet in its two widely different conditions. A mass of soft iron acts as a magnet—a most potent magnet—so long, but only so long, as it remains in connection with the galvanic battery. Break the connection, and your magnet subsides into an inert mass of soft iron. The off-hand plan of transplanting into the vernacular a terminology dissevered from its roots is but an imitation of the child who with impatient eagerness extemporises a garden by sticking in the ground flowers plucked from his father's

bushes. Such floriculture may look imposing at the moment, but only to children.

Some advocate of the easily constructed and useless sham-vernacular—where "transliteration" claims the honours of "translation"—will probably exclaim, in indignation at my uncompromising exposure of its rootlessness—"Well then—you, who pretend that everything both can, and ought to, be honestly translated, as you call it,—tell me—right off—on the moment—and without a moment's pause or reflection—how will you translate this, and this, and this, and that, and ten hundred thousand other things?" I reply, that my recorded and standing protest against the indolent impatience which I so much deprecate, suggests, of itself, the reason for my answering no one of these questions until I shall have given it such patient, careful, and studious consideration as may perhaps enable me to answer it worthily.

A futile challenge anticipated.

We have seen that the writer on whom I have been animadverting says, "I cannot imagine any one proposing to translate all the nomenclature and terminology of the arts and sciences." But why, in this way, trust everything to *imagination?* If the man who proposes to undertake the task brings forward a fair sample of that task already executed, then a candid examination of the work done might peradventure help the lagging "imagination." If, on the other hand, it can be shown that the work is not worthily executed—*that* may furnish reason for frowning on the undertaking—but not so the objector's lack of imagination. This is just another and a very noticeable phasis

Imagination no legitimate substitute for candid examination.

of that "indolent impatience" of which I complain, and
which Lord Bacon has limned with such keen master-
strokes at the opening of the 88th aphorism of the
Novum Organum. "At longe majora a pusillanimitate,
et pensorum, quae humana industria sibi proposuit, par-
vitate et tenuitate, detrimenta in scientias invecta sunt.
Et tamen (quod pessimum est) pusillanimitas ista non
sine arrogantia et fastidio se offert." Which we may
English thus :—" But far greater detriments have been
brought upon the sciences through pusillanimity, and the
littleness and slenderness of the tasks which human in-
dustry has proposed to itself. And yet (what is the
worst of it) this same [*ista*] pusillanimity presents itself
not without arrogance and disdain."

Difficulty
no reason for
shirking a sa-
cred duty.

Our objector urges as an objection to undertaking the task of translating the language of
European science into the Indian dialects, that
it is not an "*easy*" one. But it is not in the hope of
finding it an *easy* task that any man, competent to judge
of the case at all, is likely to devote himself to the
solution of such a problem, or to meddle with the solution at all. From this long controversial digression, let
us revert to the handmaid of chemistry, viz., mineralogy.

Mineralogy.

For the exposition of mineralogy, we find a
good number of terms ready to our hand ; but there are
many more which we must ourselves devise. Where
two different minerals, *e.g.* talc and mica, are confounded
under one name, *abhraka*, we distinguish them by specify-
ing their most characteristic or most obvious difference.
Seeing that mica is elastic, and talc not, we designate
them as *sthitisthāpaka-visishta* and *sthitisth^apaka-rahita*,

severally. Where the European name alludes to the structure—as in the case of granite—we preserve the allusion, as in our term *kanochchaya-prastara*, "the rock which is an agglomeration of grains." Of course the explanatory "*prastara*" can be dropped when the pupil is familiar with the term, just as the word "rock" in "trap-rock," is habitually dropped in English. Names that convey no sense—names simply denotative—as "basalt," we render by some obvious character of the thing denoted. "*Basalt*," we render *krishna-prastara*, "black-rock." It may be objected that many rocks (Obsidian in particular), are black, no less than basalt is. I reply, that European mineralogists and geologists name a certain rock "*Greenstone*," (*harita-prastara*), without regard to the fact that many other stones are green. Greenstone is the most important of the rocks that are green, and basalt of those that are black. Why should *we here* be required to attain a precision of nomenclature which has not been attained in Europe, and which, on principles of philosophical necessity, is not attainable at all? In conclusion, as regards naming the minerals, where there is no native name, and nothing suggestive in the European name, and no very marked characteristic property, as is the case with "gypsum," we may designate the mineral by reference to its chemical composition. Thus "gypsum" is *chūrna-gandhakāyitātmaka-prastara*, "the rock which consists of sulphate of lime."

The additional conception of *life* gives occasion for the next in the order of the sciences, viz., vegetable physiology, with its ancillary section of

Vegetable physiology and botany.

natural history, named botany. Here we find some terms ready to our hand. For example, cryptogamic plants are classed under the head of *vanaspati*, while the phanero-gamic are termed *vānaspati*. The Hindūs, however, have fallen into the error of ranging the *fig* among the crypto-gamic. The "stamens" and "pistils," not discriminated from each other apparently by Hindū physiologists, we distinguish into *paurusha-kesara*, "the male filaments," and *straina-kesara*, "the female filaments."

Animal phy-
siology and
zoology. The next of the sciences is marked off by the introduction of the additional conception of *sensation*. Here we have animal physiology, with its ancillary section of natural history, termed zoology. For the more obvious parts of the body we of course find names ready to our hand. For the more minute parts, names will have to be adapted. Where the Hindūs, for example, have not discriminated the nerves from the veins, we must designate the former by some such term as *mastishka-tantu*, "thread of cerebral matter." "Chyme" and "chyle" are not discriminated by the Hindūs. They can be easily distinguished in our terminology by prefix-ing to the established name for both, viz., *dhātupa*, the specification of its being the "prior," or "the latter," *pūrva* or *uttara*.

Zoological
divisions. In dividing the animal kingdom into its four provinces, we call the "vertebrata" *prishthavanśa-viśishta*, those "distinguished by a back-bone;" the "mollusca," *komala-śarīra-viśishta*, "dis-tinguished by a soft body;" the "articulata," *kānda-viśishta*, "distinguished by their sections;" and the "radiata," *samānāvayavāvritta-nābhi-viśishta*, "distinguished by a centre with similar members disposed around it."

All the sciences which we have thus hastily Geology. run through, are put in requisition by *geology*. As for the terms to be employed in the exposition of geology, the mineralogical ones have been already discussed. Of things organic, belonging specially to geology, I shall cite only two examples, each to illustrate a principle. The "mammoth," whose name is to us simply denotative, or non-significant, I speak of as the *prāchīnakālika hastin*, "the elephant of the old world." The "Ichthyosaurus," on the other hand, whose name is connotative, I render in accordance with the connotation, and denominate the *matsya-makara*, the "fish-lizard."

Furnished with the knowledge supplied by the sciences which we have reviewed, the Physical geography. inquirer will next ask, what, in consequence of all these entities and agencies, is the actual aspect of the globe on which we dwell? He desires instruction in physical geography. When we have once thoroughly secured right terms in all the sciences which we have been considering, the question of terminology for the exposition of physical geography presents few difficulties. While we endeavour to give an accurate general conception of the contour of the land and water of the globe, we must take care to proportion the minuteness of detail to the historical importance of the several regions. We must not waste upon Tierra del Fuego or Nootka Sound the fulness of detail which may be due to the plateau of Central Asia, or the valleys of the Euphrates and the Nile. Physical geography is the legitimate introduction

to civil history, and our teaching of it ought to be re-
gulated by the consideration of what we intend to teach
of civil history.

Civil History. Since, in the department of Civil History,
I have nothing which I wish at this moment to suggest in the matter of terminology, I shall here content
myself with remarking that our first exposition ought
to be rigidly bare of ornament and flourish. The historical series, let me add, must be so constructed that
no allusion shall anywhere occur which the perusal of
what went before does not qualify the attentive reader
to understand. This obvious precaution has hitherto
been much neglected.

Political Eco- From history we advance to one of the
nomy. considerations which the perusal of history
should naturally suggest to the thoughtful reader. Certain courses of conduct appear to have enriched a nation,
—other courses to have kept a nation poor, or to have
reduced it to poverty. What are those courses severally ? Adam Smith's reply to the question was given
under a title which I should have no objection to adopt,
giving the science the name of *deśa-dhana-vriddhihrāsa-
kāraṇa vidyā,—i.e.*, "The Science of the Causes of the
Increase and the Decrease of the Wealth of Nations."
Whether a name moulded on this view of the question
be adopted, or a name moulded on Whately's stricter
view of the science as "The Theory of Exchanges"—
ādana-pratidāna-vidyā — let us at all events sink the
hideous *pālitikal ikānami*, with which the hybrid treatises have hitherto puzzled India.

Following the thread of connection among   Ethics.

the sciences, we find that a fresh consideration inevitably meets us. The wealth of a nation, as of an individual, may be increased by practices against which political economy offers no remonstrance, but yet against which there is *something* in the human soul that revolts. For example, the wonderful and beneficial results of the division of labour are among the most attractive of the subjects offered to our contemplation at our entrance upon the study of political economy; but when we find this division and subdivision carried out to such an extent, that a human being becomes a mere machine for the sole and life-long performance of some such labour as the pointing of a pin, a mournful feeling comes over us, and we cannot help asking, " *ought* this to be exactly as it is?" The word "ought" embodies a new conception,—the essential conception on which is based the science of ethics. But how are we to translate the word? I confess that I find here very much more difficulty than in the physical sciences. The superficial observer may flatter himself that there is no difficulty in the case; but that is because he has not looked far enough beneath the surface to discern the difficulty. "Conscience," "duty," "moral obligation,"—where are the words to convey (except in most delusive semblance) what we really understand by those terms? The difficulty, however, is not purely philological. Let us hear Mr. Trench again (*On the Study of Words*, p. 8). "Nothing, I think, would more strongly bring before us what a new power Christianity was in the world, than to compare the meaning which so many words possessed before

Peculiar difficulty in rendering ethical terms.

its rise, and the deeper meaning which they obtained, so soon as they were assumed by it as the vehicles of its life, the new thought and feeling enlarging, purifying, and ennobling the very words which they employed." Apparently we must abide in hope that such influence will eventually raise *dhārmika*, for example, to a real as well as an etymological equivalence with " moral;" for which, at present, it is but a sorry substitute. At all events, I presume it is not likely that here the system of make-believe translation will venture on a suicidal "reductio ad absurdum" by attempting to press *kānshinss* and the *māral sinss* into the service of the sham-vernacular.

Natural Theology. Still another consideration arises out of the moral one last adverted to. *Why* do we feel this obligation in regard to right and wrong? Be the answer what it may, all experience shows that the human mind turns instinctively towards a Ruler, to whom we feel ourselves under the obligation that we do always what is right, and abstain from what is wrong. Again the consideration of the external world points to the fact of there being One Almighty Governor, But the question is not to be taken for granted. The decision, to a thoughtful mind, would be much more satisfactory if supported by evidence. The evidence lies abundantly around us,—the evidence of the being of a God, — the evidence which, in recent times, has appropriated the name of *Natural Theology*.

Revelation. Natural Theology closes the series of our secular teaching, leading onward to those more solemn subjects, for which the secular curriculum may be regarded, in its highest aspect, as being preparatory. The conclusion reached by Natural Theology compels the thinking mind to ask the question, "Has the God of nature anywhere, except in nature, revealed himself to man?" The answer to this question we offer to the Hindū in our Scriptures. But his compatriots, he replies, have scriptures of their own. True, we rejoin; but scriptures resting their claims only on the futile ground of self-assertion. Of our own, we tender him the evidences, historical and internal. But the missionary will exclaim—"It is the peculiarity of the Gospel that it is preached to the poor;—and must every poor villager go through all this course of training before he can reasonably become a Christian?" I reply, that such is not at all my meaning. The question on the lip of the uneducated masses is always, "Have any of the chief priests or rulers believed on him?" When those who are educated shall come to be won over, the uneducated masses will follow. The baptism of a Clovis entails that of armies and of crowds. "But are we not to follow the example of our Lord?" Let us see what is the example here meant. It is that conveyed, we presume, in the reply to the interrogatory of the Baptist—"The blind receive their sight, and the lame walk, the lepers are cleansed, and the deaf hear, the dead are raised up, and the poor have the Gospel preached to them." If this were designed as our example, why confine ourselves to the last in the list of marvellous works? Is it because, out of the signs of the Divine mission here co-ordinately enumerated,—out of the six instances of work accomplished in suspension of the

18

ordinary laws of nature,—the last only, when we have *no* power to suspend the laws of nature, can be imitated without risk of obvious and glaring failure ? When our missionaries can raise the dead, or give sight to the blind, then they may hopefully attempt the conversion of a nation by the non-natural process of leavening the lowest first. This much-misunderstood matter has been handled in the clearest and fullest manner by the Rev. John Penrose, in his Bampton Lecture of the year 1803, a book quoted from in our Introduction, and which every missionary would do well to read and ponder. Far be it from me to wish that the poor should receive one atom less of attention than they receive at present; but it is not from this quarter—as the enormous aggregate of avowed missionary failure might suggest — that any *infectious* extension of the faith will emanate, in an age when miracles have ceased and ought not to be counted on.

THE END.

STEPHEN AUSTIN, PRINTER, HERTFORD.

For EU product safety concerns, contact us at Calle de José Abascal, 56–1°,
28003 Madrid, Spain or eugpsr@cambridge.org.

www.ingramcontent.com/pod-product-compliance
Ingram Content Group UK Ltd.
Pitfield, Milton Keynes, MK11 3LW, UK
UKHW010346140625
459647UK00010B/872